Motor Vehicle Engineering

The UPK for NVQ Level 2

Tom Denton, BA, AMIRTE, Cert. Ed.

THOMSON

LEARNING

Australia • Canada • Mexico • Singapore • Spain • United Kingdom • United States

THOMSON

LEARNING

Motor Vehicle Engineering - The UPK for NVQ Level 2

Copyright © Tom Denton 1997

The Thomson Learning logo is a registered trademark used herein under licence.

For more information, contact Thomson Learning, Berkshire House, 168-173 High Holborn, London, WC1W 7AA or visit us on the World Wide Web at:
http://thomsonlearning.co.uk

British Library Cataloguing-in-Publication Data
A catalogue record for this book is available from the British Library

ISBN 1-86152-709-8

First edition published 1997 by Macmillan Press Ltd

Reprinted 2001 by Thomson Learning

Printed by ZRINSKI d.d., Croatia

Contents

Preface

I have a theory:

'A car has an engine and some other bits to make the wheels go round. When it breaks down or needs a service, it will in most cases be taken to a garage for repairs. The garage will operate normal company systems to fix the car and make a profit.'

What I mean by this is that different qualifications and courses come and go, but my theory will still be good! So, what you will find in this book will be relevant for quite some time, no matter what.

I still enjoy learning new things about vehicles and the motor trade in general. I hope you enjoy your career as much as I have, and still do today.

I would very much welcome comments from students and lecturers. You can visit my website at

  http://ourworld.compuserve.com/homepages/tom_denton/

I will be offering technical updates, advice about using this book for new or changed qualifications, and information about future titles. I will also be supplying new and updated learning tasks. All suggestions are welcome!

Tom Denton 1997

Acknowledgements

Thanks are due to the following companies who have supplied information and / or given permission to reproduce photographs and diagrams. Figure numbers are as listed:

AA Photo Library   3.11, 3.12, 3.13, 4.13, 4.14, 5.4, 5.5, 5.6, 5.9, 5.10, 5.11, 5.15, 5.16, 6.4, 6.5, 7.2, 7.3, 7.6, 7.9, 7.11, 7.13, 7.16, 9.3, 10.6, 10.7, 11.3, 11.4, 11.7, 11.8, 11.11, 12.3, 12.4, 12.6, 12.9, 12.10, 12.11, 12.13, 12.14, 12.15, 12.17, 13.1, 13.2, 13.3, 13.6, 13.8, 13.10, 13.11, 13.12, 13.16, 14.2, 14.7, 14.8, 14.9, 14.13, 14.15, 14.16, 20.26

Autodata Ltd.   1.5, 17.3

Citroën UK Ltd.   15.8, 15.10

Draper Tools Ltd.   2.3, 3.6

Ford Motor Company Ltd.   4.6, 4.7, 4.9, 5.14, 6.1, 8.1, 9.12, 10.5, 10.9, 15.33, 16.4, 16.7

GenRad Ltd.   20.35

Glass's Information Services Ltd.   19.7

Kelvedon Car & Service Centre   19.8, 19.9

Lucas Ltd.   3.14, 6.6, 9.4, 9.6, 9.9, 9.10, 15.11, 15.12, 15.14, 15.15, 15.16, 15.19, 15.23, 15.26, 20.9

Mazda Cars UK Ltd.   14.10, 16.1

Robert Bosch GmbH   1.3, 2.5, 8.6, 8.7, 8.9, 9.5, 9.7, 9.15, 15.9, 15.13, 15.21

Robert Bosch Press Photos   6.2, 6.8, 6.9, 6.10, 6.11, 6.12, 15.17, 15.30, 15.37

Rover Cars Ltd.   4.8, 4.11, 4.12, 4.15, 5.1, 5.2, 5.3, 5.7, 5.8, 7.5, 7.12, 7.14, 8.8, 9.1, 9.11, 11.5, 11.6, 11.12, 13.4, 13.5, 13.7, 13.9, 13.14, 15.1, 15.7, 15.29, 15.32, 16.3, 16.6, 16.8, 16.9

RS Components Ltd.   3.4

SAF Suspension   12.7

Snap-on Tools Inc.   2.4, 3.15, 4.10, 5.19, 9.14, 10.10

Sun Electric UK Ltd.   6.16

Sykes-Pickavant Ltd.   7.17, 15.38

Unipart Group Ltd.   3.1, 3.9, 7.10, 8.5, 10.2, 13.15, 15.5

Yokohama Ltd.   14.12, 14.14

Thanks again to the listed companies. If I have used any information or mentioned a company name not listed here, my apologies and acknowledgements. I would also like to thank contributors to the Automobile Forum on CompuServe. I am also grateful for the help of a colleague, Dave Roberts, for increasing my UPK of NVQs.
Last, but by no means least, thank you to my family: Vanda, Malcolm and Beth; it's good to be back – again.

NVQ level 2
underpinning knowledge

This table refers you to the most relevant pages or general area relating to the UPK statements. Many of these statements overlap, so you will have to refer to several areas.

Unit no.	Unit title and UPK statements	Page numbers
A1–G	**Contract with customers to provide for their vehicle needs**	
A1.1	Vehicle test programmes	227, 230
	Courses of action	245
	Customer relations	244, 245, 252
	Estimating costs and times	247
	Company services	241, 243, 244
	Resources available	243
A1.2	Requirements of a contract	255
	Warranty schemes	249
	Recording systems	231, 235
	Documentation requirements	248, 249
	Limits of authority	253
A6–G	**Reinstate the cleanliness of the vehicle**	
A6.1	Properties of exterior cleaning materials	NVQ 3 book
	Use of tools and equipment	NVQ 3 book
	Safety precautions	NVQ 3 book
A6.2	Properties of vehicle interior cleaning materials	NVQ 3 book
	Use of tools and equipment	NVQ 3 book
	Safety precautions	NVQ 3 book
A7–L	**Routinely service the vehicle to maintain optimum performance**	
A7.1	Reasons for regular or special vehicle inspections	227, 233
	General legislative requirements for road vehicles	10, 17, 164, 234
	Interpretation of vehicle data	229, 235
	Purposes of vehicle inspection records	231
	Requirements of customer contracts	255
A7.2	Reasons for regular adjustment	233
	Interpretation of data	229, 235
	Effects of incorrect adjustments	239
	Identification codes and grades of lubricants	116
	Use of parts lists and identification codes	246
	Reasons for servicing records	230, 235
A8–L2	**Identify faulty components/units which affect system performance**	
A8.1	Planned systematic procedures for testing	62, 77, 89, 98, 112, 123, 137, 151, 164, 180, 212, 225, 230
	Interpretation of test data and instructions	62, 77, 89, 98, 112, 123, 137, 151, 164, 180, 212, 225, 229, 230
	Use of test equipment	33, 62, 77, 89, 98, 112, 123, 137, 151, 164, 180, 212, 225, 230
A8.2	Operating principles of vehicle systems	36, 45, 64, 80, 92, 100, 115, 126, 139, 153, 166, 182, 215

Introduction and welcome!

1 Introduction

Start here! Hello! This book will help you understand and learn the background knowledge needed for your NVQ **level 2** in motor vehicle engineering. The term used to describe this is 'underpinning knowledge' or 'UPK' for short. The NVQ in motor vehicle engineering is a very practical subject. This book does not try to cover the practice in detail. However, in order to carry out practical work to national standards, a good background knowledge is essential.

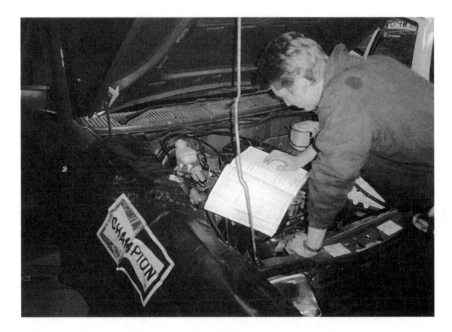

Figure 1.1 You need background knowledge for your practical work

You can study the contents of this book in any order you like, but it is not intended to be a 'self learning' study pack. It is best used in conjunction with a course of study. You will also find it a useful reference for looking up information as required.

To obtain your NVQ you will need to show your assessor that you can do the work and that you have the necessary UPK. This is where you will need this book. Because our chosen subject is now so wide ranging, you will also need to look at other sources of information. These other sources will be some or all of the following:

- your college teacher or assessor
- data books

- workshop manuals
- other textbooks, magazines and newspapers
- CD ROM information
- videos and cassettes
- your workplace supervisor or experienced work mates.

Figure 1.2 Sources of information

KEY WORDS

- All words in the table
- Sources of information

The fine details of the UPK you need will vary depending on your particular situation at work. However, the basic facts are the same for all motor vehicle systems and workshop operation methods.

Good luck with your work and studies, and remember: in order to get anything out of it, you will have to put something in!

As a final incentive, just check the newspaper job adverts and note that the top technicians earn very good money. This may be several years away yet, but it is worth putting in the effort now.

Terminology

NCVQ	National Council for Vocational Qualifications
MITSC	Motor Industry Training Standards Council. The people who set our standards, sometimes called the lead body
NVQ	National Vocational Qualification
UPK	Underpinning knowledge – most of which you will learn from this book
Evidence	Material to prove you can do something
Assessor	The person who will assess and advise you in gaining your NVQ
Portfolio	The collection of evidence which is cross referenced. Usually a ring binder
Standards	The lists of units, elements and performance criteria, set by MITSC
Units	Main parts required to build up to an NVQ. About six or seven units is normal
Elements	Each unit is split into elements to further explain what is needed
Performance criteria	Each element has many performance criteria which state exactly what you must be able to do
Range statements	These describe the range of subjects or systems you will cover in the performance criteria

What is an NVQ and why do you need one?

National Vocational Qualifications (NVQs) were designed to meet the modern and ever changing needs of our industry. They are also important in that a national standard has been set so that we are all working towards the same thing!

The aim of NVQs is to enable you to do your job. This is, of course, what an employer wants and therefore will help you get a good job.

Figure 1.3 Modern test equipment in use

'Vocational' means related to the work you do, but the qualification still requires a large amount of understanding about motor vehicle technology. Working in one particular garage or dealership specialising in one make of car, you will probably become quite good at fault finding the fuel or ignition system. This is because you know the systems well, have seen it all before and have all the information you need. When a different type of car comes in for you to repair a similar fault, you need to understand the underpinning principles to be able to carry out your work and earn the good money you deserve.

In the motor industry NVQs exist at different levels. These reflect the level of work you are or will be doing.

- NVQ level 1: basic tasks mostly under supervision
- NVQ level 2: diagnose and repair faults to unit level
- NVQ level 3: diagnose and repair detailed faults plus some degree of supervision of others
- NVQ level 4/5: Certificate in Management (IMI).

An NVQ is made up of a number of units. Each unit has a number of elements (usually two, three or four). These elements have lists of 'performance criteria'. These are the heart of your NVQ: they specify what you must be able to do. There is also a list of the UPK and the range of vehicles and/or systems as appropriate to each unit.

The qualification is awarded when you have collected enough evidence to show that you can meet all the requirements of all the units at your level. It is possible to gain credit for individual units, but most students aim at the complete qualification. Many students find the language used in the standards confusing – well it is! The reason is to keep the standards up to date with modern practices and different work situations without having to constantly change the wording. So we are stuck with it!

LEARNING TASK

➡ Look back at the key words. Explain each one to a friend, and/or write out a short description to keep as evidence.

2   Motor vehicle NVQ units and what they mean

Introduction   In this section I will give you my interpretation of the NVQ units, but you should check with your assessor who will be able to be more specific about details as they relate to you. Each unit covers many more situations than the examples given here, but these will serve as a useful guide. Depending on the qualification you are aiming at, you may not need to achieve all the units.

NVQ units – a simplified interpretation

Unit	Interpretation	Example
Unit A1–G Contract with customers to provide for their vehicle needs	You must be able to meet customers, deal with their problems, answer questions and understand the issues of a contract	Meet a customer at reception, find out what the problem is, quote a price and book the car into the workshop
Unit A8–L2 Identify faulty components/units which affect system performance	When a car has a problem, you must be able to find the cause or reason	The car you are working on makes a grinding or rumbling noise, but only when going round sharp left hand bends. It's probably a wheel bearing, but which one?
Unit A9–L2 Remove and replace vehicle components/units	This is the main part of our work, together with the previous unit: remove faulty parts and replace with new. It means following repair procedures such as in a workshop manual	Renew the wheel bearing identified above
Unit A11–L Prepare new, used or repaired vehicles for customer use	Inspect a vehicle and make sure it is safe, clean and suitable for a customer to use	Carry out a pre-delivery inspection (PDI)
Unit A12–G Maintain effective working relationships	Get on well at work with your customers, work mates supervisor and boss	You must be able to accept instructions and work well as part of a team
Unit A13–G Maintain the health, safety and security of the working environment	Deal with toxic materials in the correct way, follow sensible safety procedures and look after customers' property	Clean brakes with proper solvents, use axle stands after jacking up a vehicle and lock the customer's car when parking it outside the workshop
Unit A7–L Routinely service the vehicle to maintain optimum performance	You must be able to carry out all types of service as specified by the vehicle manufacturers	Carry out a full service
Unit A8–L3 Identify faults which affect system performance	To be able to carry out tests and use fault finding procedures to find out why the vehicle is not performing as it should	Use diagnostic equipment to diagnose why the engine misfires at high speed
Unit A9–L3 Rectify faults in vehicle systems	Once a fault has been diagnosed as above, you must be able to fix it!	Again as above, once the high speed misfire is diagnosed as, say, the rotor arm tracking, you must be able to replace it
Unit A10–LH Augment vehicle systems to meet customer requirements	'Augment' means to do work which improves on the original vehicle	Fitting alloy wheels and spot lights
Unit A6–G Reinstate the cleanliness of the vehicle	To be able to valet a car	A complete wash and wax polish and the interior upholstery cleaned

The following units are required for qualification:

Vehicle mechanical and electronic systems unit replacement (light vehicle level 2)	Vehicle mechanical and electronic systems maintenance and repair (light vehicle level 3)
A1–G	A7–L
A8–L2	A8–L3
A9–L2	A9–L3
A11–L	A10–LH
A12–G	A11–L
A13–G	A12–G
Additional unit A7–L (optional)	A13–G
	Additional unit A1–G (optional)
	Additional unit A6–G (optional)

Collecting evidence for your portfolio

KEY WORDS

- Evidence
- Assessments

Because no national examinations are set for an NVQ, you have to collect evidence which shows you can meet the standards. This will usually be collected in a ring binder or similar. The evidence has to be cross referenced to show that it covers all the criteria in the standards. Some performance criteria may require more than one piece of evidence. When you register for your NVQ, the awarding body (where your certificate will come from, such as City & Guilds) will supply lists of the standards and 'tick boxes' to help you. Your assessor will give lots of help and guidance, but you can make a start by collecting evidence from both work and college.

'Evidence' can come from many sources, for example:

- job cards showing work you have done in a garage
- tasks you have carried out while an assessor is observing
- results of tests or examinations
- answers to verbal questions
- written statements made by an expert witness, for example your employer ('witness testimony')
- previous certificates
- photographs
- examples of your work
- videos.

In most cases the types of evidence you supply will be those towards the top of this list. However, if the evidence is good and can be proved, any type can be used. We all have different needs and situations. Your assessor will advise you what is best in your case. It is also important to note that evidence should come from a task completed after training has taken place, not a training exercise itself.

Figure 1.4 Collecting evidence for your portfolio

How to use this book The previous section talked about 'evidence'. This meant evidence that you can meet the NVQ standards, by being able to do the work and also showing an understanding of vehicle technology and workplace systems. This book will help with your understanding, or underpinning knowledge (UPK).

An important thing to understand about an NVQ is that it is not a course at a training centre or college, it is a qualification by assessment. The assessment will in many cases follow your learning programme.

Figure 1.5 Refer to technical information to ensure the job is done correctly

One way to learn from a book is to read it all the way through! But by the time you get to the end, you've probably forgotten what was at the beginning. To really learn you need to study each part slowly and in detail. You will find that most of the chapters do not relate directly to a particular NVQ unit. This is because an understanding of the vehicle in particular and the motor trade in general is required for almost all of the units.

If you flick through the book you will notice that each chapter (including this one) is generally laid out in the same way.

Each chapter starts with an introduction (Start here!) and then covers terminology, the words and abbreviations you will need to know. The next parts deal with the subject in more depth. Towards the end of each main section the key words are highlighted. These are then followed by learning tasks related to the same section.

The idea is that after reading each main section and carrying out the learning tasks, you will have a better understanding of the subject you have just read about. At the very end of each chapter you will again find key words and more learning tasks. UPK statements from the standards are listed at the front of the book together with references to the chapters and sections. These statements will help you to see which areas you have covered. As you complete the learning tasks, you will be able to generate some evidence of UPK for your portfolio. If you do not understand specific areas, you can study the chapter again. It is quite normal to study some chapters more than once.

Good luck with your studies!

LEARNING TASKS

➡ Look back at the key words. Explain each one to a friend, and/or write out a short description to keep as evidence.

➡ Check that you understand what you need to do to gain an NVQ.

2 Your good health and safety

1 Introduction

Start here! It is tempting to think that health and safety is a boring subject. Well, it's not half as boring as spending months in hospital, the rest of your life in a wheelchair or doing time in prison! These three things are all possible if health and safety rules are not followed. Health and safety plays an important part in most of the NVQ units. You will have to learn quite a few new things in this chapter, but you will also come to realise that most of them are common sense.

KEY WORDS

- All words in the table
- Fault
- Blame

'Health and safety is the responsibility of everyone in the workplace.'

Just think how the following example would affect many people besides yourself. Working on a customer's car, you jack up the front, 'forget' to use axle stands. Next you remove the wheels. Whilst sitting on the floor with

Figure 2.1 Stands must be placed under a suitable part of the body, such as a suspension mounting

your legs under the car, a leaking seal on the jack finally gives in and the car drops on to your legs. Later in hospital you find out that you have a broken ankle on one leg and the knee cap on the other is shattered.

- How could this accident affect you? Apart from suffering severe pain, you are likely to lose money from being off work. In extreme cases you may never be able to work again.

- How could this accident affect your employer? Your employer could be in serious trouble if he or she contributed in any way to the accident by not following regulations. At the very least the employer will lose money while you are off and will be put to a great deal of trouble sorting out the problems.

- How could this accident affect your work mates? If the health and safety inspection which would follow such an accident found other problems, the workshop may be closed down. Your mates might lose their jobs. At the very least they would have to work harder to make up for you being off work.

- How could this accident affect your family? Depending how serious your injuries are, your family may have to look after you for a long time or even for life. The least that will happen is that they will be very upset and put to a great deal of trouble visiting or looking after you.

■   Whose fault was the accident? Not mine! Somebody else's! In the end it can only ever come back to one person. You! The blame could be spread out a bit, the jack should not have been used if it was leaking. Maybe your employer should have noticed this. You should have been trained to use axle stands. Maybe your supervisor should have stopped you. But there is only one person who could have stopped you getting hurt. You!

'It's cool to be smart and safe'

Terminology

HASAW	Health and Safety at Work Act. The Act is designed to make us all aware of workplace dangers
COSHH	Control of Substances Hazardous to Health. This is to ensure that an individual or a company takes responsibility for hazardous substances such as old engine oil or cleaning fluids
EPA	Environmental Protection Act. This Act puts very tight controls on the way a business is allowed to affect the environment
Health and Safety Inspectorate	A government agency who make sure the HASAW is followed
Health and safety audit	An inspection carried out in a workshop, for example, to check for anything which may not comply with regulations
Risk assessment	As part of an inspection you may examine, say, a wheel free ramp. The risks in using this equipment should be assessed and then reduced as much as is reasonably possible
PPE	Personal protective equipment

LEARNING TASKS

➡ Look back at the key words. Explain each one to a friend, and/or write out a short description to keep as evidence.
➡ Make a simple sketch of a workshop and clearly mark possible causes of accidents.

2   Health and safety regulations

What does the Health and Safety at Work Act mean?

The Health and Safety at Work Act 1974 places a strict duty on employers to ensure, so far as is reasonably practicable, safe working conditions and the absence of risks to health in connection with the use, handling, storage and transport of articles and substances.

KEY WORDS

■ Construction and Use Regulations
■ MOT
■ Risk assessment

The Act places a statutory duty on employers to have a declared safety policy for a business in which more than five people are employed.

First a company safety policy must be established and a safety committee formed. The committee should consist of members with specialised knowledge of the risks of a particular area, such as the workshop or offices. The chairperson of the committee should be a senior member of the company.

The Act does not specify what you should do; it merely provides the framework in which you should operate and establishes the Health and

Safety Executive and the Health and Safety Commission. The Act regulates all working methods. Its importance cannot be overemphasised: no working methods may be used that can be seen to be a health or safety hazard to employees.

The Act can be split into two areas.

1. Employers have a duty to safeguard the health, safety and welfare of their employees.

2. Employees have a duty to safeguard themselves and their work mates.

Each of these areas can be briefly summarised as follows; note in each case how you can apply the 'common sense' approach to safety. The employer must provide the following:

- safe place of work with safe access and exits
- safe working environment and appropriate welfare arrangements
- safe systems of work
- safe plant, equipment and tools
- safe methods of storing, handling and moving goods
- a procedure for reporting accidents and an accident book
- a safety policy
- information, instruction, training and supervision where appropriate.

As an employee you must:

- co-operate with your employer to comply with the HASAW
- take care of your own health and safety as well as that of your work mates
- not interfere with or misuse any health and safety items.

Health and Safety Inspectorate

The Health and Safety Inspectorate is a government agency responsible for ensuring that companies comply with the health and safety laws. It has the following tasks:

- to inspect work places to ensure that the HASAW and other safety laws are being observed
- to investigate the causes of serious accidents
- to prosecute anyone found breaking the laws (employer or employee).

The Inspectorate has many powers, including the right to enter your workshop and inspect it to make sure the law is being followed. If any problems are found, the Inspectorate can carry out one or all of the following:

- Issue an improvement notice – this gives the owner of the premises a set time to do something, for example to put up warning notices.
- Issue a prohibition notice – this says that the work being carried out in a particular place must stop until the problem is put right. For example, a ramp may have to be repaired and tested before it is used again.
- Prosecute the person breaking the law – either the employer or the employee. For example, after a serious accident the Inspectorate can take the case to court, where very large fines and/or imprisonment can be the result.

Anybody, including employees, can ask the Inspectorate to look into cases involving the health and safety laws.

Figure 2.2 A motor vehicle workshop

Other safety acts, rules and regulations

The HASAW is the most important Act, but many other rules and regulations affect the workplace. This shows how important the wellbeing of workers is considered to be. You do not have to learn this section off by heart, but you must be aware that a variety of legislation exists. You may see notices displayed in your workshop which relate to some of the items on the following list. You should read these notices.

- The Electricity at Work Regulations
- The Health and Safety (First Aid) Regulations
- Petroleum (Consolidation) Act 1928
- Petroleum (Mixtures) Orders 1929 and 1947
- Weights and Measures Act 1963
- Fire Precautions Act 1971
- Highly Flammable Liquids and Liquefied Petroleum Gases Regulations 1972
- Abrasive Wheel Regulations 1974
- Control of Pollution Act 1974
- Protection of Eyes Regulations 1974
- Health and Safety at Work Act 1974
- Fire Precautions (Factories, Offices, Shops and Railway Premises) Order 1976
- Control of Pollution (Special Wastes) Regulations 1980
- Classification, Packaging and Labelling of Dangerous Substances Regulations 1984
- Road Vehicle Construction and Use Regulations 1986
- Control of Substances Hazardous to Health (COSHH) Regulations 1988
- Environment Protection Act 1990
- Management of Health and Safety at Work Regulations 1992
- Provision and Use of Work Equipment Regulations 1992

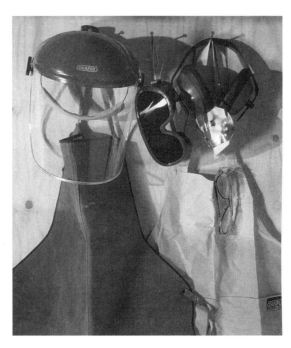

Figure 2.3 Personal protective equipment (PPE)

- Personal Protection Equipment at Work (PPE) Regulations 1992
- Manual Handling Operation Regulations 1992
- Workplace (Health, Safety and Welfare) Regulations 1992.

The HASAW is the most important Act, as it places duties on the employer and employee. However, you can check details of any of the others in your local library. They do make rather heavy reading though, so if you are in any doubt, ask your supervisor or teacher.

Personal protective equipment (PPE)

Personal protective equipment, such as safety clothing, is very important. Some people think it clever or tough not to use protection. They are very likely to die or be injured long before you! Some risks are obvious: you could burn or cut yourself when holding a hot or sharp exhaust! Other things, such as breathing in brake dust or working in a noisy area, do not produce immediately noticeable effects but could affect you later in life.

Fortunately the risks to workers are now quite well understood and we can protect ourselves before it is too late. In the following table I have listed a number of items classed as PPE (personal protective equipment) together with suggested uses. You will see that the use of most items is plain common sense. Where a hazard has been identified, your employer should by law supply suitable equipment.

Equipment	Notes	Example uses
Ear defenders	Must meet appropriate standards	When working in noisy areas or if using an air chisel
Face mask	For individual personal use only	Dusty conditions. When cleaning brakes or if preparing bodywork
High visibility clothing	Fluorescent colours such as yellow or orange	Working in traffic, e.g. to attend a breakdown

Equipment	Notes	Example uses
Leather apron	Should be replaced if it is holed or worn thin	When welding or working with very hot items
Leather gloves	Should be replaced when they become holed or worn thin	When welding or working with very hot items and also if handling sharp metalwork
Life jacket	Must meet current standards	Use when attending vehicle breakdowns on ferries!
Overalls	Should be kept clean and be flame proof if used for welding	These should be worn at all times to protect your clothes and skin. If you get too hot, just wear shorts and a T-shirt underneath
Rubber or plastic apron	Replace if holed	Use if you do a lot of work with battery acid or with strong solvents
Rubber or plastic gloves	Replace if holed	Gloves must always be used when using degreasing equipment
Safety shoes or boots	Strong toe caps are recommended	Working in any workshop with heavy equipment
Safety goggles	Keep the lenses clean	Always use goggles when grinding or when any risk of eye contamination. Cheap plastic goggles are much easier to come by than new eyes!
Safety helmet	Must be to current standards	For some types of under vehicle work
Welding goggles or welding mask	Check the goggles are suitable for the type of welding. Gas welding goggles are *not* good enough when arc welding	You should wear welding goggles or use a mask even if you are only assisting by holding something

Good working practice – identifying and reducing hazards

Working in a motor vehicle workshop is a dangerous occupation if you do not take care. If you're aware of the hazards, it is easy to avoid the danger. The hazards in a workshop are from two particular sources; firstly from you, such as caused by:

- carelessness – particularly whilst moving vehicles
- drinking or taking drugs – these badly affect your ability to react to dangerous situations
- tiredness or sickness – these will affect your abilities to think and work safely
- messing about – most accidents are caused by people fooling about
- not using safety equipment – you have a duty to yourself and others to use safety equipment
- inexperience – or lack of supervision. If in doubt, ask.

The second source of hazards are the surroundings in which you work. They may have:

- bad ventilation
- poor lighting
- noise
- dangerous substances stored incorrectly
- broken or worn tools and equipment
- faulty machinery

- slippery floors
- untidy benches and floors
- unguarded machinery
- unguarded pits.

The following table lists some of the hazards you will come across in a vehicle workshop. Also listed are the risks of these hazards and ways we can reduce the risks. This is called risk assessment.

Hazard	Risk	Action
Power tools	Damage to the vehicle or personal injury	Understand how to use the equipment and wear suitable protective clothing, for example gloves and goggles
Working under a car on the ramp	The vehicle could roll or be driven off the end	Ensure you use wheel chocks
	You can bang your head on hard or sharp objects when working under the car	Set the ramp at the best working height, wear protection if appropriate
Working under a car on a jack	The vehicle could fall on top of you	The correct axle stands should be used and positioned in a secure place
Compressed air	Damage to sensitive organs such as ears or eyes. Death, if air is forced through the skin into your blood stream	Do not fool around with compressed air. A safety nozzle prevents excessive air forces
Dirty hands and skin	Oil, petrol, diesel and other contaminants can cause serious health problems. This can range from dermatitis to skin cancer	Use a good quality barrier cream and wash you hands regularly. Do not allow dirt to transfer to other parts of your body. Good overalls should be worn at all times and in some cases gloves
Exhaust fumes	Poisonous gases such as carbon monoxide can kill. The other gases can cause cancer or at best restrict breathing and cause sore throats	Only allow running engines in very well ventilated areas or use an exhaust extraction system
Engine crane	Injury or damage can be caused if the engine swings and falls off	Ensure the crane is strong enough (do not exceed its safe working load, SWL). Secure the engine with good quality sling straps and keep the engine near to the floor when moving across the workshop
Cleaning brakes	Brake dust (especially from older types made of asbestos) is dangerous to health	Only wash clean with proper brake cleaner
Petrol	Fire or explosion	Keep all petrol away from sources of ignition. Do not smoke when working on a vehicle
Degreaser	Damage to skin or damage to sensitive components	Wear proper gloves and make sure the solvent will not affect the items you are washing
Spillage such as oil	Easy to slip, fall and be injured	Clean up spills as they happen and use absorbent granules
Battery electrolyte (acid)	Dangerous on your skin and in particular your eyes. It will also rot your clothes	Wear protective clothing and take extreme care

Hazard	Risk	Action
Welding a vehicle	The obvious risk is fire, but electric welders such as a MIG welder can damage sensitive electronic systems	Have fire extinguishers handy, remove combustible materials such as carpets and ensure petrol pipes are nowhere near. The battery earth lead must also be disconnected
Electric hand tools	The same risk as power tools but also the danger of electric shocks. particularly in damp or wet conditions. This can be fatal	Do not use electric tools in damp or wet conditions. Electrical equipment should be inspected regularly by a competent person
Driving over a pit	Driving into the pit	The pit should be covered; or get a friend to guide you and drive very slowly
Broken tools	Personal injury or damage to the car. For example a file without a handle can stab into your wrist. A faulty ratchet could slip	All tools should be kept in good order at all times. This will also make the work easier

Moving loads Injuries in a workshop are often due to incorrect lifting or moving of heavy loads. Heavy and large components (e.g. engines and gearboxes) can cause injury when being removed and refitted. A few simple precautions will prevent you from injuring yourself, or others.

- Never try to lift anything beyond your capability – get a mate to help. How much you can safely lift will vary, but always get help if lifting heavy or difficult loads.
- Whenever possible use an engine hoist, a transmission jack or a trolley.
- Lift correctly, using your legs, and keep your back straight.
- When moving heavy loads on a trolley, get help and position yourself so you will not be run over if you lose control.
- The best option in all cases is simply to avoid manual handling where possible.

Figure 2.4 Engine crane and other lifting equipment

Vehicle safety Vehicle safety and the associated regulations can be very complicated. However, for our purposes we can consider the issue across two main areas, construction and use of the vehicle.

Construction of the vehicle

Before a vehicle can be constructed a prototype has to be submitted for type

Figure 2.5 Vehicles must be in a safe condition to be used on the road

approval. This means the vehicle has to pass very stringent tests and that it has to meet all current safety requirements. Different countries have different systems, so some modifications to a car may be necessary if it is to be imported or exported. The European Union (EU) has published many 'directives' which each member country must incorporate into its own legislation. This has helped to standardise many aspects. In the UK the Road Vehicles Construction and Use Regulations 1986 ensure certain standards are met. If you become involved in modifying a vehicle, e.g. for import, you may need to refer to the details of these regulations.

Many other laws exist relating to the motor vehicle and the environment. These are about emissions and pollution. Environmental laws change quite often, so it is important to keep up to date.

The Department of Transport states that all vehicles over three years old must undergo an annual safety check to ensure they comply with the current legislation. First set up by the Ministry of Transport, it continues to be known as the MOT test. It now includes checks relating to environmental laws.

Driving and operating the vehicle

To drive a vehicle on the road you must have an appropriate driving licence and insurance; the vehicle must be taxed (or have trade plates fitted) and must be in safe working order. The highway code must be observed.

LEARNING TASKS

➡ Look back at the key words. Explain each one to a friend, and/or write out a short description to keep as evidence.

➡ Read the important parts of any notices in your workshop.

➡ Write a short explanation about how to lift and carry an engine weighing 50 kg.

➡ Write a short explanation about the safety aspects of changing brake shoes.

3   Look after yourself, your workshop and your work mates

Safety procedures

In this section you will learn how you can 'contribute to the limitation of damage to persons or property in the event of an accident or emergency'. When you know the set procedures to be followed, it is easier to look after yourself, your workshop and your work mates. You need to:

■ know who does what during an emergency.

■ know the fire procedure for your workplace, the different types of fire extinguisher and their uses

■ know who is responsible for keeping the accident book and the procedure for reporting an accident.

The rest of this section examines these points in more detail.

When things do go wrong!

If an accident does occur in your workplace the first bit of advice is 'Keep calm and don't panic'! The HASAW states that for companies above a certain size:

■ first aid equipment must be available

■ employers should display simple first aid instructions

■ fully trained first aiders must be employed.

Figure 2.6 Make sure you know what to do in case of an accident such as electric shock

You need to know where first aid equipment is located in your workplace, familiarise yourself with the first aid instructions and know who to ask for help. The following table shows how to react if a serious accident occurs.

Action	Notes
Assess the situation	Stay calm, it's important to take a few seconds to think
Remove the danger	If the person was working with a machine, turn it off. If someone is electrocuted, switch off the power before you hurt yourself. Even if you are unable to help with the injury, you can stop it getting worse
Get help	If you are not trained in first aid, get someone who is and/or phone for an ambulance
Stay with the casualty	If you can do nothing else, the casualty can be helped if you stay with him or her. Also say that help is on its way and be ready to assist. You may need to guide the ambulance
Report the accident	All accidents must be reported. Your company is legally bound to have an accident book, so that steps can be taken to prevent the accident happening again. Also, if the injured person claims compensation, a record of the accident exists – no one can deny it happened!
Learn first aid	If you are in a very small company why not get trained now, before the accident?

Fire! Accidents involving fire are very serious. First of all call the fire brigade or get somebody else to do it; do not assume it has been done. Then:

- get safe yourself and shout 'FIRE!'
- help others to get safe
- only fight the fire if it does not put you or others at risk.

'It's easy to rebuild a car or a workshop – it's not easy to rebuild you'

Of course it's far better not to let a fire start in the first place! Three things start a fire and keep it burning:

- Fuel – this can range from the obvious such as petrol to piles of rubbish or a car interior.
- Heat – a match or lighter, a spark from a cigarette or heat from a welding torch. Also electrical sparks or a spark caused by dropping a steel object.
- Oxygen – the air contains about 20% oxygen.

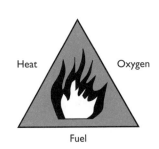

Figure 2.7 The fire triangle

These are often called the fire triangle. Unless all three are present, a fire will not start or burn. There are two lessons to be learnt here: how to prevent the fire (best option) and how to put out a fire. To prevent the fire you must never allow all three things to come together. Any two – such as a welding torch held in the air, or petrol spilt on a cold floor – do not cause a problem. The welding torch next to the spilt petrol, on the other hand, would cause a fire!

In the event of a fire your workplace should have a set procedure, so that you know:

1. how the alarm is raised
2. what the alarm sounds like
3. what to do when you hear the alarm
4. your escape route from the building
5. where to assemble
6. who is responsible for calling the fire brigade.

If it is safe to do so, you should try and put out a small fire. Extinguishers and a fire blanket should be provided. Remember: the object is to remove one side of the 'triangle', and the fire will go out. But this is not quite as obvious as it first seems. If you put enough water on a fire, it will cool down and go out. However, spraying water on an electrical circuit could kill you!

Figure 2.8 Different types of fire extinguishers

Spraying water on a petrol fire could spread it about and make the problem far worse. This means that a number of different fire extinguishers are needed. These are colour coded to allow easy recognition and are listed in the following table.

Colour	Type	How it works	Used on	DANGER
Red	Water	Removes the heat	Wood, paper, fabrics etc	Do not use on electrical or flammable liquid fires
Black	Carbon dioxide (CO_2)	Removes the oxygen	Electrical or flammable liquid fires	
Green	Vaporising liquid (Halon BCF)	Removes the oxygen	Electrical or flammable liquid fires	
Blue	Dry powder	Removes the oxygen and some heat	All fires, in particular flammable liquids and gases	
Cream	Foam	Removes the oxygen and some heat	Flammable liquids	Do not use on electrical fires
Red blanket	Fire proof blanket	Smothers the fire	Smother a fire such as a person's clothes	

All extinguishers have instructions written on them. Read them now before it is too late! European regulations are set to make all fire extinguishers green with coloured bands but the colours will be the same.

Reporting requirements

All accidents must be reported, and your company is legally bound to have an accident book. Accidents do not have to involve injury. If you report that a leaking jack seal caused a car to fall, even if no harm was done, you could prevent another, potentially serious, accident. The book allows a record to be kept so that steps can be taken to prevent the accident happening again. All accidents, no matter how small, should be reported. Even a scratch can become infected and become more serious, but you should use your common sense.

If an injured person claims compensation at some future time, the accident book provides a record of what happened. The book should be kept by a responsible person.

LEARNING TASKS

➡ Look back at the key words. Explain each one to a friend, and/or write out a short description to keep as evidence.

➡ Examine your workshop and look for ways in which fires could start. Where are the exits, the alarm and the extinguishers? Make a simple sketch of what you find.

➡ Write short notes to explain how to reduce the risk of fire in a workshop.

4   Looking after the workshop and equipment

Keep it clean   There are three main reasons for keeping your workshop and equipment clean and tidy:

1. It makes it a safer place to work.

2. It makes it a better place to work.

3. It gives a better image to your customers.

Servicing and fixing motor vehicles can be a dirty job. But if you clean up after any dirty job, your workshop is a much more pleasant place to work. The HASAW Act makes the employer provide a safe and clean place of work. Further requirements are contained in the Factories Act.

■ The workshop and floor should be uncluttered and clean to prevent accidents and fires as well as maintaining the general appearance.

■ Your workspace reflects your ability as a technician. A tidy workspace equals a tidy mind, equals a tidy job, equals a tidy wage when you are qualified.

■ Hand tools should be kept clean as you are working. Your tools are expensive – look after them and they will look after you.

■ Large equipment should only be cleaned by a trained person or a person under supervision. Obvious precautions are to ensure equipment cannot be operated while you are working on it and to use only appropriate cleaning methods. For example, would you use a bucket of water or a brush to clean down an electric pillar drill? I hope you answered 'the brush'!

Cleaning materials   In motor vehicle workshops many different cleaning operations are carried out. This means a number of different materials are required. I have split the materials into three different types. The manufacturer's instructions printed on the container must be followed at all times.

Figure 2.9 Cleaning materials

Material	Purpose	Notes
Detergents	Mixed with water for washing vehicles etc. Also used in steam cleaners for engine washing etc	Some industrial detergents are very strong and should not be allowed to come into contact with your skin
Solvents	To wash away and dissolve grease and oil etc. The best example is the liquid in the degreaser or parts washer which all workshops will have	**Never** use solvents such as thinners or petrol because they are highly inflammable. Suitable PPE should be used, for example gloves etc
Absorbent granules	To mop up oil and other types of spills. They soak up the spillage after a short time and can then be swept up	Most granules are a chalk or clay type material which has been dried out

Some extra notes about solvents:

- They may attack your skin.
- Many are flammable.
- The vapour given off can be dangerous.
- They may cause serious problems if splashed into eyes.
- Take extra care.
- Read the label.

The COSHH (Control of Substances Hazardous to Health) Regulations say that all materials should carry a description of how to use them and that the dangers should also be spelled out on the packaging. You should not use any cleaning materials unless trained.

Safety regulations and warning signs

Regulations, in particular the HASAW Act, were covered in some detail earlier. Try to remember the following:

- identify hazards
- remove them, or
- reduce the risk as much as possible and bring the hazard to everyone's attention.

This is normally done by using signs or markings. There is a standard system of signs used to mark hazards. This consists of three types of signs:

Danger warning

Instructions

Directions

Figure 2.10 Examples of warning signs

Function	Notes	Background colour	Foreground colour
Danger warning	E.g. open pit or fire risk	Yellow	Black
Instructions	E.g. use safety goggles when operating this machine	Blue	White
Directions	Escape routes or location of safety equipment such as first aid	Green	White

Disposing of hazardous materials and environmental protection

Protecting the environment is an important aspect of our work that is now backed up by regulations. In a workshop these regulations relate mostly to engine oil and solvents used for cleaning or painting:

1. Disposal methods must not breach current regulations.
2. Use of solvents should be kept to a minimum.
3. Gaseous emissions should be kept to a minimum.

You and your employer are responsible for your waste. It is no longer acceptable to just dump things. Only licenced contractors can dispose of certain materials. Failure to comply can mean heavy fines or even prison.

LEARNING TASKS

➡ Look back at the key words. Explain each one to a friend, and/or write out a short description to keep as evidence.

➡ Examine a workshop and make a note of the different cleaning materials.

➡ Write a short explanation about how to dispose of waste oil.

3 Nuts and bolts – tools and equipment

1 Introduction

Start here!

KEY WORDS

■ All words in the table

This chapter is really about joining things together. The correct methods of joining must be used in the construction and repair of a modern motor vehicle. Joining can cover many aspects, ranging from simple nuts and bolts to very modern and sophisticated adhesives.

The choice of a joining method for a repair will depend on the original method used as well as consideration of the cost and strength required.

Joining method	Example	Notes
Pins, dowels and keys	Clutch pressure plate to the flywheel	Used for strength and alignment in conjunction with nuts or bolts in most cases
Riveting	Some brake shoe linings	This involves metal pegs which are deformed to make the joint
Compression fitting	Wheel bearings	Often also called an interference fit. The part to be fitted is slightly too large or small as appropriate. Pressure has to be used to make it fit
Shrinking	Flywheel ring gear	The ring gear is heated to make it expand and is then fitted in position. As it cools it contracts and holds firmly in place
Adhesives	Body panels and sound deadening	Adhesive, or glue, is now very popular as it is often cheap, quick, easy and waterproof. Also, when two items are bonded together, the whole structure becomes stronger
Nuts, screws, washers and bolts	Just about everything!	Metric sizes are now most common, but many other sizes and thread patterns are available. This is a very convenient and strong fixing method
Welding	Exhaust pipes and boxes	There are several methods of welding, oxy-acetylene and MIG being the most common. The parts to be joined are melted so they mix together and then set in position
Brazing	Some body panels	Brazing involves using high temperatures to melt brass which forms the join between two metal components
Soldering	Electrical connections	Solder is made from lead and tin. It is melted with an electric iron to make it flow into the joint
Clips, clamps and ties	Hoses cables etc	Hose clips, for example, are designed to secure a hose to say the radiator and prevent it from leaking

2 Joining methods

Introduction

Methods of joining are described as permanent (e.g. welding) or non-permanent (e.g. nuts and bolts). The difference is that the permanent methods would cause some damage if the joint had to be undone.

Nuts, bolts and locking devices

The nut and bolt is by far the most common method of joining two components together. Figure 3.1 shows examples of screws, bolts and nuts. The head of the bolt is usually a hexagon, Allen socket or a Torx® drive. Smaller bolts can also have a screwdriver type head, namely a slot, cross or Pozidrive.

KEY WORDS

- Interference fit
- MIG, OA, MAG, MMA
- Wetting
- Heat sink
- Metric thread

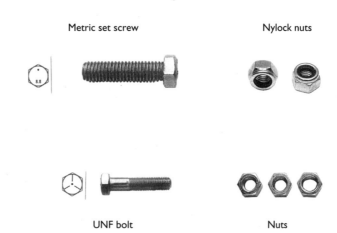

Metric set screw   Nylock nuts

UNF bolt   Nuts

Figure 3.1 Examples of screws, bolts and nuts

The material used to make a nut or bolt depends on the application. For example, sump bolts will be basic mild steel, whereas the long through bolts on a Rover K series engine are made from quite sophisticated high tensile steel.

The size of the nut and bolt will, of course, depend on the size of components to be secured. Thread sizes used to be a problem, but now most nuts and bolts are metric. Figure 3.2 shows a metric thread profile. Metric nuts and bolts are described as follows:

M10 × 1.5

The M means metric, the 10 means the bolt diameter and the 1.5 is the pitch of the thread. Be careful, though – you can get coarse or fine threads (different pitch) metric bolts, as well as older types such as AF or Whitworth.

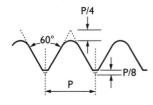

Figure 3.2 Metric thread profile

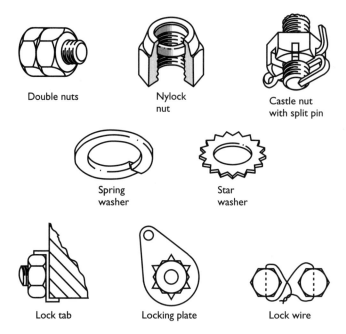

Figure 3.3 Various locking devices

When joining with nuts and bolts, flat washers and in many cases some type of locking device are commonly used. In fact, metric threads are quite good at locking in position as they are, but extra devices are often used for safety. Vibration is the main cause of bolts coming loose. Of course they should always be tightened to the correct torque in the first place! Figure 3.3 shows a selection of locking devices.

Another common method of securing threads is to use a locking compound such as 'Loctite'. This is in effect an adhesive which sticks the threads together. When the correct compound is applied with care, it is a very secure way of preventing important components from working loose.

Adhesives A very wide range of adhesives is used in today's automotive industry. The number of applications is increasing constantly, replacing older methods such as welding. There are too many types of adhesives to cover here, but most of the basic requirements are the same. Manufacturers' instructions must **always** be followed because:

- many adhesives give off toxic fumes and must be used with care
- most types are highly flammable
- adhesives are often designed for a specific application.

Adhesives also have a number of important terms associated with them:

- cleanliness – surfaces to be joined must be clean
- cure – the process of setting often described as 'going off'
- wetting – this means that the adhesive spreads evenly and fully over the surface
- thermo-setting – meaning that heat is required to cure the adhesive
- thermo-plastic – melts when heated
- contact adhesive – makes a strong joint as soon as contact is made
- 'super glue' – cyanoacrilate adhesive which bonds suitable materials in seconds, including skin – take care!

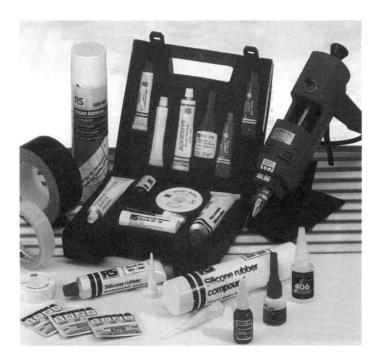

Figure 3.4 Examples of adhesives

Adhesives have many advantages, which is why they are becoming more widely used:

- even stress distribution over the whole surface
- waterproof
- good for joining delicate materials
- no distortion when joining
- a wide variety of materials can be joined
- neat, clean join can be made with little practice.

Always choose the correct type of adhesive for the job in hand. For example, an adhesive designed to bond plastic will not work when joining rubber to metal. And don't forget: if the surfaces to be joined are not clean, you will make a very good job of bonding dirt to dirt instead of what you intended!

Soldering   Soft soldering is a process used to join materials such as steel, brass, tin or copper. It involves melting a mixture of lead and tin to act as the bond. A common example of a soldered joint is the electrical connection between the stator and diode pack in an alternator. Figure 3.5 shows this process using the most common heat source, which is an electric soldering iron.

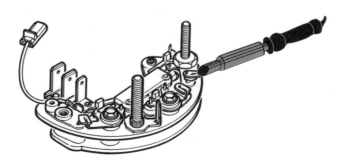

Figure 3.5 Soldering a diode pack in an alternator

The process of soldering is as follows:

1. Prepare the surfaces to be joined by cleaning and using emery cloth or wire wool as appropriate.
2. Add a flux to prevent the surfaces becoming dirty with oxide when heated, or use a solder with a flux core.
3. Apply heat to the joint and add solder so it runs into the joint.
4. Complete the process as quickly as possible to prevent heat damage.
5. Use a heat sink if necessary.

Like many other methods, soldering is easy after a bit of practice. Take time to do this in your workshop. Note that some materials such as aluminium cannot be soldered by ordinary methods.

Brazing

Brazing is a similar process to soldering, but a higher temperature is needed and a different filler is used. The materials to be joined are heated to red heat and the filler rod (bronze brass or similar), after being dipped in flux, is applied to the joint. The heat from the materials is enough to melt the rod, which flows into the gap and makes a good strong, but slightly flexible joint.

Brazing is only used on a few areas of the vehicle body. Less heat is required than for fusion welding (see next section). Dissimilar metals such as brass and steel can also be joined.

Welding

Welding is a method of joining metals by applying heat, in some cases combined with pressure. A filler rod of a similar metal is often used. The welding process joins metals by melting them, fusing the melted areas and then solidifying the joined area to form a very strong bond. Welding technology is widely used in the automotive industry.

The principal processes used today are gas and arc welding, in which the heat from a gas flame or an electric arc melts the faces to be joined. Figure 3.6 shows a welding process in action.

Several welding processes are used:

■ Gas welding uses a mixture of acetylene and oxygen which burns at a very high temperature. This is used to melt the host metal with the addition of a filler rod if required (OA or oxy-acetylene).

Figure 3.6 Welding process in action

■ Shielded metal-arc welding uses an electric arc between an electrode and the work to be joined; the electrode has a coating that decomposes to protect the weld area from contamination and the rod melts to form filler metal (MMA or manual metal arc).

■ Gas-shielded arc welding produces a welded joint under a protective gas (MIG or metal inert gas).

■ Arc welding produces a welded joint within an active gas (MAG or metal active gas).

■ Resistance welding is a method in which the weld is formed by a combination of pressure and resistance heating from an electric current (spot welding).

■ Other, specialised types of welding include laser-beam welding, which makes use of the intensive heat produced by a light beam to melt and join the metals, and ultrasonic welding; this creates a bond by applying high-frequency vibration while the parts to be joined are held under pressure.

Shrinking

When parts have to be fitted by shrinking, they first have to be heated so they expand, or cooled so they contract. In both cases the component to be fitted must be made to an exact size. If parts fitted in this way are to be removed, they are usually destroyed in the process. For example, a flywheel ring gear has to be cut through with a hacksaw to remove it.

For a hot shrink fitting the part will have a smaller internal diameter than the one on which it is to be fitted. It is important not to overheat the components, otherwise damage will occur. An oven is best, but a welding torch may be used with great care. When the component has been heated and has therefore expanded, it is placed in position at once. It will then cool and make a good tight joint.

Figure 3.7 The hot shrinking process: ring gear and flywheel

Cold shrinking is very similar, except the component to be fitted is made very slightly larger than the hole in which it is to be fitted. A cylinder head valve insert is one example. The process is the opposite of hot shrinking. The component is cooled so it contracts, after which it is placed in position where it warms back up and expands, making a secure joint. Cold shrinking is normally a specialist job, but it is possible to buy aerosols of carbon dioxide under pressure which can be used to make a component very cold (dry ice).

Compression fitting

Many parts are fitted by compression or pressure. Bearings are the most common example. The key to compression fitting is an interference fit. This means that the component, say a bearing, is very slightly larger than the hole in which it is to be fitted. Pressure is therefore used to force the bearing onto place. Suspension bushes are often also fitted in this way.

The secret is to apply the force in a way which does not make the components go together on an angle. They must be fitted true to each other. Figure 3.8 on page 30 shows a wheel bearing being fitted.

Riveting

Riveting is a method of joining metal plates, fabric to metal or brake linings to the shoes. A rivet, a metal pin with a head at one end, is inserted into matching holes in two overlapping parts. The other end is struck and formed into another head, holding the parts together. This is the basic principle of riveting, but many variations are possible.

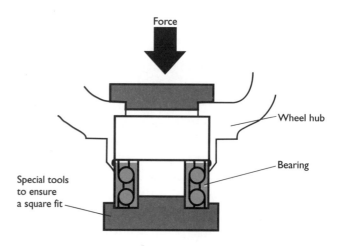

Figure 3.8 Compression fitting a wheel bearing

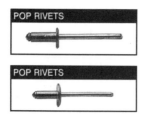

Figure 3.9 Different types of rivets

Figure 3.9 shows two different pop rivets, one of the most common types of rivets for motor vehicle use. These are hollow rivets which are already mounted on to a steel pin. The rivet is placed through the holes in the parts to be joined. Then a special rivet gun grips the pin and pulls it with great force. This causes the second rivet head to be formed. When the pin reaches a set tension it breaks off, leaving the rivet securely in place. The great advantage of this method is that you can work 'blind' – you don't need access to the other side of the hole!

LEARNING TASKS

➡ Look back at the key words. Explain each one to a friend, and/or write out a short description to keep as evidence.

➡ Examine a real system and make a simple sketch to show five different joining methods. Label the main parts of each.

➡ Make two lists of joining methods, one for permanent and the other for non-permanent techniques.

3   Preventing leaks

Gaskets

KEY WORDS

■ Gasket
■ Instant gasket
■ Oil seal

Gaskets are used to make a fluid- or pressure-tight seal between two component faces. The best example of this is the cylinder head gasket, which also has to withstand very high pressures and temperatures. Gaskets are often used to make up for less than perfect surfaces and therefore act as a seal between the two. Also, as the temperature changes, the gasket can take up the difference in expansion between the two components.

Gaskets are made from different materials depending on the task they have to perform.

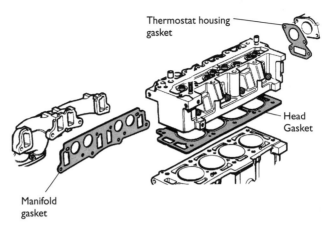

Thermostat housing gasket

Head Gasket

Manifold gasket

Figure 3.10 Cylinder head and other types of gaskets

Gasket material	Examples of where used
Paper or card	General purpose such as thermostat housings
Fibre	General purpose
Cork	Earlier type rocker covers
Rubber – often synthetic	Water pump sealing ring
Plastics – various types	Fuel pump to engine block
Copper asbestos or similar	Exhaust flange: note safety issues of asbestos
Copper and aluminium	Head gaskets
Metal and fibre compounds with metal composites	Head gaskets

The general rules for obtaining a good joint, with a gasket or otherwise, are as follows:

- cleanliness of the surfaces to be joined
- removal of burrs from the materials
- use of the correct materials
- follow manufacturers' instructions (such as tighten to the correct torque in the correct sequence)
- safe working (as always!).

Sealants

Many manufacturers are now specifying the use of sealants in place of traditional gaskets. The main reason for this is a better quality of joint. Liquid sealants, often known as instant gasket, are a type of liquid rubber which forms into a perfect gasket as the surfaces are mated together. The three major advantages of this technique are:

- easier to apply
- a perfect seal is made with very little space being taken up
- adhesive bonding effect reduces fretting due to vibration and hence is less likely to leak.

Figure 3.11 shows a sealant being applied. A major advantage for the repair trade is that a good selection of jointing sealants means you can manufacture a gasket on the spot at any time! Note the manufacturers' recommendations, however, as only the correct material must be used.

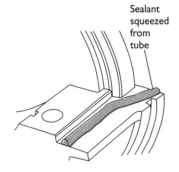

Sealant squeezed from tube

Figure 3.11 Liquid sealant being applied

Oil seals

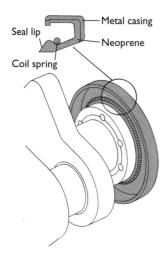

Seal lip
Metal casing
Neoprene
Coil spring

Figure 3.12 Radial lip oil seal

The most common type of oil seal is the neoprene (synthetic rubber) radial lip seal. The seal is fitted into a recess and the soft lip rubs against the rotating component. The lip is held in place by a spring. Figure 3.12 shows this type of seal; note how the lip faces the oil so that any pressure will cause the lip to fit more tightly rather than allow oil to be forced underneath. Figure 3.13 shows a valve stem oil seal, which prevents oil entering the combustion chamber past the inlet valves.

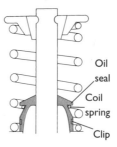

Oil seal
Coil spring
Clip

Figure 3.13 Valve stem oil seal

LEARNING TASKS

➡ Look back at the key words. Explain each one to a friend, and/or write out a short description to keep as evidence

➡ Make a simple sketch to show a radial lip type of oil seal.

➡ Examine a real system and note where different types of gaskets are used. Can you say why a particular type is employed?

4 Tools and equipment

Equipment

Your work largely consists of removing, refitting and adjusting components to ensure the vehicle system operates within specification. To do this you will use a variety of tools and equipment:

■ measuring equipment – such as a micrometer

■ hand instruments – such as a spring balance

■ electrical meters – such as a multimeter.

The use, care, calibration and storage of this equipment will vary with different types. Always read the manufacturers' instructions carefully before use, or if you have a problem. Here are some general guidelines:

■ Follow manufacturers' instructions.

■ Handle with care – do not drop; keep the instrument in its box.

■ Ensure regular calibration – check for accuracy.

■ Understand how to interpret results – if in doubt ask!

Hand tools

Using hand tools is something you will learn by experience, but an important first step is to understand the purpose of the common types. This section therefore starts by listing some of the more popular tools, with examples of

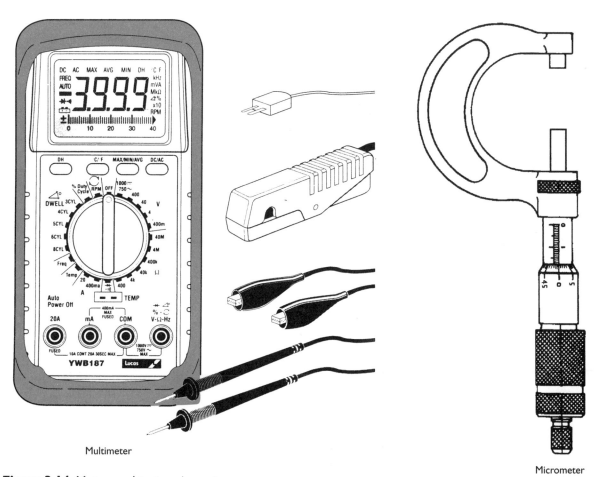

Multimeter

Micrometer

Figure 3.14 Meters and test equipment

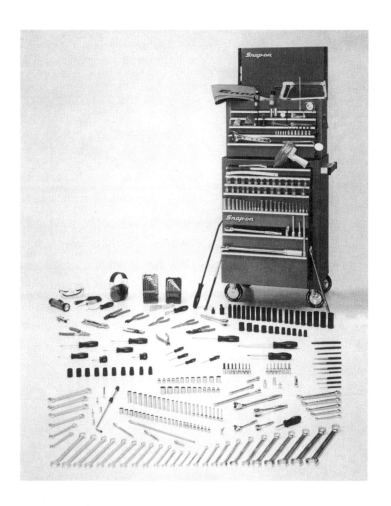

Figure 3.15 A selection of hand tools

their use, and ends with some general advice and instructions. Practise until you understand the use and purpose of the following tools when working on vehicles:

Hand tool	Uses and/or notes
Adjustable spanners	An ideal stand-by tool and useful for holding one end of a nut and bolt
Open-ended spanners	Use for nuts and bolts where access is limited or a ring spanner can't be used
Ring spanners	The best tool for holding hexagon bolts or nuts. If fitted correctly, it will not slip and damage either you or the bolt head
Torque wrenches	Essential for correct tightening of fixings. Most wrenches can be set to 'click' when the required torque has been reached. Many fitters think it is clever not to use a torque wrench. Good technicians realise the benefits
Socket wrenches	Often contain a ratchet to make operation far easier
Hexagon socket spanners	Sockets are ideal for many jobs where a spanner can't be used. A socket is often quicker and easier than a spanner. Extensions and swivel joints are also available to help reach awkward bolts
Air wrenches	These are often referred to as wheel guns. Air driven tools are great for speeding up your work; but they are very powerful, so it is easy to damage components. Only special, extra strong, high quality sockets should be used
Blade screwdrivers	Simple common screw heads. Use the correct size!
Pozidrive and cross-head screwdrivers	Better grip, particularly with the Pozidrive. But learn not to confuse the two very similar types. The wrong type will slip and damage will occur
Torx®	Similar to a hexagon tool like an Allen key but with further flutes cut in the side. It can transmit good torque
Special purpose wrenches	Many different types are available. Mole grips, for example, are very useful tools: they hold like pliers but can lock in position
Pliers	These are used for gripping and pulling or bending. They are available in a wide variety of sizes: from snipe nose for electrical work to engineers' pliers for larger jobs such as fitting split pins
Levers	Used to apply a very large force to a small area. Incorrectly applied, it is easy to damage a component
Hammers	Everybody's favourite tool! Anybody can hit with a hammer, but how hard and exactly where is a great skill to learn!

General advice and instructions for the use of hand tools:

- Only use a tool for its intended purpose.
- Always use the correct size tool for the job you are doing.
- Whenever possible, pull a wrench rather than pushing.
- Do not use a file or similar without a handle.
- Keep all tools clean and replace them in a suitable box or cabinet.
- Do not use a screwdriver as a pry bar.
- Look after your tools and they will look after you!

LEARNING TASKS

➡ Look back at the key words. Explain each one to a friend, and/or write out a short description to keep as evidence.

➡ Make a simple sketch to show how a torque wrench should be used.

➡ Read about the different types of tools available in a catalogue. Note the prices and consider the advantages compared to the cost.

4 Vehicle layouts

1 Introduction

Start here! This chapter is a general introduction to the car as a whole. Over the years many unusual designs have been tried, some with more success than others. The most common is, of course, a rectangular vehicle with a wheel at each corner! 'Light vehicles' fall in one of five groups:

1. front engine driving the front wheels
2. front engine driving the rear wheels
3. front engine driving all four wheels
4. rear engine driving the rear wheels
5. mid engine driving the rear wheels.

The most common layout these days is the front engine, front wheel drive vehicle. This will be examined in more detail in a later section.

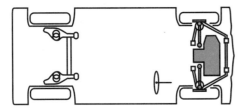

Figure 4.1 Front engine driving the front wheels

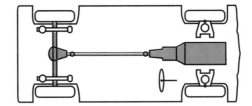

Figure 4.2 Front engine driving the rear wheels

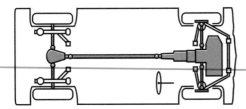

Figure 4.3 Front engine driving all four wheels

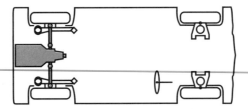

Figure 4.4 Rear engine driving the rear wheels

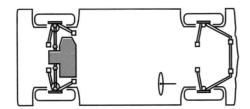

Figure 4.5 Mid engine driving the rear wheels

Terminology

FWD	Front wheel drive
RWD	Rear wheel drive
AWD	All wheel drive
4WD	Four wheel drive
Light vehicle	Normally classified as a car or van of less than three tonnes
Light vehicle types	These range from small two seater sports cars to quite large people carriers (such as the Ford Galaxy). Also included are light commercial vehicles such as vans and pick-up trucks.
Vehicle systems	A set of related components on the vehicle. For example, all components used to make the brakes work are described simply as the 'braking system'. Most vehicle systems are covered in some detail in this book as separate chapters

A bit of history!   As you learn more about the fascinating world of the motor car, you will keep meeting 'new' technologies. I have included a list of events and dates for you to see that some new ideas are not as 'new' as you first thought! You don't need to learn this bit, it is for interest only.

1769	Cugnot built a steam tractor in France.
1801	Trevithick built a steam coach.
1860	Lenoir built an internal combustion gas engine.
1876	Otto improved the gas engine.
1885	Daimler developed a petrol engine and fitted it to a bicycle.
1885	Benz fitted his petrol engine to a three wheeled carriage.
1886	Daimler fitted his engine to a four wheeled carriage to produce a four wheeled motorcar.
1891	Panhard and Levassor started the present design of cars by putting the engine in front.
1896	Lanchester introduced epicyclic gearing now used in automatic transmission.
1899	Jenatzy broke the 100 kph barrier in an electric car.
1901	The first Mercedes took to the roads.
1904	Rigolly broke the 100 mph barrier.
1906	Rolls-Royce introduced the Silver Ghost.

Figure 4.6 A very old vehicle

1908	Ford used an assembly line production to manufacture the Model T.
1911	Cadillac introduced the electric starter and dynamo lighting.
1913	Ford introduced the moving conveyor belt to the assembly line.
1920	Duesenberg began fitting four wheel hydraulic brakes.
1922	Lancia used a unitary (all in one) chassis construction and independent front suspension.
1927	Segrave broke the 200 mph barrier in a Sunbeam.
1928	Cadillac introduced the synchromesh gearbox.
1934	Citroën pioneered front wheel drive in their 7CV model.
1938	Germany produced the Volkswagen Beetle.
1948	Jaguar launched the XK120 sports car and Michelin introduced a radial ply tyre.
1950	Dunlop announced the disc brake.
1951	Buick and Chrysler introduced power steering.
1952	Rover's gas turbine car set a speed record of 243 kph.
1954	Bosch introduced fuel injection for cars.
1955	Citroën introduced a car with hydropneumatic suspension.
1957	Wankel built his first rotary petrol engine.
1959	BMC (now Rover Cars) introduced the Mini.
1966	California brought in legislation regarding air pollution by cars.
1970	Gabelich drove a rocket powered car, 'Blue Flame', to a new record speed of 1 001.473 kph.
1972	Dunlop introduced safety tyres, which seal themselves after a puncture.
1979	Barrett exceeded the speed of sound in the rocket engined 'Budweiser Rocket' (1 190.377 kph).
1980	The first mass produced car with four wheel drive, the Audi Quattro.
1981	BMW introduced the on-board computer.
1983	Richard Noble set an official speed record in the jet engined 'Thrust 2' (1 019.4 kph).
1983	Austin Rover introduced the Maestro, the first car with a talking dashboard.
1987	The solar powered 'Sunraycer' travelled 3 000 km.
1988	California's emission controls aim for use of zero emission vehicles (ZEVs) by 1998.
1989	The Mitsubishi Gallant was the first mass produced car with four wheel steering.
1990	Fiat of Italy and Peugeot of France launched electric cars.

Figure 4.7 A very new vehicle

1991   European Parliament voted to adopt stringent control of car emissions.

1992   Japanese companies developed an imaging system which views the road through a camera.

1993   A Japanese electric car reached a speed of 176 kph.

1995   Greenpeace designed its own environmentally friendly car capable of doing 67–78 miles to the gallon (100 km per 3–3.5 litres).

1996/7   to date. The story continues with **you!**

LEARNING TASKS

➠   Look back at the key words. Explain each one to a friend, and/or write out a short description to keep as evidence.

➠   Examine real motor vehicles and make a simple sketch to show the system layout of each type.

---

2   Vehicle layouts

Front engine

KEY WORDS

- Front engine
- Rear engine
- Mid engine

A vehicle design with the engine at the front has a number of advantages:

- protection in case of a front end collision
- easier engine cooling because of the air flow
- cornering can be better if the weight is at the front.

Front wheel drive adds further advantages, particularly if the engine is mounted sideways on (transversely):

- more room in the passenger compartment
- power unit can be made as a complete unit
- drive acts in the same direction that the steered wheels are pointing.

Rear wheel drive from a front engine was the method used for many years. Some manufacturers have continued its use, BMW for example. A long propeller shaft from the gearbox to the final drive, which is part of the rear axle, is the main feature. The propshaft has universal joints to allow for suspension movement. This layout has some advantages:

- weight transfers to the rear driving wheels when accelerating
- complicated constant velocity joints, such as used by front wheel drive vehicles, are not needed.

Four wheel drive combines all the good points mentioned above but makes the vehicle more complicated and therefore expensive. The main difference with four wheel drive is that an extra gearbox, known as a transfer box, is needed to link the front and rear wheel drive.

Rear engine, rear wheel drive

The rear engine design has not been very popular, but it was used for the best selling car of all time – the VW beetle. The advantages are that weight is placed on the rear wheels, giving good grip, and that the power unit and drive can all be one assembly. One downside is that less room is available for luggage in the front. The biggest problem is that handling is affected because there is less weight on the steered wheels. Flat type engines are the most common choice for this type of vehicle.

Mid engined vehicles

Mid engine is used to describe any vehicle where the engine is between the axles, even if it is not in the middle! Fitting the engine in the mid position of a car has one major disadvantage: it takes up space inside the vehicle. This makes it impractical for most 'normal' vehicles. However, the weight distribution is very good. This makes it the choice of high performance vehicle designers. A good example is the Ferrari Testerosa.

LEARNING TASKS

➠ Look back at the key words. Explain each one to a friend, and/or write out a short description to keep as evidence.

➠ Write a short explanation about the advantages and disadvantages of the 'key word' vehicle types.

---

3 Vehicle systems (front engine, front wheel drive)

Detailed layout

Front engine, front wheel drive is now the most common, so this will be used for a more detailed explanation. However, all layout designs have similar major components which operate in much the same way.

KEY WORDS

■ Vehicle system
■ Power train
■ Braking
■ Steering
■ Suspension

The main systems of a front engine, front wheel drive car are as follows:

■ power train consisting of: engine, clutch, gearbox, final drive and drive shafts (engine and transmission system combined)

■ braking system

■ steering system

■ suspension system.

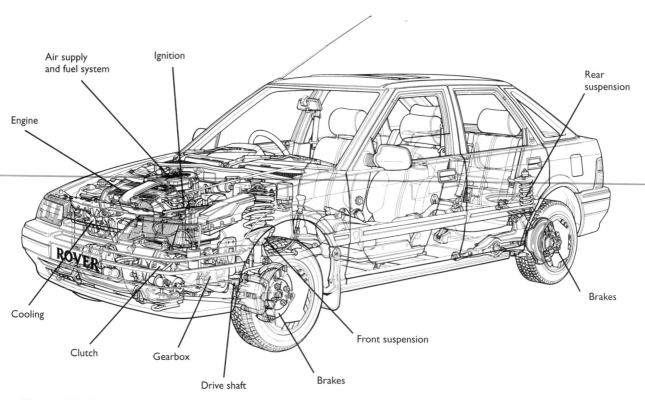

Figure 4.8 Systems layout of a front engine, front wheel drive car

Power train   There are various groupings of engine, clutch, gearbox and final drive. The basic power flow, meaning the way in which energy is passed through the system, is as follows. The pistons push on connecting rods which are on cranks, just like a cyclist's legs driving pedals. This makes the crankshaft rotate. Power is passed through the clutch and then straight through a gearbox (in fourth gear). The output of the gearbox is linked to the final drive. This then applies the power to the front wheels through drive shafts. These shafts have joints so they can move with the steering and suspension. The details can now be considered further.

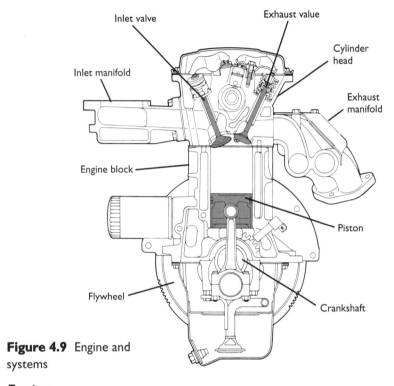

Figure 4.9 Engine and systems

Engine

A fuel–air mixture enters through an inlet manifold and is fired in each cylinder in turn. This expands and pushes down on the piston. The spent gases leave via the exhaust system. The power is applied to the crankshaft. The pulses of power from each piston are smoothed out by a heavy flywheel. Power leaves the engine through the flywheel which is fitted on the rear of the rotating crankshaft and passes to the clutch.

Clutch

The clutch allows the driver to disconnect drive from the engine and move the vehicle off from rest. It can be thought of as being in two separate sections:

1. The flywheel and clutch cover are bolted together so the cover always rotates with the engine. A pressure plate and clutch springs are mounted on the cover.
2. The gearbox shaft is fixed so that it rotates with the driven plate but it can slide slightly. The clutch, or driven plate has friction linings.

The clutch is engaged when the pedal is up because the clutch springs and pressure plate hold the driven plate against the flywheel. This makes the drive pass to the gearbox.

To disengage the clutch, the pedal is pressed down. A release bearing makes the pressure plate move back away from the flywheel and frees the driven plate from the flywheel. No drive is now passed to the gearbox.

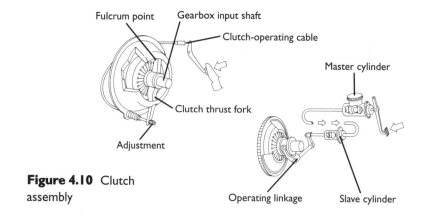

Figure 4.10 Clutch
assembly

As the car moves off, the clutch is engaged slowly to prevent the car jerking
or to prevent a sudden force being applied to the mechanical components.

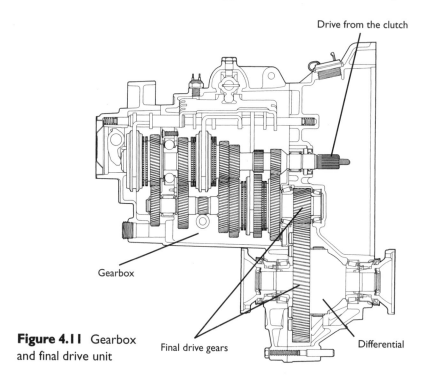

Figure 4.11 Gearbox
and final drive unit

Gearbox

A gearbox is needed because an engine produces power only when turning
quite fast. The gearbox allows the driver to keep the engine at its best speed.
When the gearbox is in neutral, power does not leave it. When the gearbox is
in first gear, power is transferred from a small to a larger gear and then out
to the final drive. Different stages of speed reduction (second and third gear)
are created using different sizes of gear. Less speed out of the gearbox has a
higher turning force (torque) because the engine is running faster. Fourth
gear normally makes the output shaft turn at the same speed as the engine.
Fifth gear makes the output shaft run faster than the engine for economical
higher speed driving.

Final drive

The final drive assembly of a front wheel drive vehicle has two main tasks:

■   Further speed reduction of about 4:1. This is the output gear to pinion
    ratio which will vary with different types of vehicles and engines.

■ Different speeds to the drive shafts are made possible by a unit called the differential. This is needed because the road wheels turn at different speeds when the vehicle is cornering .

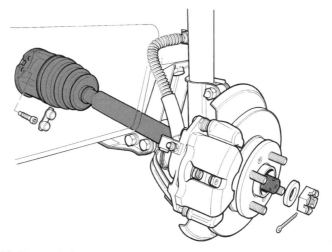

Figure 4.12 Drive shaft

Drive shafts

The two drive shafts each have two constant velocity (CV) joints. They are heavy duty steel shafts and simply pass the drive to the wheels. The joints are needed because the movement of the steering and suspension changes the position of the wheels.

Braking system

Hydraulic brakes are used to slow down or stop the vehicle. The hand brake uses a mechanical linkage to operate parking brakes. The main brakes work on all four wheels, the hand brake usually just on the rear.

The hydraulic principle is that foot pressure on the brake pedal pushes fluid under pressure to all four wheels. Braking materials (friction linings) are pressed against rotating surfaces, slowing them down and thereby slowing down the vehicle.

Discs, normally on the front, are gripped between pads of friction lining. Drums, normally on the rear, are gripped on their inside surfaces by shoes

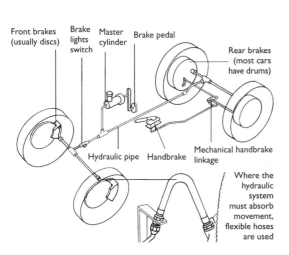

Figure 4.13 Layout of the braking system

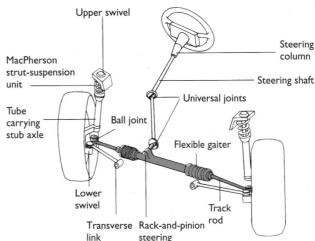

Figure 4.14 Rack and pinion steering

covered with friction lining. This is the most common arrangement, but some vehicles have all drums or all discs.

Steering system

Both front wheels are linked mechanically and must turn together to provide steering control. Figure 4.14, on page 43, shows a rack and pinion. The steering wheel is linked to the pinion; as this is turned, it moves the rack to and fro. This moves both the wheels. Some vehicles have power assisted steering which uses a pump driven by the engine to make turning the steering wheel easier. Some very modern systems use small electric motors for this task.

Suspension system

The suspension system has the following main tasks:

- absorb road surface faults (shocks) to give a comfortable ride
- keep the tyres in contact with the road surface
- resist braking and steering forces
- allow for different loads of passengers and luggage.

Figure 4.15 shows a single trailing arm with coil springs and damper on the rear, and a strut with a coil spring and built in damper on the front. Many variations of design are used, but the principle is the same.

Tyres also absorb road shock and play a very important part in road holding. Most of the remaining shocks and vibrations are absorbed by springs in the driver's and passengers' seats.

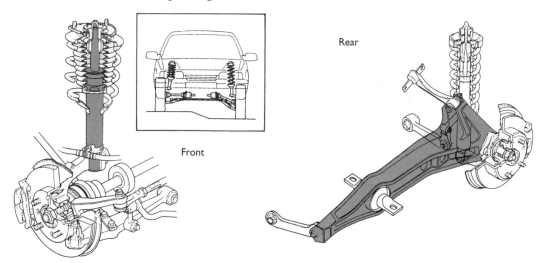

Rear

Front

Figure 4.15 Suspension system with front struts and rear trailing arms

Summary

In this chapter I have outlined some of the important systems on the vehicle. You need to understand the basic layouts before moving on to examine things in more detail. Read and work through this chapter again if necessary. Keep up the good work!

LEARNING TASKS

➡ Look back at the key words. Explain each one to a friend, and/or write out a short description to keep as evidence.

➡ Examine real systems on a vehicle and note the layout and position of the components.

5 Engines

1 | Introduction

Start here! The engine is a device for converting stored energy into useful work or movement. Vehicles with electric engines are being developed quite quickly, but most vehicle engines use a fuel as their energy store. The fuel is burnt to produce heat energy, which is then converted into movement. With internal combustion the fuel is burnt inside; if it is burnt outside, as with a steam engine, it is called external combustion. Most car engines work by a reciprocating action of the pistons (back and forwards in a straight line), but just a few are rotary, such as a gas turbine or Wankel engine.

Learning about engines and other technology is as much about learning new words as it is about understanding complicated techniques. Once you know the words it is easier to understand how an engine works. The following list explains some of the terms associated with engines.

Figure 5.1 A modern car engine

KEY WORDS

- Reciprocating
- Particulates
- Internal combustion
- Spark ignition
- Compression ignition

Terminology

Top dead centre (TDC)	A piston is at its top or highest position in the cylinder. ATDC means 'after top dead centre' and BTDC means 'before top dead centre'
Bottom dead centre (BDC)	A piston is at its bottom or lowest position in the cylinder. ABDC means 'after bottom dead centre' and BBDC means 'before bottom dead centre'
Bore	The internal diameter of a cylinder
Valve timing	The mechanical timing of the inlet and exhaust valves so that they open just at the right time to allow the operating cycle (e.g. four stroke) to work at its most efficient

Terminology

Stroke	The distance a piston moves from BDC to TDC
Swept volume (SV)	This means the volume in each cylinder between the piston at TDC and BDC
Capacity	The number of cylinders multiplied by the swept volume. For example, a four cylinder engine with a swept volume of 500 cc has a capacity of 2000 cc or 2 litres
Clearance volume (CV)	The space above the piston when it is at TDC. This is mostly the combustion chamber
Compression ratio	This is the total volume or the cylinder (SV + CV), compared to just the clearance volume. It can be calculated by (SV + CV) ÷ CV
SI	Spark ignition. This describes all petrol engines – the petrol is ignited by a spark
CI	Compression ignition. This describes all diesel engines – the fuel is ignited by heat caused by high compression

Petrol or diesel The most common source of power for motor vehicles is the petrol engine. It was introduced by the German engineers Karl Benz and Gottlieb Daimler in 1885. This petrol engine is a complicated machine made up of about 150 moving parts! It is a piston engine, in which one or more pistons move up and down in cylinders. The fuel is ignited by a spark, hence the term spark ignition. The motion of the pistons rotates a crankshaft, at the end of which is a heavy flywheel. From the flywheel the power is transferred to the car's driving wheels via the clutch, gearbox and final drive.

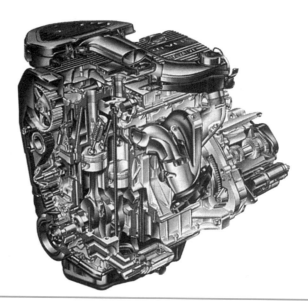

Figure 5.2 Petrol engine

The design of the diesel engine was first explained in England by Herbert Akroyd in 1890; it was applied practically by Rudolf Diesel in Germany two years later. The diesel engine is similar to the petrol or spark ignition engine. It burns a lightweight fuel oil normally referred to as 'diesel'. The diesel engine operates by compressing air until it becomes sufficiently hot to ignite the fuel. It is a piston engine, like the petrol engine, but only air is taken into the cylinder. The fuel is injected into the cylinder, where it burns, forcing the piston down on its power stroke. This is called compression ignition because it is the heat caused by the compression which ignites the fuel.

Diesel engines tend to be considered 'cleaner' than petrol engines because they do not need lead or similar additives; they also produce fewer gaseous pollutants. However, they do produce high levels of the tiny black carbon

Figure 5.3 Diesel engine

particles called particulates, which are thought to be carcinogenic (cancer causing) and may aggravate or even cause asthma. You will be able to make up your own mind about this issue as you learn more about the technology.

2 Engine operation

KEY WORDS

- Spark ignition four stroke cycle
- Compression ignition four stroke cycle
- Spark ignition two stroke cycle
- Compression
- Mixture
- Air–fuel ratio
- Exhaust gas
- Induction

Imagine (don't try this out though!) filling a room with a mixture of petrol and air – then striking a match! What would happen? Why do the windows all blow out? Why does the house explode? As the petrol and air mixture burns or reacts it expands very rapidly, particularly if the mixture is at a good air–fuel ratio. The ideal ratio for use in most engines is about 15:1. This means that for each gram of petrol about 15 grams of air are used. This amount of air takes up quite a lot of space (a large volume). It is this expanding effect when petrol and air burn which, when controlled within an engine, can produce so much power to move the car. The product of the reaction is the exhaust gas.

Spark ignition four stroke cycle

The engine components are combined to use the power of expanding gas to drive the engine. The term 'stroke' means the movement of a piston from TDC to BDC or the other way round. Figure 5.4 shows diagrams to help explain the SI four stroke cycle.

1. Induction stroke – the fuel–air mixture is forced into the cylinder through the open inlet valve because, as the piston moves down, it makes a lower pressure. It is often acceptable to say the mixture is drawn into the cylinder.

2. Compression stroke – as the piston moves back up the cylinder, the fuel–air mixture is compressed to about an eighth of its original volume because the inlet and exhaust valves are closed. This is a compression ratio of 8:1, which is typical for many normal engines.

3. Power stroke – at a suitable time before top dead centre, the compressed mixture is ignited by a spark at the plug. The mixture now burns very quickly, and the powerful expansion pushes the piston back down the cylinder. Both valves are closed.

4. Exhaust stroke – the final stroke occurs as the piston moves back up the cylinder and pushes the spent gases out of the now open exhaust valve.

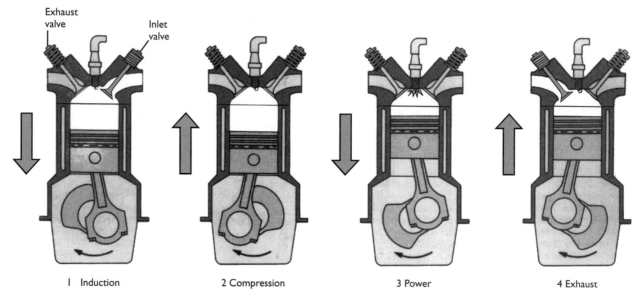

Figure 5.4 SI four stroke cycle

Compression ignition four stroke cycle

The engine components are combined to use the power of expanding gas to drive a compression ignition engine. Note that the operation cycle of the four stroke diesel is very similar to the spark ignition system. Figure 5.5 shows diagrams to help explain the CI four stroke cycle.

1. Induction stroke – air is forced into the cylinder through the open inlet valve because, as the piston moves down, it makes a lower pressure. It is often acceptable to say the air is drawn into the cylinder.

2. Compression stroke – as the piston moves back up the cylinder, the fuel–air mixture is compressed (in some engines to about a sixteenth of its original volume) because the inlet and exhaust valves are closed. This is a compression ratio of 16:1, which causes a large build up of heat.

3. Power stroke – at a suitable time before top dead centre, very high pressure atomised diesel fuel (at about 180 bar) is injected into the combustion chamber. The mixture burns very quickly, and the powerful expansion pushes the piston back down the cylinder. The valves are closed.

4. Exhaust stroke – the final stroke occurs as the piston moves back up the cylinder and pushes the spent gases out of the now open exhaust valve.

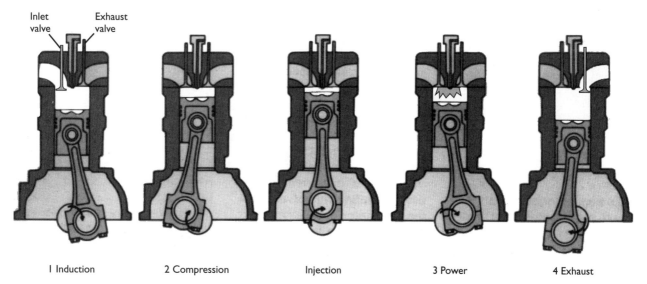

Figure 5.5 CI four stoke cycle

Spark ignition two stroke cycle

The two stroke cycle operates in a similar way to the four stroke cycles described above. However, two operations take place during each stroke. The piston covers or uncovers ports as it moves up and down from TDC to BDC. This opening and closing of the ports is similar to the opening and closing of valves. Figure 5.6 shows diagrams to explain the two stroke cycle.

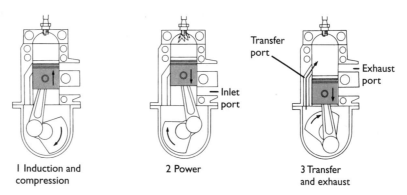

Figure 5.6 SI two stroke cycle

As the piston rises, it closes all the ports to the combustion chamber and compresses the mixture into the chamber. At the same time this causes a lower pressure in the crankcase, which 'draws' in new mixture underneath the piston.

The compressed mixture is ignited at a suitable point, and the expansion pushes the piston back down the bore. This forces fresh fuel–air mixture from the crankcase to the cylinder when the transfer port opens. With the help of the incoming mixture, the expanding spent gases leave the cylinder by the exhaust port.

LEARNING TASKS

➠ Look at the key words. Explain each one to a friend and/or write out a short description to keep as evidence.

➠ Make a simple sketch to show what is meant by compression ratio.

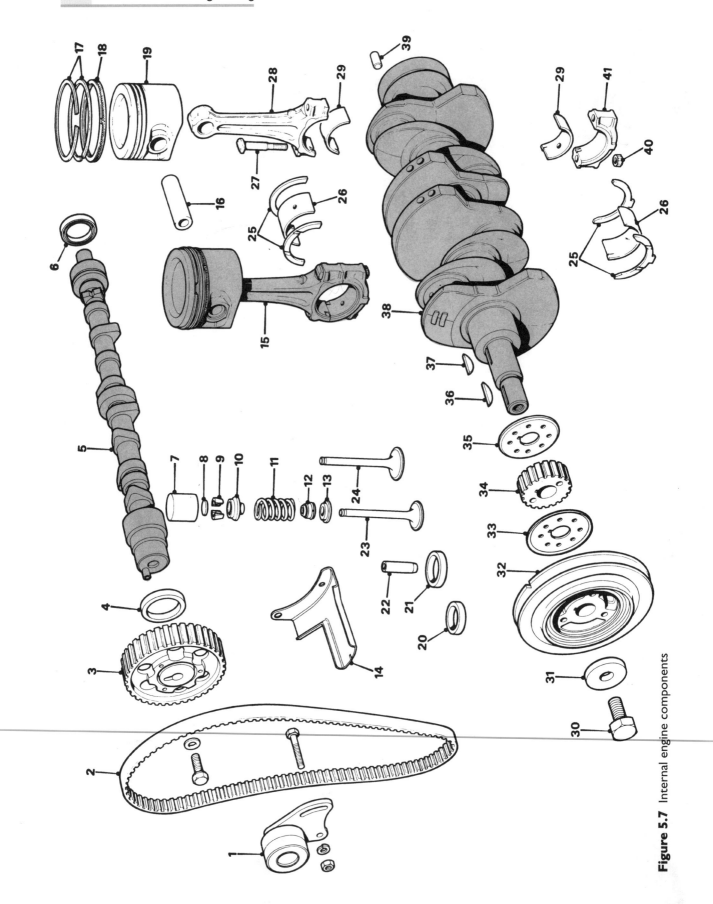

Figure 5.7 Internal engine components

3   Engine components

Name and purpose of the main parts

Figure 5.7 shows the internal components of a typical modern engine. Their function and properties are described in the following table.

No.	Name	Function	Properties
1	Timing belt tensioner	Ensures the timing belt remains at the correct tension. The tension can be measured with a gauge. A good guide is if it can be twisted 90° in the middle of its longest run	Contains a sealed ball bearing as it has to run at high speed
2	Timing belt	Drives the camshaft and in some engines a distributor drive and/or a water pump. On small diesel engines it drives the rotary fuel injection pump	Flexibility, long lasting and oil resistant
3	Camshaft gear	Turns the camshaft. It has double the number of teeth of the crank gear, so it turns the camshaft at half engine speed	Has a mark which must be aligned when fitting a belt
4	Camshaft front oil seal	Prevents oil leaking	Radial lip seal is the most common type
5	Camshaft	Driven by the belt or chain in some engines, opens the exhaust and inlet valves	Must be well lubricated to prevent wear
6	Camshaft rear oil seal	Prevents oil leaking	Radial lip seal is the most common type
7	Tappet	Follows the profile (shape) of the cam and pushes the valve open. Most modern engines have hydraulic tappets	Many types have a plunger built in which automatically takes up any free play
8	Shim	Used to adjust the valve clearance by fitting different sizes	Different sizes are available
9	Collets	Fix the cup to the valve stem	Easy to lose!
10	Cup	Works the valve spring as the valve is opened	
11	Spring	Closes the valve	Some performance engines use two springs
12	Valve stem oil seal	Prevents oil entering the exhaust or inlet ports	'Plastic' seal often with a small spring to keep a tight fit to the valve stem
13	Seat	Fitting for the stem oil seal	
14	Deflector	Deflects dust, water etc	
15	Connecting rod and piston	The heart of the engine. Pressure caused by the burning mixture forces the piston down. This force is transferred to the connecting rod which makes the crank rotate	The 'con' rod is often made of forged steel
16	Gudgeon pin	Connects the 'little end' of the connecting rod to the piston	The pin has to withstand 'shear' forces

No.	Name	Function	Properties
17	Compression rings	These ensure that the piston makes a gas tight seal in the cylinder bore	Piston rings are easy to break when fitting as they are made of very hard brittle material such as cast iron
18	Oil control ring	This special design of piston ring ensures that oil on the walls of the cylinder does not pass the piston and enter the combustion area	This ring is always the lowest on the piston
19	Piston	The engine shown has four pistons. Note the slight hollow in the top which forms part of the combustion chamber. The lower part of the piston is called the skirt	The piston must withstand many forces and high temperatures. It is made of aluminium alloy
20	Exhaust valve seat insert	Makes a gas tight seal with the exhaust valve. On older engines this was part of the cylinder head	It is a very hard material to prevent burning
21	Inlet valve seat insert	Makes a gas tight seal with the inlet valve. The valve seats can be replaced if necessary	It is a very hard material to prevent burning
22	Valve guide	A simple tube for the valve to slide up and down in when operating	The valve guides can be replaced if necessary
23	Exhaust valve	Opened by the cam and closed by a spring, this valve allows spent gases to pass into the exhaust port, then the manifold and finally into the exhaust pipe	The head of the valve is cut at an angle of 45° or 30° to make a perfect seal with the valve seat
24	Inlet valve	Opened by the cam and closed by a spring, this valve allows the fuel–air mixture from the carburettor or injection system to pass from the inlet manifold into the cylinder	When overhauling the 'top end' of an engine, the valves are often lapped in to the seats using an abrasive compound
25	Crankshaft thrust washers	Sometimes called thrust bearings, they control the end to end position (float) of the crankshaft	Often made of steel backed with copper and covered with white metal such as a mix of tin and aluminium
26	Main bearing shell	The main shells are the bearings in which the crankshaft rotates	Often made of copper covered with white metal such as a mix of tin and aluminium
27	Connecting rod bolt	This bolt simply joins the two parts of the con rod	It must be strong in tension
28	Connecting rod	Transfers the reciprocating (back and forth in a straight line) movement of the piston into rotation of the crank	Drop forged and machined steel
29	Big end bearing shell	Made in two halves, hence the name shell; forms the bearings in the big end of the con rod	Often made of steel backed with copper and covered with white metal such as a mix of tin and aluminium
30	Pulley bolt	Simple bolt to secure the pulley and gear to the crank	

No.	Name	Function	Properties
31	Washer	Spreads the load of the bolt	
32	Pulley and vibration damper	The pulley allows a drive belt to transfer power to engine ancillaries such as the alternator, power steering, air conditioning or water pump	The outer and inner parts are joined with rubber to damp vibrations caused by piston movements
33	Gear flange	Helps the drive belt sit correctly	
34	Crankshaft gear	Drives the cambelt. It has half the number of teeth of the camshaft gear (item 3)	Will only fit on in one position
35	Gear flange	Helps the drive belt sit correctly	
36	Pulley and gear key	Woodruff keys to transfer drive from the crank to the pulley and gear	This type of key is used in numerous places
37	Oil pump key	Drives the oil pump	
38	Crankshaft	The big ends are offset from the main bearings. The front and rear are aligned, as are the two in the middle. This makes pistons 1 and 4 reach TDC together. The same is true for pistons 2 and 3 (counting from the front of the engine)	Drop forged and accurately machined steel alloy
39	Flywheel dowel	A peg to ensure the flywheel is aligned correctly on the rear of the crankshaft	Mild steel
40	Connecting rod nut	Secures the cap to the connecting rod	
41	Connecting rod cap	The lower half of the con rod which is split in two so that it can be assembled round the crankshaft	Must be accurately machined

Figure 5.8 shows an exploded view of a typical engine's main external parts and ancillary components. Their function and properties are described in the table.

No.	Name	Function	Properties
1	Timing belt cover	Protects the belt and prevents anyone touching the belt when it is rotating	Moulded plastic or thin steel
2	Timing belt cover back plate	To secure the belt cover	
3	Steady rod	Holds the inlet manifold steady at the rear	
4	Manifold heater	On this engine an electric heater warms the manifold when the engine is first started. This makes the engine run more smoothly when cold	Switches off when the engine is warm
5	Inlet manifold	Directs fuel–air mixture to the inlet ports in the cylinder head	Cast aluminium alloy or on some very new engines plastic!
6	Carburettor support bracket	Support is often needed for many components because of vibration when the engine is running	

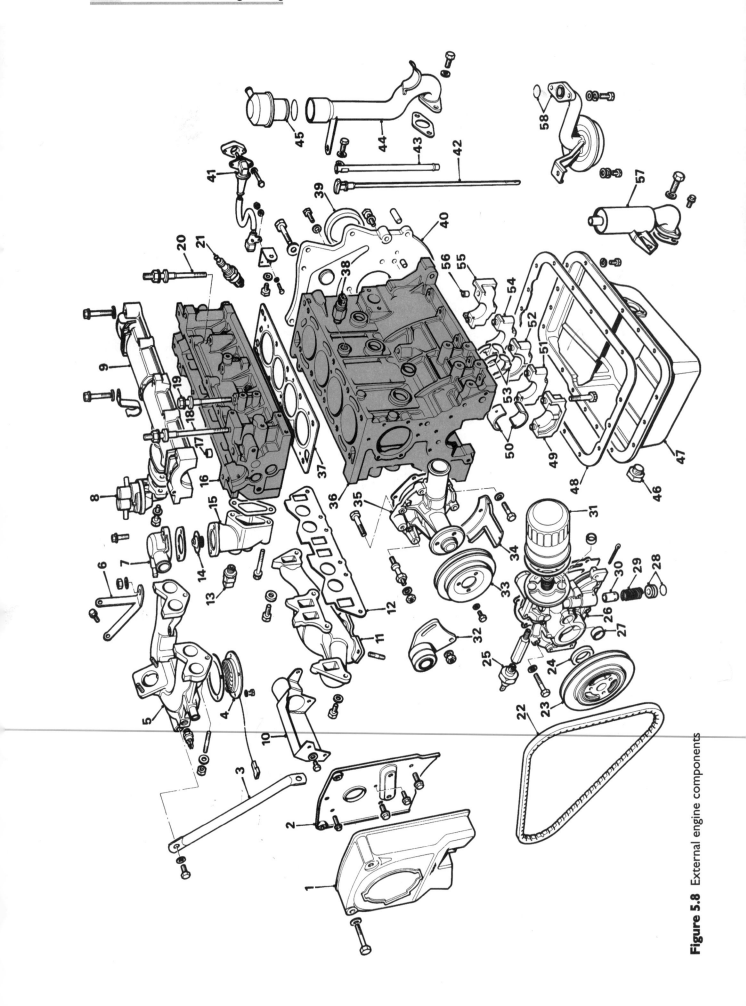

Figure 5.8 External engine components

No.	Name	Function	Properties
7	Thermostat outlet	A water connection to the radiator. Part of the cooling system	
8	Fuel pump	The pump, which in this case is driven from the camshaft, pumps fuel from the tank to the carburettor	Injection systems have a separate electrical fuel pump
9	Camshaft cover	Top cover; in this case also contains the cam bearings	Often this is just a 'tin' cover
10	Hot box	A pick up for the air intake fitted round the exhaust manifold	Engine runs better if the air is at a set higher temperature
11	Exhaust manifold	Connects the exhaust ports in the cylinder head to the exhaust down pipe	Cast iron is used in most cases. It is very hot when running!
12	Manifold gasket	A good gas tight seal is necessary between the manifold and cylinder head	Gaskets are used in many places to ensure tight seals for gas, fuel, oil, air or water
13	Coolant thermistor	Sends a signal to the temperature gauge and also to the engine control electronics	
14	Thermostat	Controls the temperature of the cooling system	
15	Thermostat housing	Part of the cooling system	
16	Cylinder head	The 'top end' part of the engine. Its main parts are the combustion chambers, inlet and exhaust ports, camshaft or rockers and valve gear support and the inlet and exhaust valve assemblies	Cast iron or now more often cast aluminium alloy because of its better heat transfer properties
17	Dowel	Ensures correct location of the camshaft cover	Dowels are used for similar purposes in many parts of the vehicle
18	Cylinder head stud – long	Secures the head to the main engine block	Must be strong in tension
19	Cylinder head bolt	Secures the head to the main engine block	Studs or bolts often have to be replaced when refitting the cylinder head because they are made to stretch when tightened
20	Cylinder head stud – short	Secures the head to the main engine block	Studs with nuts, or head bolts, must be tightened in the correct sequence and to the correct torque
21	Spark plug	Ignites the fuel–air mixture in the cylinder with a high voltage spark.	Has to withstand very high temperatures and pressures
22	Drive belt or alternator belt	On this engine the belt drives a water pump and an alternator	'V' belts or 'poly V' belts are used

No.	Name	Function	Properties
23	Crankshaft pulley	Transfers drive from the crank to the alternator and water pump in this case	
24	Oil seal	Prevents oil leaking from the engine	Lip type seals are the most common
25	Oil pressure switch	Operates a light to warn the driver if oil pressure is less than a set limit which would cause serious engine damage	
26	Oil pump	Oil is picked up from the sump and delivered under pressure to many parts of the engine	A number of types are used, see Chapter 10
27	Oil pump plug	Seals a hole in the pump	
28	Plug and 'O' ring	Seals the pressure relief valve	
29	Oil pressure relief valve spring	Provides a set tension for the valve	
30	Oil pressure relief valve plunger	Oil is held at a set pressure within the engine by this valve. If pressure goes above a limit (set by the spring tension), the plunger moves and allows oil to return to the sump	
31	Oil filter cartridge	Cleans the oil as it circulates round the engine	Should be changed at regular intervals
32	Timing belt tensioner	Keeps the timing belt at a set tension	
33	Water pump pulley	Drives the water pump	
34	Deflector	Deflects contamination	
35	Water pump	Circulates coolant round the engine. The areas which require most cooling are the combustion chambers in the cylinder head	Cast aluminium alloy or even plastic
36	Cylinder block	Largest and heaviest engine component. It contains many machined surfaces to allow other components to be fitted. The main parts are the cylinder bores, the machined flat surface for the head to be fitted and the crank bearing surfaces	Most engine are cast iron, but if cylinder liners are used other materials can be utilised
37	Cylinder head gasket	A very high quality seal is required as the combustion pressures in the cylinders are very high. Also the oil and water ways must not leak	See Chapter 3 for further details
38	Knock sensor	Sends a signal to the engine control electronics if the mixture burns too quickly and causes combustion knock or detonation	It changes the timing – not used on all engines
39	Crankshaft rear oil seal	Prevents oil leaking from the rear of the engine onto the flywheel and clutch	

No.	Name	Function	Properties
40	Gearbox adapter plate	Different gearboxes can be fitted to one type of engine	Basically a steel plate with holes in it!
41	Crankshaft sensor	Tells the engine control electronics the speed and position of the engine	
42	Dipstick	For testing oil level in the sump	Marked with maximum and minimum oil levels
43	Dipstick tube	Holds the stick in a convenient position	Must be sealed to prevent oil leaks
44	Oil filler tube	Access to top up or refill the oil	
45	Oil filler cap	Acts as a seal but also a breather for the inside of the engine	Many engines run the inside at a pressure lower than atmospheric
46	Sump plug	To drain the oil at services	A washer prevents leaks
47	Oil sump	Holds the oil, often about four litres	
48	Oil sump gasket	Seals the sump to the engine block	Plastic/rubber are most common. Cork was and is still used in some cases
49 to 55	Main bearing caps, front, intermediate, centre and rear Main shells (50)	Hold the crank and allow it to rotate at high speed within the bearing shells. Caps should only be fitted in the original position if engine is being rebuilt	Often made of steel backed with copper and covered with white metal such as a mix of tin and aluminium
53	Thrust washers	Controls crank position	
56	Dowel	Ensures correct location of bearing caps	
57	Oil separator	Prevents oil being drawn into the engine breather and then into the intake	
58	Oil strainer and 'O' ring	Prevents large bits of dirt or metal entering the oil pump	Primary oil filter on the end of the pick up pipe

Cylinder layouts   Great improvements can be made to the performance and balance of an engine by using more than one cylinder. There are three possibilities for cylinder layout:

■   In line or straight (Figure 5.9). The cylinders are in a vertical, inclined or horizontal straight line.

■   Vee (Figure 5.10). The cylinders are in two rows at a set angle. The actual angle varies but is often 60° or 90°.

■   Opposed (Figure 5.11). The cylinders are in two opposing, usually horizontal rows.

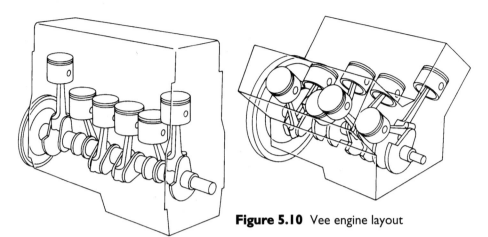

Figure 5.10 Vee engine layout

Figure 5.9 In line or straight engine layout

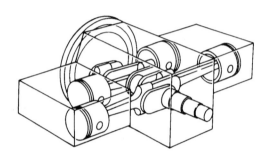

Figure 5.11 Opposed engine layout

By far the most common arrangement, used by all manufacturers in their standard family cars, is the straight four. Larger cars make use of the Vee configuration. The opposed layout, whilst still used, is less popular. Engine firing order is important. This means the order in which the power strokes occur. It is important to check in the workshop manual or data book when working on a particular engine.

Camshaft drives

The camshaft is driven by the engine in one of three ways: gear drive, chain drive or by a drive belt. The last of these is now the most popular as it tends to be simpler and quieter. Note that in all cases the cam is driven at half the engine speed. This is done by the ratio of teeth between the crank and cam cogs: 1:2 or, say, 20 crank teeth and 40 cam teeth.

- Camshaft drive gears (Figure 5.12). Gears are not used very often on petrol engines, but are used on larger diesel engines where they ensure a good positive drive from the crankshaft gear to the camshaft.
- Camshaft chain drive (Figure 5.13). Chain drive is not as popular now as it used to be. The problems with it are that a way must be found to tension the chain and also provide lubrication. A typical chain tensioner is shown.
- Camshaft drive belt (Figure 5.14). Camshaft drive belts have become very popular. The main reasons for this are that they are quieter, do not need lubrication and are less complicated. They do break now and then, but this is usually due to lack of servicing. Cam belts should be renewed at set times, for example on a 48 000 mile service.

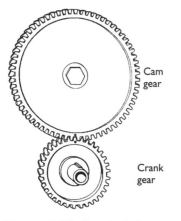

Figure 5.12 Camshaft drive gears

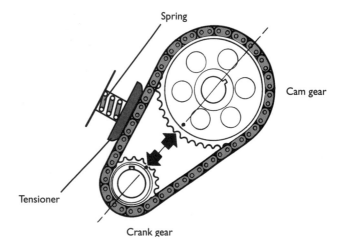

Figure 5.13 Camshaft chain drive and tensioner

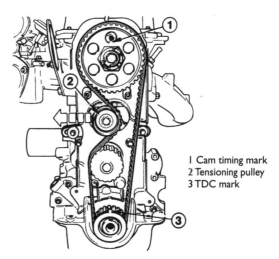

1 Cam timing mark
2 Tensioning pulley
3 TDC mark

Figure 5.14 Camshaft drive belt

Valve mechanisms

A number of methods are used to operate the valves. Three common types are shown with a basic explanation of each.

- Overhead valve with push rods and rockers (Figure 5.15). This method is now less popular than it used to be, but many vehicles still on the road are described as overhead valve (OHV). As the cam turns, it moves the follower, which in turn pushes the push rod. The push rod moves the rocker, which pivots on the rocker shaft and pushes the valve open. As the cam moves further, it allows the spring to close the valve.

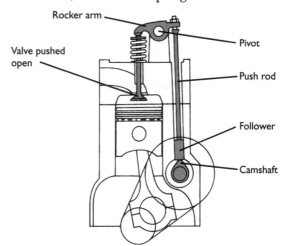

Figure 5.15 Overhead valve with pushrods and rockers

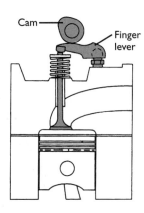

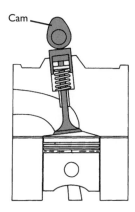

Figure 5.16 Overhead cam with followers

Figure 5.17 Overhead cam, direct acting and with automatic adjusters

- Overhead cam with followers (Figure 5.16). Using an overhead cam (OHC) reduces the number of moving parts. In the system shown here the lobe of the cam acts directly on the follower, which pivots on its adjuster and pushes the valve open.

- Overhead cam, direct acting and automatic adjusters (Figure 5.17). Most new engines now use an OHC with automatic adjustment. This saves repair and service time and keeps the cost to the customer lower. Systems vary between manufacturers, some use followers and some have the cam acting directly on to the valve. In each case, though, the adjustment is by oil pressure. The valve is operated by a type of plunger which has a chamber where oil can be pumped under pressure. This expands the plunger and takes up any unwanted clearance.

Valve clearance adjustment is very important. If too large, the valves will not open fully and will be noisy. If the clearance is too small, the valves will not close and no compression will be possible. When an engine is running, the valves become very hot and therefore expand. The exhaust valve clearance is usually larger than the inlet, because it gets hotter. Regular servicing is vital for all components, but the valve operating mechanism in particular needs a good supply of clean oil at all times.

Valve and ignition timing

Valve timing is important. Figure 5.18 shows the degrees of rotation of the crankshaft during the four stroke cycle, from when the valves open to when they close. The actual position in the cycle of operation when valves open and close depends on many factors and will vary slightly with different designs of engine. Some cars now control valve timing electronically. The diagram is marked to show what is meant by valve lead, lag and overlap. Ignition timing is marked on the diagram. Note how this changes as engine speed changes. This is discussed further in Chapter 9.

The valve timing diagram (Figure 5.18) shows that the valves of a four stroke engine open just before and close just after the particular stroke. Looking at the timing diagram, the piston is nearly at the top of the exhaust stroke when the inlet valve opens (IVO). The piston reaches the top and then moves down on the intake stroke. Just after starting the compression stroke the inlet valve closes (IVC). The piston continues upwards and, at a point several degrees before top dead centre, the spark occurs and starts the mixture burning.

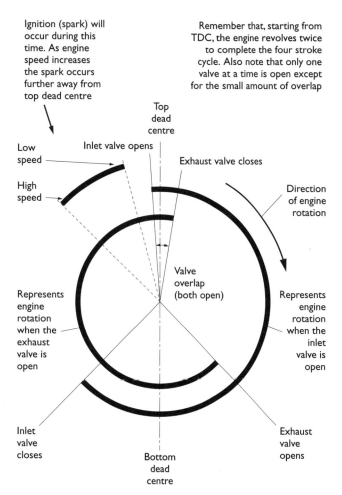

Figure 5.18 Valve timing diagram with ignition timing

The maximum expansion is 'timed' to occur after top dead centre, therefore the piston is pushed down on its power stroke. Before the end of this stroke, the exhaust valve opens (EVO). Most of the exhaust gases now leave because of their very high pressure. As it moves back up the cylinder, the piston pushes the rest of the spent gases out. Just after the end of this stroke the exhaust valve closes (EVC) and the inlet has already opened, ready to start the cycle once again.

The valves open and close like this to make the engine more efficient by giving more time for the mixture to enter and the spent gases to leave. The outgoing exhaust gases help to draw in the fuel–air mixture from the inlet. Overall, this gives the engine a better 'volumetric efficiency'.

LEARNING TASKS

➡ Look back at the key words. Explain each one to a friend, and/or write out a short description to keep as evidence.

➡ Make a simple sketch to show two types of valve operating mechanisms.

➡ Look up in a workshop manual how to adjust valve clearances.

4 Diagnostics

Systematic testing

Working through a logical and planned systematic procedure for testing a system is the only reliable way to diagnose a problem. I suggest you always try to use these six stages of fault finding:

1. Verify the fault.
2. Collect further information.
3. Evaluate the evidence.
4. Carry out further tests in a logical sequence.
5. Rectify the problem.
6. Check all systems.

For example, if the reported fault is excessive use of engine oil, you could proceed as follows:

1. Question the customer to find out how much oil is being used.
2. Examine the vehicle for oil leaks and blue smoke from the exhaust.
3. For example, oil may be leaking from a gasket or seal; if no leaks are found, the engine may be burning the oil.
4. A compression test, if the results were acceptable, would indicate a leak to be the most likely fault. Clean down the engine and run for a while; the leak might show up.
5. For example, change the gasket or seals.
6. Run through an inspection of vehicle systems, particularly those associated with the engine. Double check the fault has been rectified and that you have not caused any other problems.

Test equipment

Always refer to the manufacturers' instructions appropriate to the equipment you are using.

Compression tester

With this device the spark plugs are removed and the tester screwed or held in to each spark plug hole in turn. The engine is cranked over by the starter and the gauge will read the compression or pressure of each cylinder.

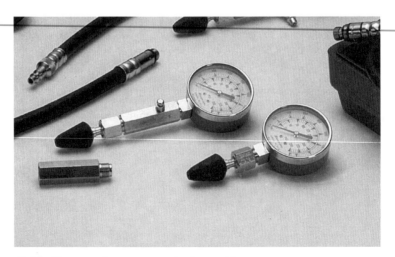

Figure 5.19 Compression tester and adaptor kit

Cylinder leakage tester

A leakage tester uses compressed air to pressurise each cylinder in turn by a fitting screwed into the spark plug hole. The cylinder under test is set to TDC compression. The percentage of air leaking out and where it is leaking from helps you determine the engine condition. For example, if air is leaking through the exhaust pipe, then the exhaust valves are not sealing. If air leaks into the cooling system, then a leak from the cylinder to the water jacket may be the problem (blown head gasket is possible).

Test results The following table shows some of the information you may have to get from other sources such as data books or a workshop manual.

Test carried out	Information required
Compression test	Expected readings for the particular engine under test. For example, the pressure reach for each cylinder may be expected to read 800 kPa ± 15%
Cylinder leakage test	The percentage leak allowed for the tester you are using; some allow about 15% leakage as the limit.

Fault diagnosis

Symptom	Possible causes of faults	Suggested action
Oil consumption	Worn piston rings and/or cylinders	Engine overhaul
	Worn valve stems, guides or stem oil seals	Replace valves (guides if possible) and oil seals
Oil on engine or floor	Leaking gaskets or seals	Replace appropriate gasket or seal
	Build up of pressure in the crankcase	Check engine breather system
Mechanical knocking noises	Worn engine bearings (big ends or mains for example)	Replace bearings or overhaul engine; also check the oil pressure
	Incorrect valve clearances or defective automatic adjuster	Adjust clearances to correct settings or replace defective adjuster
	Piston slap on side of cylinder	Engine overhaul required now or quite soon
Vibration	Engine mountings loose or worn	Secure or renew
	Misfiring	Check engine ancillary systems such as fuel and ignition

LEARNING TASKS

➡ Practise fault finding on real vehicles.

➡ Make a list of steps you would take to find some of the faults causing the symptoms listed in the table.

6 Fuel system

1 Introduction

Start here!

All vehicle fuel systems consist of the carburettor or fuel injectors, the fuel tank, the fuel pump and the fuel filter, together with connecting pipes. Working with these components requires care and skill, just like on any other system, with one major difference!

'Safety first'

With petrol and diesel there is a serious risk of explosion – take extra care. In particular, injection systems pressurise the fuel, so you must always follow manufacturers' instructions before removing any parts.

As we have discussed in other chapters, an engine works by the massive expansion of an ignited fuel–air mixture, acting on a piston. The job of the fuel system is to produce this mixture at just the right ratio to run the engine under all operating conditions. There are three main ways this is achieved:

- Petrol is mixed with air in a carburettor.
- Petrol is injected into the manifold or throttle body to mix with the air.

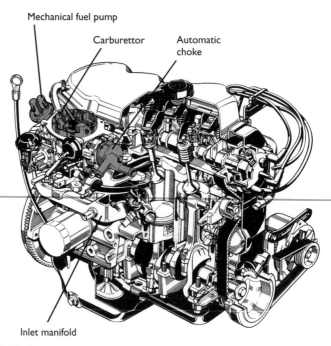

Mechanical fuel pump

Carburettor

Automatic choke

Inlet manifold

Figure 6.1 Carburettor system

■   Diesel is injected under very high pressure directly into the air already in
the engine combustion chamber.

Each of these techniques is looked at in more detail later in this chapter.

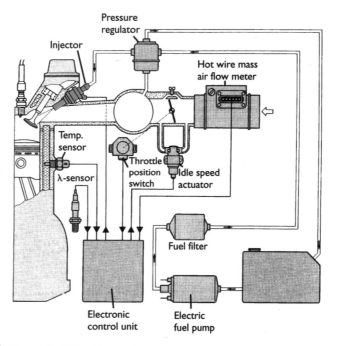

Figure 6.2 Petrol fuel injection system

Fuel-injection system with distributor-type pump
1   Fuel tank
2   Fuel line
3   Fuel filter
4   Distributor-type fuel-injection pump
5   Pressure line
6   Injection nozzle
7   Fuel-return line

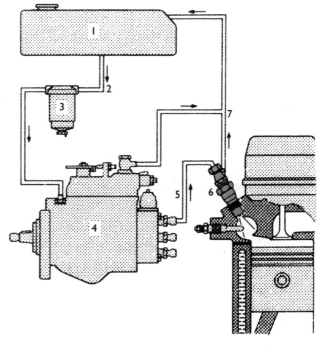

Figure 6.3 Diesel injection system

Terminology

Fuel	The source of energy. Petrol and diesel are known as hydrocarbon (HC) fuels, as they contain hydrogen and carbon
Fuel tank	Simply a supply tank to allow a suitable quantity to be carried. Normally made of mild steel or plastic
Fuel filter	Most fuel is quite clean, but very small particles of dirt can damage fuel injectors or carburettor jets. Paper is used to filter the fuel
Fuel lift pump (carburation engines)	On most vehicles the fuel tank is lower than the engine and carburettor. The lift pump lifts the fuel to where it is needed. The lift pump is usually driven by the engine camshaft, but a few are electric
Fuel pressure pump (injection engines)	Fuel is sprayed out of injectors into the manifold or throttle body in fuel injection engines. The fuel needs to be under pressure to do this
Fuel lines	These are simple plastic or metal pipes joining the tank to the pump, to a filter and then the carburettor
Air filter	Large amounts of dust or dirt taken into the engine would cause wear and damage. The filter prevents this by trapping the contamination. Most filters are made from paper
Venturi	This is defined as a narrowing of a passage such as in a carburettor. When air is forced through a smaller area, it speeds up. This causes the air pressure to become lower
Throttle	Some form of control is needed over the amount of air entering an engine. More air means more petrol, which means greater engine speeds. The throttle is a simple disc which, by rotating, opens or closes the way in to the inlet manifold for the air
Carburettor – fixed venturi	The carburettor is a device for mixing air and fuel. The fixed venturi type has a fixed size of venturi! This means that, as more air flows through, its speed is greater and its pressure less. This means it will take in more fuel through a fixed size jet
Carburettor – variable venturi	The carburettor is a device for mixing air and fuel. The variable venturi type has a variable size of venturi! This means that, as more air flows through, the venturi increases in size, the speed of air is constant and so is its pressure. However, the petrol jet is made to increase in size to allow in more fuel
Choke	More fuel is needed in order to start a cold engine. This is mainly because fuel condenses on the inside of the manifold, much like when you breathe on a cold window. Carburation engines use a choke to restrict the air intake, which causes more fuel to be picked up. This makes a richer mixture. The choke is often just a simple valve like the throttle
Jet	A very small orifice (hole) which controls the amount of fuel to be mixed with the air
Fuel injection	The system now used by most modern vehicles. The amount of fuel can be controlled very accurately by the engine's electronic control unit (ECU), so ensuring the most efficient mixture at all times
Multipoint injectors	Electrically controlled valves which, when activated, spray petrol into each inlet manifold tube
Throttle body injector	A single injector which is fitted in the throttle body and sprays fuel onto the throttle disc
Fuel pressure regulator	To ensure the amount of fuel injected is controlled only by the time the injectors are open for; the fuel pressure has to be kept constant
Diesel fuel injection	Used by compression ignition engines, diesel injection is a mechanical system which sprays diesel under very high pressure directly into the engine cylinder or pre-combustion chamber
Diesel injection pump	Driven by the engine, the injection pump is either a plunger type or a rotary type. It provides a metered quantity of fuel under very high pressure
Diesel injectors	Components which open under pressure to spray very fine droplets of fuel into the engine's cylinder or pre-combustion chamber

2 Carburettor system

Basic principle
The carburettor atomises a fuel such as petrol and mixes it with air in the proper ratio for combustion in an engine. Under normal conditions the ratio of air to petrol should be about 15:1 by mass (15 parts air to 1 part petrol). A higher proportion of petrol (e.g. 10:1) is called a richer mixture, and a lower proportion (e.g. 22:1) is called leaner or weaker.

A simple carburettor consists of a float chamber, a jet nozzle and an air chamber that is narrowed at one point. Such a narrowing in a chamber or tube is called a venturi.

A float valve keeps the petrol in the float chamber at a constant level. When the engine is running, the downward movement of the pistons creates a low pressure, drawing air through the carburettor. The air is accelerated by the venturi, which creates a low pressure region; the jet nozzle, which is attached in this area, draws a fine spray of petrol from the float chamber into the venturi.

The fuel in the venturi mixes with the air, much like paint is mixed in a spray gun. The mixture of petrol vapour and air is then fed to the engine cylinders, where it is ignited. A throttle valve, which is moved by the accelerator pedal, controls engine speed by regulating the amount of fuel–air mixture that enters the engine.

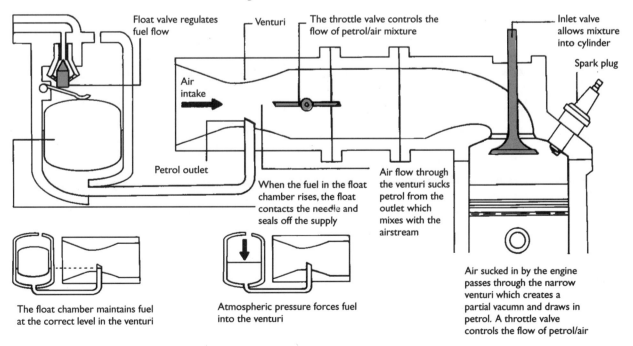

Figure 6.4 Simple carburation principle

KEY WORDS

■ All words in the tables

■ Air–fuel ratio

■ Stages of carburation

A choke valve at the inlet side of the carburettor is used to restrict the amount of air entering the chamber when the engine is cold. Less air means a richer mixture, which can be more easily ignited by the spark. As the engine warms up, the choke valve gradually opens, reducing the richness of the mixture. The choke can be operated manually or automatically.

Carburettors use various means, often called correction systems, to ensure an ideal mixture of petrol and air under different operating conditions. These conditions are often considered as the six stages of carburation:

Stage	Operating condition
Choke	The warm up stage when extra fuel is required to make the engine perform correctly. Ratio can be between 8:1 and 10:1
Idle	When the engine is ticking over or idling, usually at about 700–800 rev/min. Ratio is about 14:1
Progression	Just as the engine speed moves from idle, a little extra fuel is needed to prevent a flat spot
Acceleration	For harder acceleration a fixed amount of extra fuel is mixed in to the air stream. The ratio drops to about 12:1
Cruising or main	The normal operating condition, most fuel is from the main jet. A weaker mixture is used for reasons of economy. Ratio is about 16:1, but can be much higher for modern leaner burn engines – say 20:1
Full load	Under full load a small amount of extra fuel is admitted to provide extra power. Ratio is about 14:1

Fixed venturi carburettor

Component	Purpose
Float chamber	Contains a small amount of fuel held at a fixed level
Float	Moves down if the fuel level moves down, allowing the needle valve to open
Needle valve	Opens to allow in more fuel to keep the float chamber at a set level
Venturi	A narrowing of the air inlet passage
Main jet	The small jet to control the fuel under normal operating conditions
Idle jet	Controls the fuel under idle conditions
Progression holes	Prevent flat spots by allowing just a little more fuel as the throttle is moved from idle jets to the main jet system
Throttle pump	Sprays in extra fuel during acceleration
Emulsion tube	Pre-mixes fuel from the main jet with a small amount of air before it is mixed into the main air flow
Choke valve	An air restriction to force in more fuel when the engine is cold
Throttle valve	The means of controlling the air drawn into the engine as a way of controlling its speed

Variable venturi carburettor

There are two main types of carburettor: the fixed venturi, as described above, and the variable venturi or variable choke type. A typical example of this type is the HIF (horizontal integral float) carburettor used on many existing Rover cars (Figure 6.6). Ford produced a version called the VV (variable venturi) carburettor.

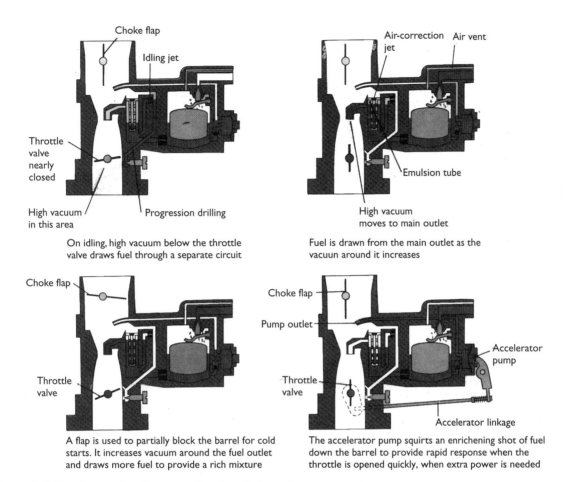

Choke flap

Idling jet

Throttle valve nearly closed

High vacuum in this area

Progression drilling

On idling, high vacuum below the throttle valve draws fuel through a separate circuit

Air-correction jet   Air vent

Emulsion tube

High vacuum moves to main outlet

Fuel is drawn from the main outlet as the vacuun around it increases

Choke flap

Throttle valve

A flap is used to partially block the barrel for cold starts. It increases vacuum around the fuel outlet and draws more fuel to provide a rich mixture

Choke flap

Pump outlet

Throttle valve

Accelerator pump

Accelerator linkage

The accelerator pump squirts an enriching shot of fuel down the barrel to provide rapid response when the throttle is opened quickly, when extra power is needed

Figure 6.5 Fixed venturi carburettor showing all the main components

The variable type uses a single jet with a tapered needle in it. As the engine draws in more air, a component lifts or moves to increase the size of the venturi. This means that the air pressure stays the same. More fuel is taken in because the tapered needle is withdrawn from the jet to make a larger hole.

This principle is quite simple in practice and can make for a very efficient carburettor without adding complicated correction systems.

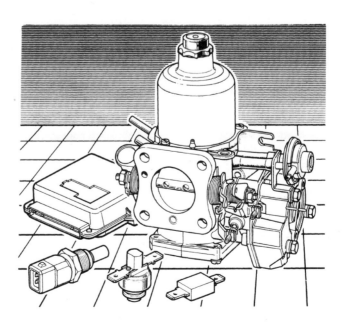

Figure 6.6 HIF variable venturi carburettor with electronic control components

3 Petrol fuel injection

Basic principle

Fuel injection is now the most popular method of supplying a precise mixture of fuel and air to the cylinders of an internal combustion engine. The fuel–air mixture is electronically calculated and controlled by the engine's electronic control unit (ECU). With fuel injection, petrol mixtures burn more efficiently. This ensures that fuel consumption is cut and the pollutants in the engine exhaust are reduced to a minimum. The small amount of poisonous emissions can then be reduced to almost zero by a catalytic converter.

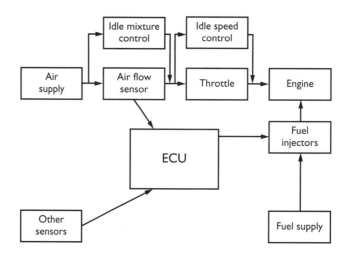

Figure 6.7 Fuel injection principle

Sensors are used to monitor engine speed and load as well as other engine operating conditions, such as temperature. The injection system for a petrol engine also uses sensors to read the amount of oxygen in the exhaust. This is an indication of how efficiently and cleanly fuel is being burned. All sensor signals are fed into a small electronic control unit or computer, usually located inside the vehicle or under the bonnet.

The injector itself is a small valve operated by a winding (solenoid). Petrol is sent under pressure from the fuel pump into the fuel rail. A signal from the ECU actuates the injector, and fuel sprays out of the valve nozzle into the inlet manifold close to the inlet valves, where it mixes with the incoming air. The ECU only controls the length of the injector pulse. Conditions such as cold starting, a warm running engine, or high altitude oxygen compensation are adjusted for by changing the length of time the injector is open.

KEY WORDS

■ All words in the table
■ Single point
■ Multi point

Figure 6.8 Fuel injection components

The following table describes the main components of the fuel injection system.

Component	Purpose
ECU	Electronic control unit. This contains a computer which takes information from sensors and controls the amount of fuel injected by operating the injectors for just the right amount of time
Air flow meter	A sensor used to tell the ECU how much air is being drawn into the engine
MAP sensor	Manifold absolute pressure sensor. This senses the pressure in the engine's inlet manifold as an indication of the load the engine is working under
Speed sensor	Engine speed is often sensed by a sensor on the front pulley or the engine flywheel
Temperature sensor	Coolant temperature is used to determine if more fuel is needed when cold. Much like the operation of the choke on carburation engines
Lambda sensor	A sensor which can tell how much oxygen is in the exhaust. This is an indication of the fuel mixture strength which can then be kept exactly right by the ECU (14.7:1)
Fuel pump	A simple device to supply fuel under pressure to the injectors. It is electrically operated and in some cases fitted inside the fuel tank

Component	Purpose
Filter	Keeps the fuel very clean to prevent injectors becoming damaged or even restricted
Fuel rail	A common connection to multi point injectors
Pressure regulator	Fuel pressure must be constant so that the amount of fuel injected is only controlled by the time the injectors are switched on
Injector	Small component containing a winding or solenoid. When energised by the ECU, the injector opens a valve. Fuel is sprayed into the inlet manifold in tiny droplets
Idle actuator	A valve operated by the ECU to control an air bypass around the throttle to set idle speed

Types of fuel injection system

There are two main types of automobile petrol fuel injection:

- Single point, or throttle body injection. This system has one injector that operates from a central point (Figures 6.9 and 6.10).
- Multi point injection. This system uses a separate injector for each cylinder (Figures 6.11 and 6.12).

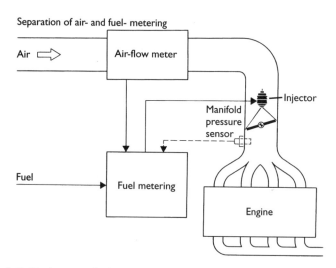

Figure 6.9 Single point fuel injection principle

Figure 6.10 Single point fuel injection system

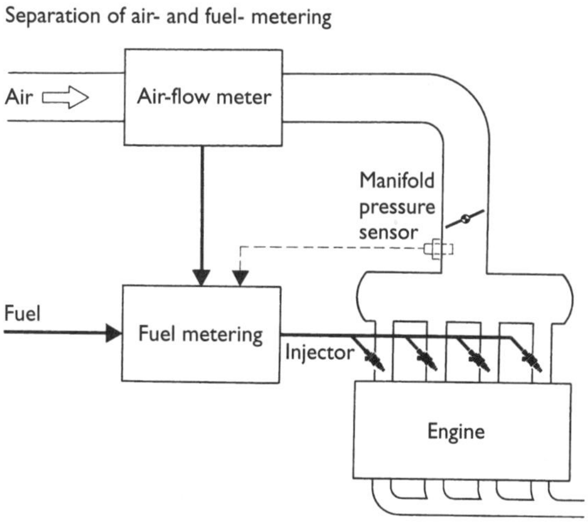

Separation of air- and fuel- metering

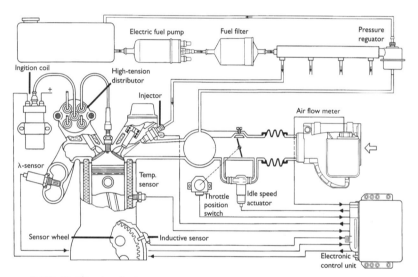

Figure 6.11 Multipoint fuel injection principle

Figure 6.12 Multipoint fuel injection system

LEARNING TASKS

➠ Look back at the key words. Explain each one to a friend, and/or write out a short description to keep as evidence.

➠ Examine a real system and make a simple sketch to show the layout of the fuel injection components.

➠ Write a short explanation about how to replace a fuel injection filter.

---

4 Diesel systems

Introduction The basic principle of the four stroke diesel engine is very similar to the petrol system. The main difference is that, as only air is drawn into the engine's cylinder, the mixture formation takes place in the cylinder's combustion chamber as the fuel is injected under very high pressure. The timing and quantity of the fuel injected is important.

Fuel is metered into the combustion chamber by way of a high pressure pump connected to injectors via heavy duty pipes. When the fuel is injected, it mixes with the air in the cylinder and will self ignite at about 800°C. This high temperature is caused by the high compression of the air and the high speed at which the fuel is made to move as it is injected.

Diesel engines do not in general use a throttle butterfly as the throttle acts directly on the injection pump to control fuel quantity. At low speeds in particular, a very high excess air factor ensures complete burning and very low emissions. Where possible, diesel engines operate with an excess air factor even at high speeds. Figure 6.13 shows a typical diesel fuel injection system. Overall, the emissions from diesel combustion are far lower than emissions from petrol combustion. The main problem area is that of particulate emissions (a type of soot).

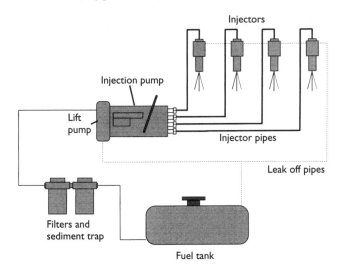

Figure 6.13 Diesel fuel injection system

Diesel system components

Figure 6.13 shows the layout of a diesel fuel injection system. The following table explains the main components.

Component	Purpose
Fuel tank	A simple supply tank usually mounted low down at the rear of the vehicle
Fuel lift pump	This pump lifts fuel from the tank to make it available to the injection pump. Some injection pumps have the lift pump built in. A mechanical pump forming part of the main injection pump or driven by the engine camshaft
Water and sediment trap	Mostly now incorporated as part of the fuel filter, a collection point for water which may be contaminating the fuel
Fuel filter	Fuel must be kept very clean, so that the injection pump and injectors are not damaged. The filters must be changed at regular intervals
Injection pump	Can be a plunger or rotary type, the latter being the most common. It supplies a high pressure metered quantity of fuel timed to the engine cycle
Injectors	High quality, high strength units which spray fuel into the combustion chambers
Leak off pipes	Excess fuel is returned to the tank by the leak off pipes

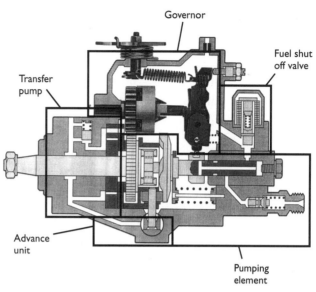

Figure 6.14 Diesel injection – rotary pump

Rotary or distributor type pump

Figure 6.14 shows a typical diesel fuel injection pump. The following table explains the main components.

Component	Purpose
Fuel shut off valve	A solenoid valve controlled by the ignition switch simply shuts off the fuel supply to stop the engine
Governor	Keeps the fuel quantity at constant levels at set speeds; this controls the engine's maximum and minimum speeds
Transfer pump	Produces pressurised fuel inside the injection pump
Pumping element	Contains a plunger which is rotated and moved back and forth. This distributes the fuel to each pipe in turn (one for each cylinder injector) and also provides the metered quantity of fuel under very high pressure
Advance unit	To change the time when the fuel is injected, the increase in transfer pump pressure forces the advance unit to move as engine speed increases

Electronic control of diesel injection (EDC)

Whilst high pressure and injection are still produced mechanically in all current systems, electronic control over the diesel injection pump has allowed many advances:

- more precise control of fuel quantity injected
- better control of start of injection
- idle speed control
- drive by wire system (potentiometer on throttle pedal)
- temperature compensation
- cruise control.

Figure 6.15 shows a distributor type injection pump used with electronic control. Ideal values for fuel quantity and timing are stored in memory maps in the electronic control unit. The injected fuel quantity is calculated from the accelerator position and the engine speed.

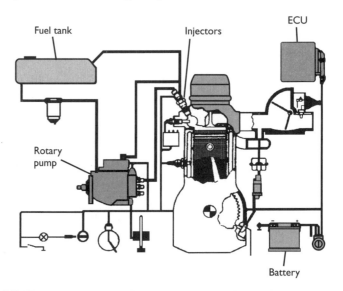

Figure 6.15 Electronic control of diesel injection with distributor pump

LEARNING TASKS

➡ Look back at the key words. Explain each one to a friend, and/or write out a short description to keep as evidence.

➡ Examine a real system and make a simple sketch of diesel fuel system components layout.

➡ Write a short explanation of the advantages and disadvantages of diesel injection.

5   Diagnostics

Systematic testing

For example, if the reported fault is excessive fuel consumption, you could proceed as follows:

1. Check that the consumption is excessive for the particular vehicle. Test it yourself if necessary.
2. Are there any other problems with the vehicle – misfiring, for example, or difficult starting?
3. If the vehicle is misfiring as well, an ignition fault may be the cause of the problem.
4. Remove and examine spark plugs, check HT lead resistance and ignition timing. Check CO emissions.
5. Renew plugs and set fuel mixture.
6. Road test vehicle for correct engine operation.

Test equipment

Always refer to the manufacturers' instructions appropriate to the equipment you are using.

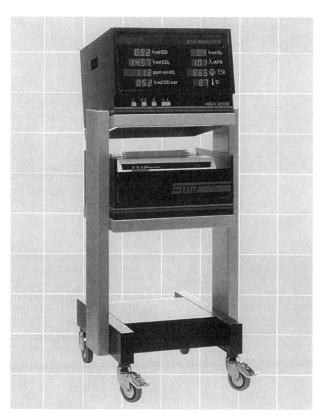

Figure 6.16 Exhaust gas analyser

Exhaust gas analyser

This is a very expensive and sophisticated piece of test equipment used to measure the make up of the vehicle's exhaust gas. The most common requirement is to measure carbon monoxide (CO). A sample probe is placed in the exhaust tail pipe or a special position before the catalytic converter (if fitted); the machine reads out the percentage of certain gases produced. A digital readout is most common. The fuel mixture can then be adjusted until the required readings are obtained.

Fuel pressure gauge

The output pressure of the fuel pump can be tested to ensure adequate delivery. The device is a simple pressure gauge, but note the added precautions necessary when dealing with petrol.

Test results

The following table shows some of the information you may have to get from other sources such as data books or a workshop manual.

Test carried out	Information required
Exhaust gas analysis	CO setting. Most modern vehicles will have settings of about 1% or less. If a 'cat' is fitted, then the readings will be even lower when measured at the tail pipe
Fuel pressure	The expected pressure readings will vary depending on the type of fuel system. Fuel injection pressure will be about 2.5 bar, whereas fuel pressure for a carburettor will be about 0.3 bar
Fuel delivery	How much fuel the pump should move in a set time. This will again vary with the type of fuel system, but 1 litre in 30 seconds is typical for some injection fuel pumps

Fault diagnosis

Symptom	Possible causes of faults	Suggested action
No fuel at carburettor or injection fuel rail	Empty tank!	Fill it!
	Blocked filter or line	Replace filter, renew/repair line
	Defective fuel pump	Renew/check it is being driven
	No electrical supply to pump	Check fuses/trace fault
Engine will not, or is difficult to, start	Choke or enrichment device not working	Check linkages or automatic actuator
Engine stalls or will not idle smoothly	Idle speed incorrectly set	Look up correct settings and adjust
	Mixture setting wrong	Look up correct settings and adjust
	Ignition problem	Check ignition system
Poor acceleration	Blockage in carburettor accelerator pump	Strip down and clean out or try a carburettor cleaner first
	Partially blocked filter	Renew
	Injection electrical fault	Refer to specialist information
Excessive fuel consumption	Incorrect mixture settings	Look up correct settings and adjust
	Driving technique!	Explain to the customer – but be diplomatic!

Symptom	Possible causes of faults	Suggested action
Black smoke from exhaust	Excessively rich mixture	Look up correct settings and adjust
	Flooding	Check and adjust carburettor float settings and operation

LEARNING TASKS

➡ Practise fault finding on real vehicles.

➡ Make a list of steps you would take to find some of the faults causing the symptoms listed in the table.

7 Cooling system

1 Introduction

Start here! When an internal combustion engine is operating, a very large amount of heat is produced. Some of this heat is converted to mechanical energy in the engine, but a large proportion is wasted. In fact, about 50% of the heat is lost down the exhaust, and about 25% is converted in the engine. The other 25% causes heat to build up around the engine. If this heat build up is not controlled, then the engine components would get so hot that they would melt or at least cause the engine to seize up due to expansion. This is where the cooling system comes in.

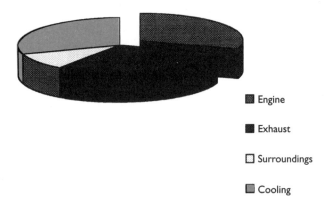

- Engine
- Exhaust
- Surroundings
- Cooling

Figure 7.1 Heat distribution from burning fuel

KEY WORDS

- All words in the table
- Radiation
- Convection

Cooling is done either by air or by water. Water cooling is the best and therefore most popular method, but a number of vehicles do rely on air cooling. The basic principle of a cooling system is that excess or unwanted heat is passed to the surrounding air by either cooling fins (air cooling) or by a radiator (water cooling).

Terminology

Coolant	The liquid used to take heat from different parts of the engine, particularly the cylinder head around the combustion area. The coolant used for most motor vehicles is a mixture of water and antifreeze
Radiator	Fitted in the air stream, the radiator allows excess heat to pass to the atmosphere. This is not as the name suggests by radiation but mostly by convection. See Chapter 20 for more details
Thermostat	A temperature controlled valve or tap to allow coolant to heat up more quickly and then be kept at a constant temperature by opening and closing automatically

Terminology

Antifreeze	An additive to a water cooling system to prevent the water freezing. The most common type is made from ethylene-glycol. Some antifreeze also helps to inhibit corrosion
Core plugs	When engine blocks are cast, holes are needed to construct water ways. Metal plugs are then used to seal these off. If the coolant freezes, the core plugs should be forced out rather than the block cracking
Air cooling	The most common car example is the VW beetle. Fins are used to dissipate the heat from the engine. A large fan is also needed to force air over the fins
Pressure cap	Fitted to the radiator or a header tank, the cap allows the coolant pressure to build up to a set level. This increases the boiling point of the coolant and reduces the risk of boiling over
Water pump	A belt driven pump used to circulate the coolant
Cooling fan	A fan driven by an electric motor or the engine. It is used to increase air flow over the engine and/or the radiator
Viscous coupling	A thermally controlled coupling between the engine drive and a cooling fan. This only allows the fan to be coupled when it is required, so reducing drag
Drive belt	Many engines now drive the water pump from the camshaft belt. Some use what became known as the fan belt, as traditionally it was used to drive the fan from the engine front pulley
Heater	Some of the excess heat is used to work the car interior heater. Water systems use a separate small radiator inside the car, together with a blower motor

LEARNING TASKS

➡ Look back at the key words. Explain each one to a friend, and/or write out a short description to keep as evidence.

➡ Examine a real cooling system to see the layout and be able to name and state the purpose of all the parts.

2 Air cooling

Air cooled system

Air cooled engines with multi cylinders, especially under a bonnet, must have some form of fan cooling and ducting. This is to make sure all cylinders are cooled evenly. The cylinders and cylinder heads are finned. Hotter areas, such as near the exhaust ports on the cylinders, have bigger fins.

Fan blown air is directed by a metal cowling so it stays close to the finned areas. Air flow is controlled by a thermostatically controlled flap. When the engine is warming up, the flap is closed to restrict the movement of air. When the engine reaches its operating temperature, the flap opens and allows the air to flow over the engine. The large cooling fan is driven from the engine by a belt. This belt must not be allowed to slip or break, because serious damage will occur. Regular servicing is important.

KEY WORDS

- Thermostatically
- Fins

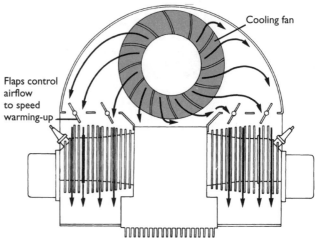

Figure 7.2 Air cooled system

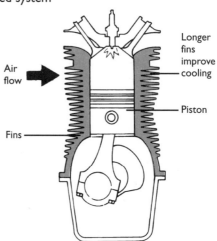

Figure 7.3 Air cooled cylinder showing cooling fins

The following table shows the advantages and disadvantages of air cooled systems.

Advantages	Disadvantages
Lighter in weight because of fewer parts	Not suitable for in-line engines due to heat build up
No leaks or freeze ups of the water	Noisier because water reduces vibrations
Operates in all climates	Fan absorbs a significant amount of power from the engine
Simpler and fewer wearing parts	

Heating With an air cooled engine car heating is not easy to arrange. Some vehicles use a heat exchanger around the exhaust pipe. Air is passed through this device, where it is warmed. With the aid of an electric motor and fan it can then be used for de-misting and heating.

LEARNING TASKS

➡ Look back at the key words. Explain each one to a friend, and/or write out a short description to keep as evidence.

➡ Make a simple sketch to show the layout of an air cooled system.

➡ Examine a real system and note its operation.

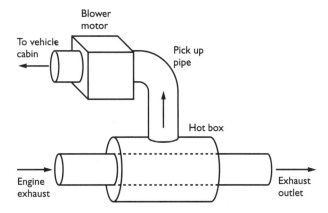

Figure 7.4 Air cooled system heat exchanger for the car heater

3   Water cooling

Full system

The main parts of a water cooling system are as follows:

1. water jacket
2. water pump
3. thermostat
4. radiator
5. cooling fan.

Water cooled engines work by surrounding the hot areas inside the engine with a water jacket. The water takes on heat from the engine and, as it circulates through the radiator, gives it off to the atmosphere. The heat concentrates around the top of the engine, so a water pump is needed to ensure proper circulation.

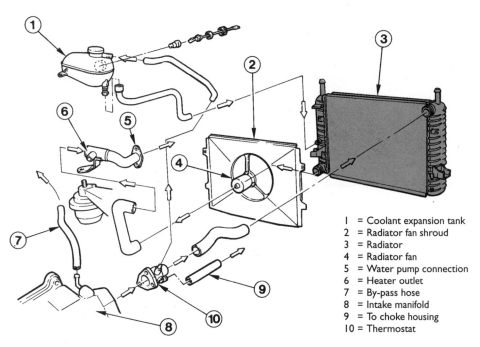

1 = Coolant expansion tank
2 = Radiator fan shroud
3 = Radiator
4 = Radiator fan
5 = Water pump connection
6 = Heater outlet
7 = By-pass hose
8 = Intake manifold
9 = To choke housing
10 = Thermostat

Figure 7.5 Water cooling system layout

When the thermostat is open, the water pump circulates water through the radiator and around the engine. When the thermostat is closed, water circulates only round the engine and not through the radiator. Forcing water around the engine prevents vapour pockets forming in very hot areas. Water circulation is assisted by the thermo-siphon action: as the water is heated, it rises and moves to the top of the radiator. This pushes down on the colder water underneath, which moves into the engine. This water is heated, rises and so on.

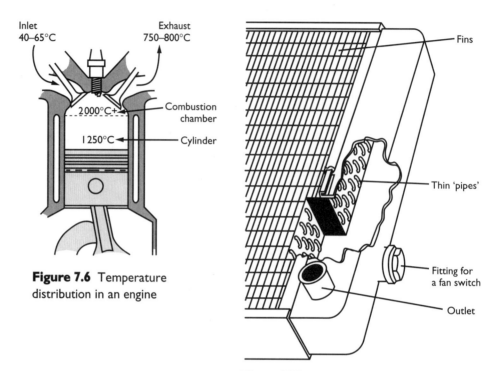

Figure 7.6 Temperature distribution in an engine

Figure 7.7 Details of radiator construction

Radiator A better name for a radiator would be a convector because it warms the air passing over it. Have a look in Chapter 20 if you need more information on this subject. Coolant from the engine water jacket passes through a hose to the radiator at the top. It then passes through thin pipes, called the radiator matrix, to the lower tank and then back to the lower part of the engine.

Many passages are used between the top and bottom tanks of the radiator, to increase the surface area. Fins further increase the surface area to make the radiator even more efficient. A cooling fan assists air flow. The heat from the coolant passes to the pipes and fins and then to the air as it is blown over the fins by a fan.

Many modern radiators are made from aluminium pipes and fins with plastic tanks top and bottom (down flow), or at each end (cross flow). The cross flow radiators with tanks at each end are becoming the most popular. The more traditional method was to use copper and brass.

Thermostat A thermostat is a temperature controlled valve. Its purpose is to allow coolant to heat up more quickly and then be kept at a constant temperature. The total coolant volume in an engine takes time to heat up. Modern engines run more efficiently when at the correct operating temperature. The thermostat prevents coolant circulation from the engine to the radiator until a set temperature is reached. When the valve opens, the coolant can circulate fully, and a good cooling action occurs because of full flow through the radiator. The constant action of the thermostat ensures that the engine temperature remains at a constant level.

Almost all modern engine use a wax capsule type thermostat, Figure 7.8. Figure 7.9 shows how this type works. If the thermostat is faulty, ensure the correct type for the engine is fitted as some work at different temperatures.

Figure 7.8 Thermostat in the cooling system

Figure 7.9 Thermostat operation

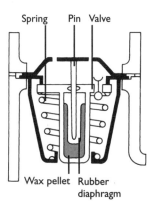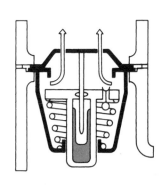

Spring Pin Valve

Wax pellet Rubber diaphragm

Wax thermostat shut: With the engine cold, a heavy coil spring closes the valve

Wax thermostat open: When hot, the wax expands, and in trying to expel the pin it opens the valve

Water pump and cooling fan

The water pump is driven by a V-belt or multi-V-belt from the crankshaft pulley or by the cam belt. The pump is a simple impeller type and is usually fitted at the front of the engine (where the pulleys are). It assists with the thermo-siphon action of the cooling system, forcing water around the engine block and radiator.

Figure 7.10 Water pumps and other cooling system parts

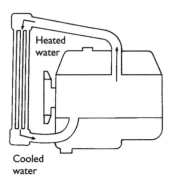

Heated water

Cooled water

Figure 7.11 Thermo-siphon effect of a cooling system

Figure 7.12 Electric cooling fan

The engine fan, which maintains the flow of air through the radiator, is mounted on the water pump pulley on older systems. Most cooling fans are now electric. These are more efficient because they only work when needed. The forward motion of the car also helps the air movement through the radiator.

Sealed systems   Cooling systems on most vehicles today are sealed or semi-sealed. This allows them to operate at pressures as much as 140 kN/m^2 (140 kPa) over atmospheric pressure, raising the boiling point of the coolant to as much as 126.6°C (remember that water boils at 100°C at atmospheric pressure (100 kN/m^2 (100 kPa)). The system can therefore operate at a higher temperature and with greater efficiency.

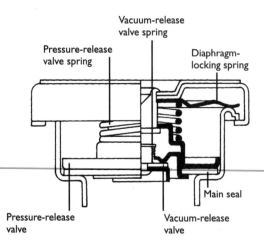

Figure 7.13 Radiator pressure cap

The pressure build up is made possible by the radiator pressure cap (Figure 7.13). The cap contains a pressure valve, which opens at a set pressure, and a vacuum valve, which opens at a set vacuum. On a semi-sealed system, air is pushed out to the atmosphere through the pressure valve as the coolant expands. Air is then drawn back into the radiator through the vacuum valve as the coolant cools and contracts. A sealed system has an expansion tank into which coolant is forced as it expands, and when the engine cools,

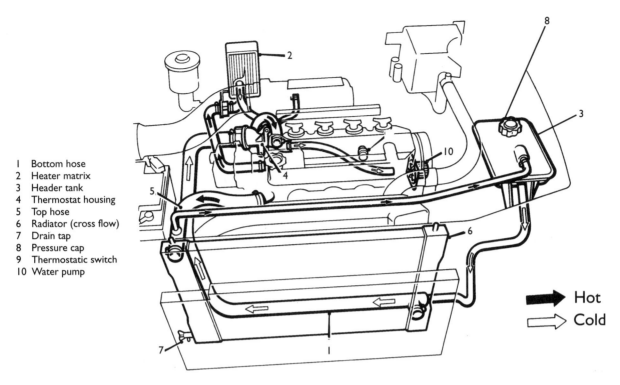

1 Bottom hose
2 Heater matrix
3 Header tank
4 Thermostat housing
5 Top hose
6 Radiator (cross flow)
7 Drain tap
8 Pressure cap
9 Thermostatic switch
10 Water pump

Figure 7.14 Semi-sealed cooling system

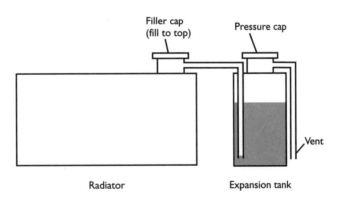

Figure 7.15 Sealed cooling system

coolant can flow from the tank back into the cooling system. Figure 7.14 shows a semi-sealed type cooling system and Figure 7.15 a sealed type.

Correct levels in the expansion tank or in an unsealed radiator are very important. If too much coolant is used, it will be expelled on to the floor when the engine gets hot. If not enough is used, then the level could become low and overheating take place.

If a pressure cap is removed from a hot system, hot water under pressure will boil the instant pressure is released. This can be very dangerous.

Heating   Heat from the engine can be used to increase the temperature of the car interior. This is achieved by use of a heat exchanger, often called the heater matrix. Due to the action of the thermostat in the engine cooling system, the coolant temperature remains nearly constant. The air being passed over the heater matrix is therefore heated to a set level.

A source of hot air is now available for heating the vehicle interior. On most modern vehicles the amount of heat reaching the inside of the car is controlled by blending. A control flap determines how much of the air being passed into the vehicle is directed over the heater matrix. Some systems use a valve to control the hot coolant flowing to the heater matrix.

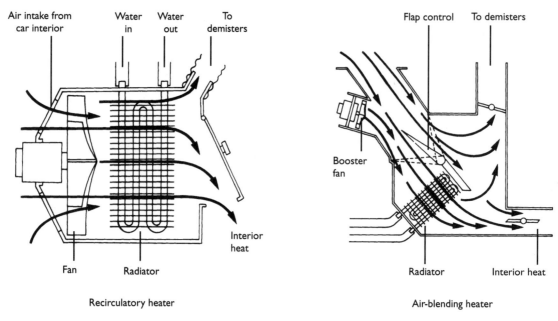

Figure 7.16 Heater system

By a suitable arrangement of flaps it is possible to direct air of the chosen temperature to selected areas of the vehicle interior. In general, basic systems allow the warm air to be adjusted between the inside of the windscreen and the driver and passenger footwells. Fresh cool air outlets with directional nozzles are also fitted.

One final facility which is available on many vehicles is the choice between fresh or recirculated air. The primary reason for this is to decrease the time taken to demist or defrost the vehicle windows and simply to heat the car interior more quickly and to a higher temperature. The other reason is that in heavy congested traffic, for example, the outside air may not be very clean.

Antifreeze The term 'antifreeze' gives a rather good clue to what it does! If the coolant in an engine was allowed to freeze, serious damage could be done to the engine due to the expansion of ice. Corrosion and scale build up can also be a problem in a cooling system, but good antifreeze will have inhibitors to prevent this. It is therefore a good idea to use antifreeze all year round.

Different percentage solutions are used for different conditions. A mixture with about 33% of antifreeze is often acceptable, but more may be required in very cold conditions. The higher the percentage, the greater the protection from freezing. Always check manufacturers' instructions. Manufacturers often recommend 50% to ensure protection continues even in the worst possible conditions. Also note that if the cooling system is topped up with water, the solution will become weaker. Most antifreeze solutions require changing or at the very least checking on a regular basis. A hydrometer measures the relative density of the liquid, which changes depending on the amount of antifreeze.

LEARNING TASKS

➡ Look back at the key words. Explain each one to a friend, and/or write out a short description to keep as evidence.

➡ Make a simple sketch to show the layout of a water cooling system.

➡ Examine a number of different real systems and note the layout of components.

➡ Write a short explanation about how to check antifreeze content.

---

4 Diagnostics

Systematic testing

FAULT FINDING

1. Verify the fault

2. Collect further information

3. Evaluate the evidence

4. Carry out further tests in a logical sequence

5. Rectify the problem

6. Check all systems

For example, if the reported fault is loss of coolant, you could proceed as follows:

1. Check coolant level and discuss with customer how much is being lost.

2. Run the engine to see if it is overheating.

3. If the engine is not overheating, a leak would seem to be most likely.

4. Pressure test the cooling system and check for leaks from hoses, gaskets and the radiator.

5. Renew a gasket or the radiator, clips or hoses as required. Top up the coolant and check antifreeze content.

6. Road test the vehicle to confirm the fault is cured and that no other problems have occurred.

Test equipment Always refer to the manufacturers' instructions appropriate to the equipment you are using.

Cooling system pressure tester

This is a pump with a pressure gauge built in, together with suitable adapters for fitting to the header tank or radiator filler. The system can then be pressurised to check for leaks. The pressure can be looked up, or it is often

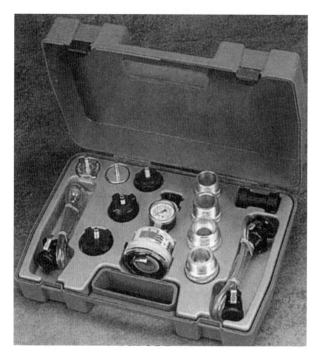

Figure 7.17 Cooling system pressure tester

stamped on the filler cap. A good way of doing this test is to pressurise the system when cold and then start the engine and allow it to warm up. You can be looking for leaks, but beware of rotating components.

Antifreeze tester

This piece of equipment is a hydrometer. It measures the relative density of the coolant (see Chapter 20). The relative density of coolant varies with the amount of antifreeze. A table can be used to determine how much more antifreeze should be added to give the required protection.

Temperature meter/thermometer

Sometimes an apparent overheating problem can be caused by the dashboard temperature gauge reading too high. A suitable meter or thermometer can be used to check the temperature. Note though that normal operating temperature is often above 90°C (hot enough to burn badly).

Test results The following table shows some of the information you may have to get from other sources such as data books or a workshop manual.

Test carried out	Information required
Leakage test	System pressure. Printed on the cap or from data books. About 1 bar is normal (100 kN/m^2)
Antifreeze content	Cooling system capacity and required percentage of antifreeze. If the system holds 6 litres, then for a 50% antifreeze content you will need to add 3 litres of antifreeze. Of course you will have to drain out enough water to make room for the antifreeze!
Operating temperature	This is about the same as the thermostat opening temperature. 88 to 92°C is a typical range

Fault diagnosis

Symptom	Possible causes of faults	Suggested action
Overheating	Lack of coolant	Top up but then check for leaks
	Thermostat stuck closed	Renew
	Electric cooling fan not operating	Check operation of thermal switch
	Blocked radiator	Renew
	Water pump/fan belt slipping	Check, adjust/renew
Loss of coolant	Leaks	Pressure test when cold and hot, look for leaks and repair as required
Engine does not reach normal temperature or it takes a long time	Thermostat stuck in the open position	Renew

LEARNING TASKS

➡ Practise fault finding on real vehicles.

➡ Make a list of steps you would take to find some of the faults causing the symptoms listed in the table.

8 Air supply and exhaust systems

1 Introduction

Start here!

KEY WORDS

- All words in the table
- Tuned manifolds

Keep it quiet! That's the main purpose of the exhaust system. You will remember that the operation of the internal combustion engine is caused by fuel–air mixture burning very rapidly. This very quick movement and burning of the gases makes them very noisy as well as hot. So we need an exhaust system with silencing built in. The exhaust system also directs the exhaust away from the vehicle, most often to the rear.

The air supplied for mixing with the fuel must be cleaned to prevent damage to delicate components; larger particles such as stones or grit must not enter the engine, otherwise serious damage would occur. Even dust would work its way into the oil and cause rapid wear to the pistons and bearings.

1 = 3-way catalytic converter
2 = Front exhaust pipe
3 = Exhaust pipe to rear muffler
4 = Exhaust pipe flange joint
5 = Heat shield
6 = HEGO-sensor

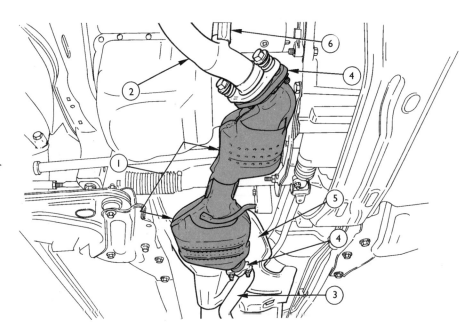

Figure 8.1 Exhaust system

Terminology

Exhaust	The spent gases and byproducts of the fuel–air mixture being burnt in an engine
Silencer (muffler)	Noise is reduced by passing the exhaust through silencers. The two main types are called 'capacity' and 'absorption'
Exhaust manifold	Joins together the exhaust ports or outlets from the engine cylinder head. This is then connected to a 'down pipe'
Exhaust emissions	All the gases and particles which make up the engine exhaust. The ones of most interest are the toxic emissions
Catalytic converter	A device which looks like an exhaust box but is used to considerably reduce toxic emissions from the vehicle
Air filter	Either a paper element or an oil bath to remove dust and dirt from the air
Inlet manifold	Used to channel the air or fuel–air mixture into the cylinder head
Hot box	An air pick up point around the exhaust manifold to allow warm air to be collected and directed to the inlet
Manifold heater	The inlet manifold can be heated either from the exhaust or in many cases by an electrical heater. This prevents fuel condensing when it is cold
High efficiency manifolds	Performance vehicles use manifolds which are tuned by being 'gas flowed'. A good example is a four branch manifold

What goes in and out of an engine?

Figure 8.2 is a representation of what happens when air and fuel are burnt in an engine. Points to note are that air consists of oxygen (O) and nitrogen (N), and that petrol is made of hydrocarbons (HC), which consists of hydrogen (H) and carbon (C). You will see that the combustion byproducts (or exhaust) largely consist of carbon dioxide, water and nitrogen. All of these are harmless to us, but the small amount of poisonous emissions produced can be dangerous.

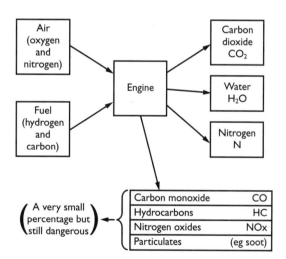

Figure 8.2 Exhaust emission byproducts

LEARNING TASKS

➡ Look back at the key words. Explain each one to a friend, and/or write out a short description to keep as evidence.

➡ Examine a real system and make a simple sketch to show the layout of the air supply and exhaust systems.

➡ Write a short explanation about why the exhaust system is so important.

2 Exhaust system

Complete system

A vehicle exhaust system directs combustion products away from the passenger compartment, reduces combustion noise and, on most modern vehicles, reduces harmful pollutants in the exhaust stream. The main parts of the system are the engine's exhaust manifold, the silencer or muffler, the pipes connecting them and possibly a catalytic converter.

Most exhaust systems are made from mild steel, but some are made from stainless steel which lasts much longer. The system is suspended under the vehicle on rubber mountings. These allow movement because the engine is also rubber mounted, and they also reduce vibration noise.

Manifolds

An exhaust manifold links the engine exhaust ports to the down pipe and main system. It also reduces combustion noise and transfers heat downstream to allow the continued burning of hydrocarbons and carbon monoxide. The manifold is connected to the down pipe, which in turn can be connected to the catalytic converter. Most exhaust manifolds are made from cast iron, as this has the necessary strength and heat transfer properties.

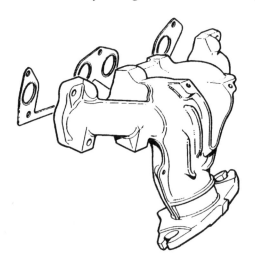

Figure 8.3 Exhaust manifold

Silencers

The silencer's main function is to reduce engine noise to an acceptable level. Engine noise is made up of its firing frequencies (the number of times per second each cylinder fires). These range from about 100 to 400 Hz (cycles/sec). A silencer reduces noise in two main ways:

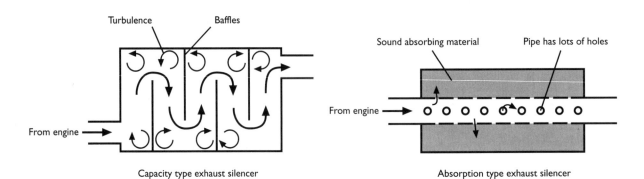

Capacity type exhaust silencer

Absorption type exhaust silencer

Figure 8.4 Two types of exhaust silencer

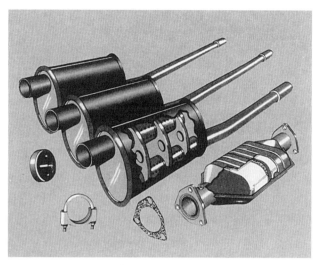

Figure 8.5 Exhaust system components

- Interior chambers using baffles are tuned to set up cancelling vibrations.
- Absorptive surfaces function like sound deadening wall and ceiling panels to absorb noise.

When the exhaust gases finally leave the exhaust system, their temperature, pressure and noise have been reduced considerably. The overall length of an exhaust system, including the silencers, can affect the smooth flow of gases. For this reason the length or the layout of an exhaust system must not be altered.

Catalytic converters

Stringent regulations in many parts of the world have made the use of a catalytic converter necessary. The three way catalyst (TWC) is used to great effect by most manufacturers. It is in effect a very simple device, which looks similar to a standard exhaust silencer box. Note that in order for the 'cat' to operate correctly, the engine must always be well tuned. This is to ensure that the right 'ingredients' are available for the catalyst to perform its function. A catalytic converter works by converting the dangerous exhaust gases into gases which are non toxic.

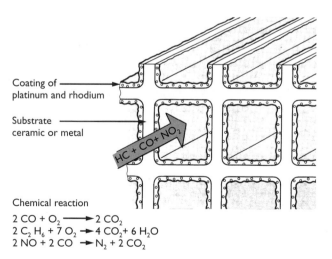

Coating of platinum and rhodium

Substrate ceramic or metal

$HC + CO + NO_2$

Chemical reaction

$2 CO + O_2 \longrightarrow 2 CO_2$
$2 C_2 H_6 + 7 O_2 \longrightarrow 4 CO_2 + 6 H_2O$
$2 NO + 2 CO \longrightarrow N_2 + 2 CO_2$

Figure 8.6 Catalytic converter and the chemical process

Figure 8.6 shows a magnified view of the inside of a catalytic converter, known as a ceramic monolith. This ceramic is a magnesium aluminium silicate and, due to the several thousand very small channels, provides a large surface area. It is coated with a wash coat of aluminium oxide, which again increases its effective surface area several thousand times. 'Noble' metals are used for catalysts. Platinum helps to burn off the hydrocarbons (HC) and carbon monoxide (CO), rhodium helps the reduction of nitrogen oxides (NOx). The whole three way catalytic converter only contains about three to four grams of these precious metals.

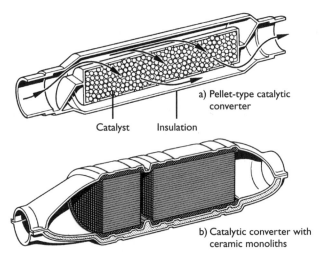

a) Pellet-type catalytic converter

Catalyst   Insulation

b) Catalytic converter with ceramic monoliths

Figure 8.7 Inside a catalytic converter

Catalytic converters can be damaged by the engine in two ways. Firstly by the use of leaded fuel which can cause lead compounds to be deposited on the active surfaces. Secondly by engine misfire which can cause the catalytic converter to overheat due to burning fuel inside the unit. Some manufacturers, BMW for example, use a system on some vehicles where a sensor checks the output of the ignition HT system; if the spark is not present, it will not allow fuel to be injected.

LEARNING TASKS

➠ Look back at the key words. Explain each one to a friend, and/or write out a short description to keep as evidence.

➠ Make a simple sketch to show the main components of an exhaust system. Label each part.

➠ Write a short explanation about the advantages of using a 'cat'.

3   Air supply system

Complete system

KEY WORDS

■ Filter
■ Resonance
■ Hot air pick up

There are three purposes of the complete air supply system:

■ clean the air
■ control air temperature
■ reduce noise.

The air cleaning is done by a filter. Air temperature is controlled by drawing air from around the exhaust manifold. When large quantities of air are

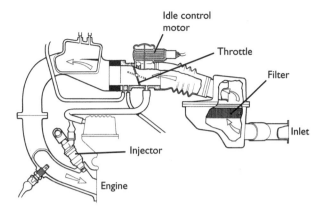

Figure 8.8 Air supply system

drawn into the engine, the air begins to vibrate and this makes it noisy. As with the exhaust system, baffles are used to stop resonance (when vibrations reach a natural level, they tend to increase and keep going). You can hear for yourself how much noise is reduced by the air intake system if you compare the noise of an engine run with the air filter in place and with it removed.

Air filters   Two types of air filter are in use, the first of these being by far the most popular:

- paper element
- oil bath and mesh.

The paper element is made of resin impregnated paper. Air filters using this type of replaceable element are used both for cars and commercial vehicles. They provide a very high filtering efficiency and reasonable service life. They can be mounted in any position available under the bonnet. Service intervals vary, so check recommendations; between 12 000 and 24 000 miles is typical.

The oil bath and mesh type of air cleaner was widely used on non turbo charged commercial vehicles. However, it is not very practical for modern low styled bonnets. Because it can be cleaned and fresh oil added, an oil bath air cleaner may still be used for vehicles operating in dusty conditions.

Figure 8.9 Paper air filters and other types of filters

Air temperature   Air temperature control is used to help the vehicle conform to emission
control   control regulations and for good driveability when the engine is cold. Good vaporisation of the fuel is the key. An automatic control is often fitted to

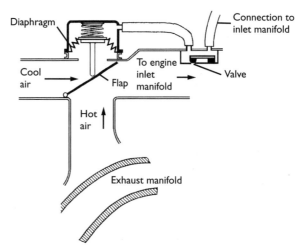

Figure 8.10 Air temperature control system

make sure that the air intake temperature is always correct. The air cleaner has two intake pipes, one for cold air and the other for hot air from the exhaust manifold or hot box. The proportion of hot and cold air is controlled by a flap which is moved by a diaphragm acted on by low pressure from the inlet manifold. The flap rests in the hot air pick up position.

A thermo-valve in the air stream senses the temperature of the air going into the engine. When a temperature of about 25°C is reached, the valve opens. This removes the connection to the manifold, which in turn increases the pressure acting on the diaphragm. The flap is now caused to move, and the pick up is now from the cool air position. The flap is constantly moving and ensures the temperature of air entering the engine remains constant. Picking up hot air when the engine is still cold can also help to prevent icing in a carburettor.

LEARNING TASKS

➡ Look back at the key words. Explain each one to a friend, and/or write out a short description to keep as evidence.

➡ Examine a real system and make a simple sketch to show all the parts of an air supply system.

4 Diagnostics

Systematic testing

FAULT FINDING

1. Verify the fault
2. Collect further information
3. Evaluate the evidence
4. Carry out further tests in a logical sequence
5. Rectify the problem
6. Check all systems

For example, if the reported fault is a noisy exhaust, you could proceed as follows:

1. Check if the noise is due to the exhaust knocking or blowing.
2. Examine the vehicle on the lift.
3. Are further tests required or is it obvious?
4. Cover the end of the exhaust pipe with a rag for a second or two to highlight where the exhaust may be blowing.
5. Renew the exhaust section or complete system as appropriate.
6. Run and test for leaks and knocking.

Fault diagnosis

Symptom	Possible causes of faults	Suggested action
Exhaust noise	Hole in pipe, box or at joints	Renew as appropriate
Knocking noise	Exhaust incorrectly positioned Broken mountings	Reposition Renew
Rich mixture/smoke	Blocked air filter	Replace
Noisy air intake	Intake trunking or filter box leaking or loose	Repair or secure as required
Poor cold driveability	Hot air pick up not operating	Check pipe connections to inlet manifold for leaks. Renew temperature valve or actuator

LEARNING TASKS

➡ Practise fault finding on real vehicles.

➡ Make a list of steps you would take to find some of the faults causing the symptoms listed in the table.

9 Ignition systems

1 Introduction

Start here!

KEY WORDS

■ Timing
■ Dwell
■ Induction
■ All words in the table

The purpose of the ignition system is to make a spark inside the cylinder, near the end of the compression stroke. This will ignite the compressed fuel–air mixture. Fundamentally all ignition systems operate in the same way.

To make a spark of electricity jump across an air gap of 0.6 mm under normal atmospheric conditions requires 2 000 to 3 000 V. To make a spark to jump across a similar gap in an engine cylinder requires over 8 000 V. For higher compression engines and weaker mixtures, a voltage up to 20 000 V may be needed!

These high voltages are dangerous. Take care and follow manufacturers' instructions.

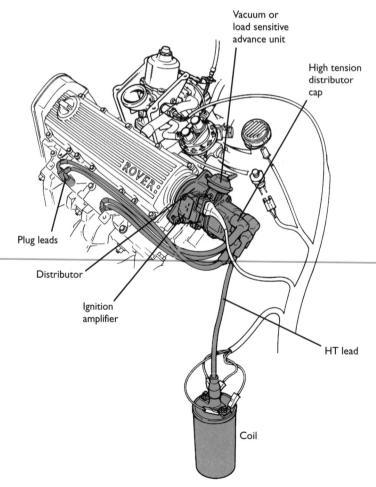

Figure 9.1 Engine showing ignition system components

The ignition system has to change the normal battery voltage of 12 V into many thousands of volts. This high voltage then has to be sent to the right cylinder, and at the right time. Most ignition systems are now electronically controlled.

Terminology

Ignition	The source which makes something start and continue burning on its own. Like putting a match to a bonfire, or of course lighting the fuel–air mixture in an engine cylinder
Electric spark	Electricity will jump through the air or other gas if the voltage pressure is large enough. Many kV are required for a spark plug in an engine. Lightning in a thunderstorm is a somewhat larger example
Low tension (LT)	An old fashioned phrase meaning low voltage
High tension (HT)	An old fashioned phrase meaning high voltage
Primary	The low voltage (battery voltage) part of an ignition system. This includes the battery, ignition switch, one winding of the coil and a triggering or switching device
Secondary	The high voltage part of the ignition system. In some cases this includes one of the coil windings, plug leads, rotor arm, distributor cap and spark plugs
Dwell angle	The angle of rotation of the engine camshaft during which time the ignition coil is switched on
Dwell percentage	The angle of rotation of the engine camshaft during which time the ignition coil is switched on as a percentage of the angle available. For example, on a four cylinder engine, four sparks are needed each time the cam rotates once. This means 90° for each, so if the dwell angle is 45° the dwell percentage will be 50% (45/90×100%)
Breakerless	A way of describing electronic ignition. The word 'breaker' refers to the older type systems which use moving contacts
Electronic ignition	The ignition coil is switched on and off by an electronic device such as a transistor
Conventional ignition	A term to be cautious with! Conventional means something like 'normal and in common use'. Therefore in this case it should mean electronic ignition, but it is usually used to refer to the older contact breaker type!

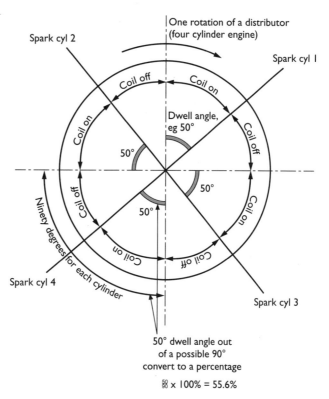

Figure 9.2 Dwell angle and percentage

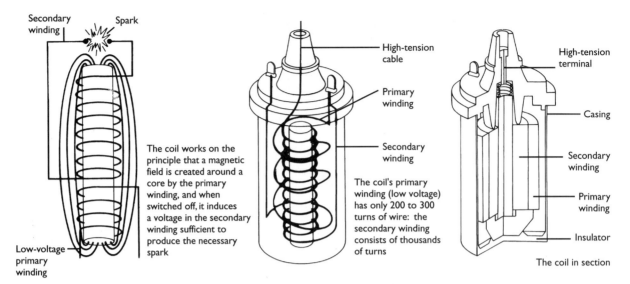

Figure 9.3 Transformer action of an ignition coil

How to make a high voltage

The most important part of the ignition system is the coil. It acts as a transformer. The coil consists of two windings around an iron core. The primary winding is connected to the battery and has only a few hundred turns of wire. The secondary winding, which is the output, has thousands of turns of thinner wire. The coil charges up from the 12 volt battery and transforms it to a high voltage (up to 20 000 volts) to ignite the fuel–air mixture in the engine. To ensure the coil is charged before the ignition point, a dwell period is required.

When the engine is running, the battery current to the coil is switched on and off by means of a transistor (or contact breakers in the distributor on older cars). As it is switched off, the collapsing current in the primary winding makes a voltage in the secondary winding. This is known as electromagnetic induction. The induced voltage in the secondary winding is typically about 15 000 to 20 000 volts. This passes to the spark plugs to create sparks. The actual spark occurs at the instant the coil is switched off.

Ignition timing

To allow the engine to work at its most efficient, the ignition should be timed to cause the maximum combustion pressure to occur about 10° after TDC. The ideal ignition timing depends on two main factors: engine speed and engine load. An increase in engine speed requires the ignition to be earlier in the cycle (timing advanced). This is because the piston moves more quickly, but the cylinder full of air–fuel mixture still requires a certain time to burn. The fuel burning rate remains almost constant.

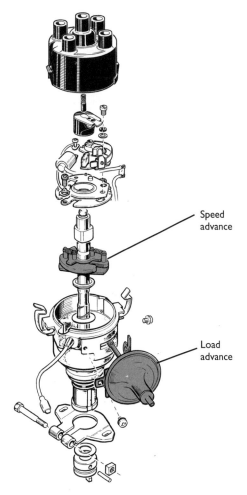

Figure 9.4 Distributor showing speed and load advance mechanism

A change in timing due to engine load (how hard the engine is working) is required because a weaker mixture is used on low load conditions, and this burns at a slower rate than a richer mixture.

Spark timing change is achieved in a number of ways. The simplest of these is a mechanical system comprising of a centrifugal advance mechanism and a vacuum or pressure control unit (Figure 9.4). The pressure in the inlet manifold is proportional to the engine load. Most modern ignition systems adjust the timing electronically.

LEARNING TASKS

➡ Look back at the key words. Explain each one to a friend, and/or write out a short description to keep as evidence.

➡ Write a short explanation about why ignition timing is so important.

2   Ignition components

KEY WORDS

- All words in the table
- Spark plug temperatures

The following table describes the main components of the ignition system.

Component	Purpose
Spark plug	Seals electrodes for the spark to jump across inside the engine combustion chamber. Must be able to withstand very high voltages, pressures and temperatures
Ignition coil	Stores energy in the form of magnetism and delivers it to the distributor via the HT lead. Consists of primary and secondary windings
Ignition switch	Provides driver control of the ignition system and other electrical systems. It is usually also used to cause the starter to crank the engine
Ballast resistor	Fitted in series with the coil primary winding, it is shorted out during starting to cause a more powerful spark. Also contributes towards improving the spark at higher speeds
Pulse generator	A device fitted on the engine crank, flywheel or in the ignition distributor. It produces a signal relative to the engine speed and position. This is used to tell the electronic module when to operate the ignition coil
Ignition module (electronic control unit or amplifier)	An electronic device, the most important part of which is a transistor to switch the ignition coil on and off at the right time. Many are now made as part of the unit which controls the fuel system as well
Contact breakers (points)	Fitted in the distributor, the contacts are operated by a cam and switch the primary ignition circuit on and off to charge and discharge the coil
Capacitor (condenser)	Stops most of the arcing as the contact breakers open. This allows for a more rapid break of primary current and hence a more rapid collapse of coil magnetism which produces a higher voltage output
HT distributor	Sends the spark from the coil to each cylinder in the engine firing order
Rotor arm	Rotates in time with the engine to point at a contact in the distributor cap. It is supplied from the coil
Distributor cap	Contains the same number of connections as engine cylinders. The rotor arm revolves inside it. Each connection to a spark plug is made by a plug lead
Plug leads	Highly insulated wires to keep the high voltage inside. They connect the distributor cap to the plugs and in many cases the coil to the cap. They are made to have a high resistance to reduce radio interference
Centrifugal advance	Changes the ignition timing with engine speed. As speed increases, the timing is advanced (made to occur earlier in the cycle). Speed sensitive advance
Vacuum advance	Changes timing depending on engine load. Load sensitive advance

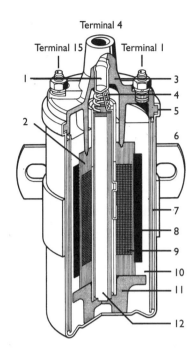

1 = High-tension connection on the outside
2 = Winding layers with insulating paper
3 = Insulating cap
4 = High-tension connection on the inside via spring contact
5 = Case
6 = Mounting bracket
7 = Metal plate jacketing (magnetic)
8 = Primary winding
9 = Secondary winding
10 = Sealing compound
11 = Insulator
12 = Iron core

Figure 9.5 Section through an ignition coil

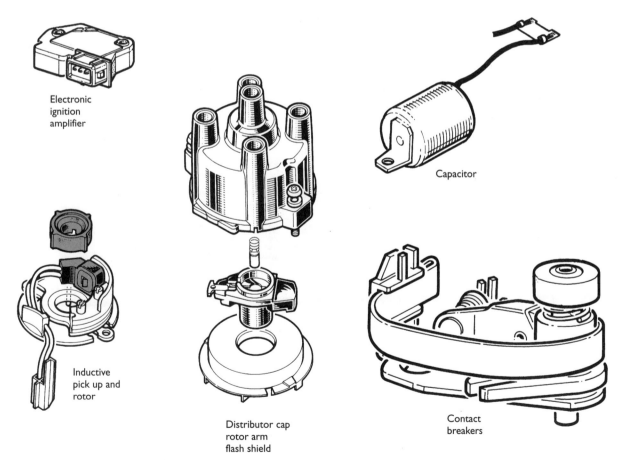

Figure 9.6 Electronic and contact breaker ignition components

Spark plugs A spark plug must allow a spark to form in the combustion chamber. In order to do this the plug has to withstand a number of severe conditions:

- very high pressures
- severe vibration
- harsh chemical environment
- voltages up to 40 kV.

Figure 9.7 shows a typical spark plug. The centre electrode is connected to the top terminal by a stud. The electrode is constructed of a nickel based alloy. Silver and platinum are also used for some applications. If a copper core is used in the electrode, it conducts heat better. The insulating material is ceramic and of a very high quality. Flash over or sparks tracking down the outside of the plug insulation is prevented by ribs which increase the surface distance from the terminal to the metal fixing.

The range of temperatures a spark plug is exposed to can vary significantly in different engines. The operating temperature of the centre electrode of a spark plug is very important. If the temperature becomes too high and it becomes red hot, ignition may occur too early. On the other hand, if the electrode temperature is too low, then carbon and oil fouling can occur as deposits are not burnt off. The ideal operating temperature of the plug electrode is between 400 and 900°C. Figure 9.8 shows how the temperature of the electrode changes with engine power output. It is for this reason that only the plugs recommended by the vehicle manufacturer must be used. They are designed to work at the ideal temperature.

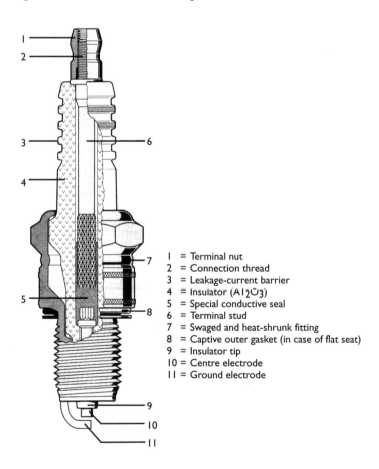

1 = Terminal nut
2 = Connection thread
3 = Leakage-current barrier
4 = Insulator (Al_2O_3)
5 = Special conductive seal
6 = Terminal stud
7 = Swaged and heat-shrunk fitting
8 = Captive outer gasket (in case of flat seat)
9 = Insulator tip
10 = Centre electrode
11 = Ground electrode

Figure 9.7 Spark plug

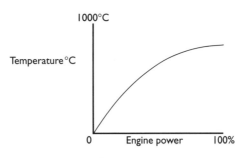

Figure 9.8 Spark plug temperature during operation

Over the years, as the power of the ignition systems driving the spark has increased, spark plug electrode gap settings have increased. The plug gap must be large enough to allow easy access for the mixture to prevent misfires, but not too large so the spark can't jump. It must therefore be set only as recommended in technical data.

LEARNING TASKS

➡ Look back at the key words. Explain each one to a friend, and/or write out a short description to keep as evidence.

➡ Write a short explanation about how to change a set of spark plugs.

---

3 Types of ignition systems

Introduction

KEY WORDS

■ Contact breaker ignition

■ Electronic ignition

■ Programmed ignition

■ Distributorless ignition

■ Direct ignition

The basic types of ignition systems can be classified as shown in the table. The techniques are explained further in the following sections.

	Contact breaker	Electronic	Programmed	Distributorless	Direct
Trigger	Mechanical	Electronic	Electronic	Electronic	Electronic
Advance	Mechanical	Mechanical	Electronic	Electronic	Electronic
Volt source	Inductive	Inductive	Inductive	Inductive	Inductive
Distribution	Mechanical	Mechanical	Mechanical	Electronic	Electronic

Contact breaker ignition

The distributor is the heart of the contact breaker ignition system. Its job is to trigger the ignition coil at the appropriate time and to distribute the high voltages the coil creates. The distributor has a shaft that runs through its middle. The shaft is driven by the engine, usually with a set of gears. In a four stroke engine, ignition occurs on every other engine revolution. The distributor therefore rotates at half the engine speed.

The distributor cam operates the contact breaker points. These are electrical contacts held together by a spring and are forced apart as the cam rotates. The contacts connect the battery to the ignition coil. This electrical circuit is known as the primary ignition circuit. Each time the contacts open, the primary circuit is interrupted and a high voltage is created in the ignition coil. This travels to the central terminal of the distributor cap. The distributor cap has one output terminal for each of the engine's cylinders.

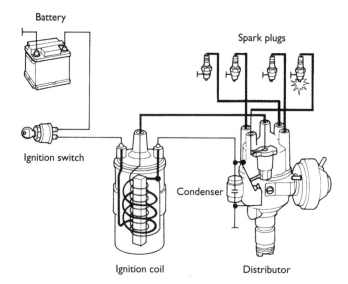

Figure 9.9 Contact breaker ignition system

The rotor arm mounted on top of the shaft is always in contact with the cap's central terminal. As the rotor spins, its arm comes into close contact with each of the outer terminals in sequence. The rotor creates a connection between the centre terminal and each outer terminal. This in turn is connected to its spark plug with well insulated wire.

At the same time as the rotor lines up with one of the outer terminals, the primary ignition circuit is opened by the contacts. The high voltage pulse travels from the coil to the distributor's central terminal, then through the rotor and an outer terminal, and finally through the plug lead to the spark plug.

Ignition occurs just before the piston reaches the top of its stroke, so the fuel–air mixture in the combustion chamber is completely burned at the top of the piston's stroke. The heat and expanding gases generated by combustion then push the piston downward. At higher engine speeds the piston travels faster and ignition must occur earlier (advanced ignition).

To provide this earlier spark, the distributor incorporates an advance mechanism. The mechanism consists of spring loaded weights that are pulled outward by centrifugal force as the engine speed increases. This alters the position of the distributor rotor and cam on the shaft and causes earlier, or advanced ignition. The vacuum (lower pressure) created in the inlet manifold also adjusts the amount of spark advance. As engine load increases, manifold pressure increases, and the distributor rotor and cam are moved to alter the timing to suit the engine load. Most distributors use both load and centrifugal advance mechanisms to adjust ignition timing. The advance mechanism described here is used for some electronic systems as well as the older contact breaker types.

Electronic ignition   Electronic ignition is now fitted almost universally to petrol driven vehicles. This is because the mechanical contacts system has three major disadvantages:

- mechanical problems with the contact breakers, not least of which is their limited lifetime

- current flow in the primary circuit is limited to about 4 A, otherwise damage to the contacts will occur or at least their lifetime will be seriously reduced
- legislation requires stringent emission limits, so the ignition timing must stay in tune for a long period of time.

These problems have been overcome by using a transistor to carry out the switching and a pulse generator to provide the timing signal. In electronic ignition systems a toothed wheel (usually one tooth per engine cylinder) takes the place of the distributor cam. In place of the contacts, a stationary sensor inside the distributor electromagnetically senses the passing of each tooth. With fewer moving parts to wear out, electronic ignition requires less maintenance and is more reliable than the older systems.

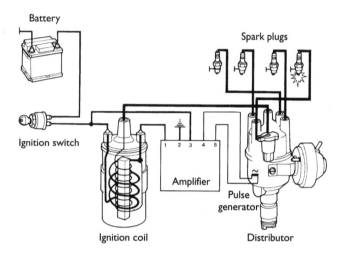

Figure 9.10 Electronic ignition system

Ignition and fuel injection are now often controlled by a single electronic control unit (ECU), providing better engine performance and efficiency. Some ignition systems may not even have distributors, but use instead a double ended coil or even a small ignition coil for each spark plug. The ignition ECU triggers the coils individually, using engine sensors to time the pulses correctly. These systems are examined briefly in the next sections.

Programmed ignition

Programmed ignition is the term used by Rover and some other manufacturers. Ford, Bosch and others call it electronic spark advance or ESA. Programmed ignition systems have a major difference compared to earlier systems, in that they operate digitally (by a computer). The best operating requirements (timing settings under different conditions) of a particular engine can be programmed in to memory inside the electronic control unit. Programmed ignition has several advantages:

- The ignition timing can be accurately matched to the individual vehicle.
- Other control input can be used, such as coolant temperature and air temperature.
- Starting is improved, fuel consumption and emissions are reduced.
- Other inputs can be taken into account, such as engine knock (incorrect ignition).
- The number of wearing components in the ignition system is considerably reduced.

1 = Programmed ignition electronic
    control unit (ECU)
2 = Coolant temperature sensor
3 = Knock sensor
4 = Crankshaft sensor and reluctor
5 = Ignition coil
6 = Ignition switch
7 = High tension distributor
8 = Fuel injection ECU

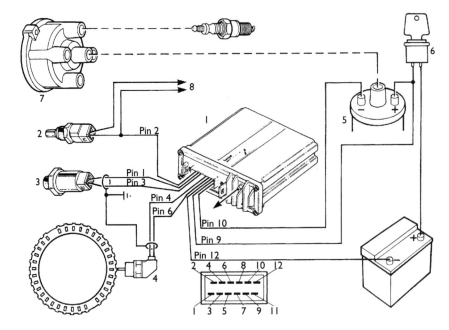

Figure 9.11 Programmed ignition system

Figure 9.11 shows the layout of the Rover programmed ignition system. In order for the ECU to work out suitable timing, certain input information is required:

■ engine speed and position – crankshaft sensor

■ engine load – manifold absolute pressure sensor

■ engine temperature – coolant sensor

■ detonation – knock sensor.

The high tension distribution is similar to a more conventional system. The rotor arm, however, is mounted on the end of the camshaft with the distributor cap positioned over the top. The distributor cap is mounted on a base plate which prevents any oil from the camshaft seal fouling the cap and rotor arm.

Distributorless ignition

Distributorless ignition, used extensively by Ford and other manufacturers, has all the features of electronic spark advance systems (programmed ignition), but by using a special type of ignition coil it outputs to the spark plugs without the need for an HT distributor.

The system is generally only used on four cylinder engines. The basic principle is that of the 'lost spark'. The distribution of the spark is achieved by using two double ended coils which are fired alternately by the ECU. The timing is determined from a crankshaft speed and position sensor as well as load and other corrections. When one of the coils is fired, a spark is delivered to two engine cylinders, either 1 and 4 or 2 and 3. The spark delivered to the cylinder on the compression stroke will ignite the mixture as normal. The spark produced in the other cylinder will have no effect as this cylinder will be just completing its exhaust stroke.

Because of the low compression and the exhaust gases in the 'lost spark' cylinder, the voltage used for the spark to jump the gap is only about 3 kV. The spark produced in the compression cylinder is therefore not affected.

1 = Electronic spark control module
2 = Pipe to inlet manifold
3 = Crank speed and position sensor
4 = Coolant temperature sensor
5 = DIS coil

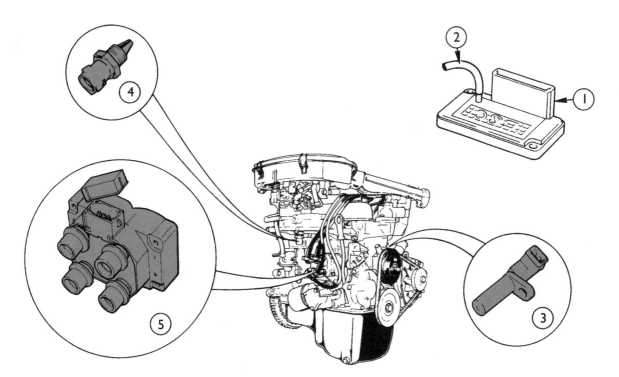

Figure 9.12 Distributorless ignition

Direct ignition   In a way direct ignition is the follow on from distributorless ignition. This system uses a coil for each cylinder. These coils are mounted directly on the spark plugs. The use of an individual coil for each plug ensures that a very high voltage, high energy spark is produced. This voltage, which can be in excess of 40 kV, provides very good ignition.

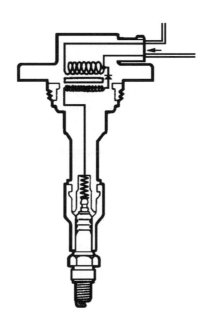

Figure 9.13 Direct ignition system

LEARNING TASKS

➡ Look back at the key words. Explain each one to a friend, and/or write out a short description to keep as evidence.

➡ Examine a real system and make a simple sketch to show the layout of ignition components.

➡ Write a short explanation about the advantages of programmed ignition.

---

4 Diagnostics

Systematic testing

For example, if the reported fault is an engine misfire, you could proceed as follows:

1. Road test or run the vehicle.
2. Check when the fault occurs: when hot, cold or all the time?
3. For example, if the fault occurs only when cold, it may be the cold start fuel system.
4. Remove and examine the spark plugs, check HT components etc.
5. Renew plug leads, for example.
6. Road test to ensure the problem has been rectified.

FAULT FINDING

1. Verify the fault
2. Collect further information
3. Evaluate the evidence
4. Carry out further tests in a logical sequence
5. Rectify the problem
6. Check all systems

Test equipment

Always refer to the manufacturers' instructions appropriate to the equipment you are using.

Multimeter

This essential tool has many uses. In the case of ignition systems, the ohmmeter function will allow you to measure the resistance of HT leads.

Timing light

A stroboscopic timing light is used to set dynamic timing. This means setting ignition timing when the engine is running. A connection is made to the battery as a power supply and a clip fits over number one plug lead. The light will now flash each time number one plug fires. The light is directed at the engine timing marks and the distributor can be moved until the appropriate marks line up when the engine is at a set speed. Timing is now set and adjusted electronically on many engines, but many cars with distributors are still in use.

Rev counter/dwell meter

This handheld tool may be part of a multimeter or a separate device. A connection is made to the ignition coil LT terminal with one wire, the other is connected to earth. The speed of the engine in rev/min and the dwell, as an angle or a percentage, can be read off and compared to data.

Figure 9.14   Ignition timing light

Engine analyser

This very expensive and complex piece of equipment is almost essential for complex fault finding of ignition as well as other electrical systems. This will be covered in detail in the level 3 book.

Test results   The following table shows some of the information you may have to get from other sources such as data books or a workshop manual.

Test carried out	Information required
Ignition timing	Ignition timing is given as a number of degrees BTDC and at a certain speed. For example, 12° BTDC at 700 rev/min (often written as 12°/700)
Lead resistance	The resistance of anything varies with length. This figure will be given as, for example, 40 kΩ/m maximum (in other words, a lead 25 cm long should be no more than 10 kΩ). Some manufacturers specify a maximum resistance for any lead of 30 kΩ
Engine speed	Simply measured in rev/min
Plug gaps	Simply measured in mm. For example 0.8 or 1 mm are common settings
Dwell	This can be as an angle, e.g. 30°, or a percentage, e.g. 50%. For a six cylinder engine these two readings would mean the same, but on a four cylinder engine they are different. Make sure you compare like with like

Fault diagnosis

Symptom	Possible causes of faults	Suggested action
Misfire	One or more plugs worn to excess or incorrectly gapped	The plugs should be renewed and/or correctly gapped
	Open circuit HT lead	Renew
	Water contamination	Clean and dry all parts. Use a water repellent

Symptom	Possible causes of faults	Suggested action
Pinking	Ignition timing too far advanced (too early in the cycle)	Timing should be checked and reset to the manufacturer's specifications
	Incorrect grade of fuel	Check and use the correct grade specified for the engine
Overheating	Timing too far retarded (too late in the cycle)	Timing should be checked and reset to the manufacturer's specifications
	Cooling system fault	Check cooling system
Poor performance	Timing incorrect	Correctly set timing
	Plugs worn	Renew
	HT lead open circuit or shorting to the engine	Renew

LEARNING TASKS

➡ Practise fault finding on real vehicles.

➡ Make a list of steps you would take to find some of the faults causing the symptoms listed in the table.

10 Lubrication

1 Introduction

Start here! Lubrication is the introduction of a substance, called a lubricant (oil, for example, to create an oil film), between two moving contact surfaces in order to reduce friction. This reduction of friction greatly reduces the wear of the surfaces and thus lengthens their service life. It also reduces the energy required for the movement. Lubrication is important in all moving parts of the vehicle, but the engine has the greatest need.

Under a microscope even the smoothest engine components have a surface that looks very rough. If these surfaces made contact, they would rub together, overheat and destroy themselves. To prevent this happening, engines have a lubrication system that pumps or drips a constant supply of oil on all the moving metal components.

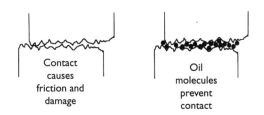

Figure 10.1 How oil prevents surface contact

Although the basic function of a lubricant is to reduce friction and wear, a lubricant may also perform a number of other tasks. It carries off generated heat, and it also helps to form a gas tight seal between piston rings and cylinders. It also carries away harmful combustion waste products. Lubrication helps to control corrosion by coating parts with a protective film. A detergent added to the lubricant helps to removes sludge deposits.

Terminology	
Oil	The lubricant! It can be vegetable, mineral or, for high performance engines, synthetic
Filter	Usually a paper element to keep the oil clean
Strainer	The primary oil filter fitted on the oil pump pickup pipe in most engines. It is simply a wire mesh
Main gallery	A drilling or casting in the engine block from where oil is distributed round the engine
Oil pressure switch	A switch to operate the oil pressure warning light. It gives a warning if oil pressure drops as this could wreck the engine very quickly
Oil pump	A device to produce oil pressure to distribute oil around the engine and force oil in between some bearing surfaces

Terminology

Pressure relief valve	A valve to limit the oil pressure by returning oil to the sump when the set pressure is reached
Crankcase ventilation/ engine breathing	System to prevent buildup of pressure in, and emissions from, the engine interior or crankcase
Viscosity	A measure of the resistance to flow of a liquid like oil (in a way the thickness of the oil). Greater viscosity means more resistance or, to be exact, a greater internal friction. This means better lubrication, as it prevents oil being squeezed out of contact surfaces. However, it is more difficult to pump and move
Viscosity index	The viscosity of oil changes with temperature. The index gives an indication of this change. A higher number means temperature has less effect on the viscosity
SAE – Multigrade oils	The higher the SAE (Society of Automotive Engineers) number, the higher the viscosity. For example, SAE 20 has a lower viscosity than SAE 40. Multigrade oils have different viscosities at different temperatures. SAE 20/40, for example, means that the oil will act like 20 or 40 depending on the temperature. Thinner oil when cold makes the engine easier to crank over, but without the special additives it would become too thin at higher temperatures. Multigrade contains an additive known as a viscosity extender to get the best of both worlds
Oiliness	The ability of an oil to cling to a surface. Important for boundary lubrication
Additives	Chemicals added to oil to improve its properties. These range from detergents for cleaning to viscosity extenders to make 'multigrade oils'

Types of oil Lubricants made from animal and vegetable products (such as whale oil or linseed oil) have been used for a very long time. Fortunately they have now been superseded by more effective mineral products, particularly by lubricants refined from petroleum. Polymer films and silicones are synthetic lubricants that have been developed to meet the demanding requirements of modern automobile systems.

The wide range of oil types now available makes it impossible to give recommendations other than the usual advice:

'Always follow manufacturers' instructions and use the correct oil.'

Figure 10.2 Examples from the range of products available

Types of lubrication   If a film of lubricant is used between the surfaces, the process is called boundary lubrication. This type of lubrication is introduced between the moving surfaces by splash feed or an oil mist. The best example is on the side of the pistons, but all sliding components use this method.

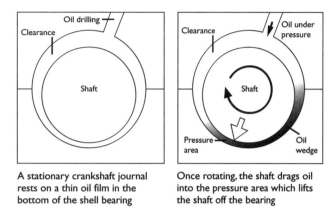

A stationary crankshaft journal rests on a thin oil film in the bottom of the shell bearing

Once rotating, the shaft drags oil into the pressure area which lifts the shaft off the bearing

Figure 10.3 An oil wedge in a big end bearing

Boundary lubrication also commonly occurs on some bearings during starting of the engine. Once the engine is moving, pressure is generated as a result of the shape and motion of the surfaces. This is known as hydrodynamic lubrication. For example, the rotation of the crankshaft in a bearing forces lubricant into the wedge shaped space between the shaft and the bearing. The clearance between the bearing and the shaft, the load on the shaft, the speed of rotation and the viscosity of the lubricant have a marked effect on this process.

Methods of   Bath lubrication or splash lubrication (used in gearboxes and rear axles) may
lubrication   be used for gears, chains, bearings and other moving parts that can be partly submerged in an oil reservoir. In the bath system the gear simply picks up oil as it dips into the reservoir and sprays or carries it to other parts along its path. The splash system increases the efficiency by attaching a special splash ring to a moving part so that the oil is splashed against other parts that need to be lubricated. This is similar to oil mist lubrication, created by the oil escaping from the engine's rotating crankshaft, where it is atomised in a stream of air.

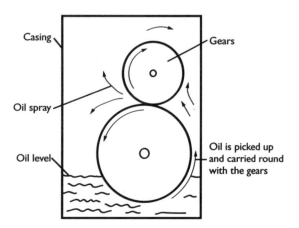

Figure 10.4 Splash feed lubrication

Force feed lubrication uses an oil pump to force the oil under pressure to the parts to be lubricated, normally the engine crankshaft and camshaft. On some high performance vehicles the mainshaft in the gearbox is pressure fed. Some parts are self lubricating and require no external lubrication; the lubricant may be sealed in against loss, as in sealed ball bearings, alternatively a porous material such as porous bronze can be used so that oil impregnated in the material can penetrate through pores to the point of contact of the moving parts. In small two stroke engines the oil is mixed in with the fuel to bring it to the moving parts inside the engine.

Although lubricating oil is used elsewhere in a car, the lubrication of the engine is of greatest importance because it reduces the friction and wear between moving metal parts and also removes heat from the engine. A supply of oil is kept in the engine crankcase. An oil pump, which is powered by the engine, forces oil from the crankcase under pressure to the cylinder block main oil gallery. Passages in the engine block channel the oil to various moving parts, such as the crankshaft and camshaft, and the oil eventually drains back down in the crankcase. An oil filter is fitted in the oil circuit to filter out metal shavings, carbon deposits and dirt. Because the filter is not completely effective, and because of prolonged exposure to high temperatures, the oil eventually becomes contaminated, decomposes, and loses its lubricating qualities. That is why routine maintenance calls for changing the oil and oil filter at regular intervals (between 6 000 and 12 000 miles is typical).

LEARNING TASKS

➡ Look back at the key words. Explain each one to a friend, and/or write out a short description to keep as evidence.

➡ Make a simple sketch to show what is meant by surface contact and how oil reduces it.

➡ Read about manufacturers' recommendations on service intervals in a workshop manual.

---

2   System layout

Lubrication system From the sump reservoir under the crankshaft, oil is drawn through a strainer into the pump. Oil pumps have an output of tens of litres per minute and operating pressures of over 5 bar at high speeds. A pressure relief valve limits the pressure of the lubrication system to between 2.5 and 4 bar. This control is needed because the pump would produce excessive pressure at high speeds. After leaving the pump, oil passes into a filter and then into a main oil gallery in the engine block or crankcase.

Drillings connect the gallery to the crankshaft bearing housings. When the engine is running, oil is forced under pressure between the rotating crank journals and the main bearings. The crankshaft is drilled so that the oil supply from the main bearings also reaches the big end bearings of the connecting rods.

The con rods are often drilled near the base so that a jet of oil sprays the cylinder walls and the underside of the pistons. In some cases the con rod

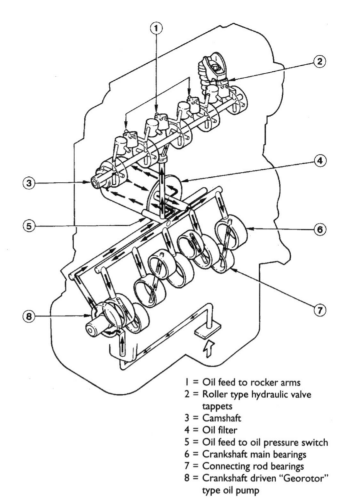

1 = Oil feed to rocker arms
2 = Roller type hydraulic valve tappets
3 = Camshaft
4 = Oil filter
5 = Oil feed to oil pressure switch
6 = Crankshaft main bearings
7 = Connecting rod bearings
8 = Crankshaft driven "Georotor" type oil pump

Figure 10.5 Engine lubrication system

may be drilled along its entire length so that oil from the big end bearing is taken directly to the gudgeon pin (small end). The surplus then splashes out to cool the underside of the piston and cylinder.

The camshaft operates at half crankshaft speed, but it still needs good lubrication because of the high pressure loads on the cams. It is usual to supply pressurised oil to the camshaft bearings and splash or spray oil on the cam lobes. On overhead camshaft engines, two systems are used. In the simplest system the rotating cam lobes dip into a trough of oil. Another method is to spray the cam lobes with oil. This is usually done by an oil pipe with small holes in it alongside the camshaft. The small holes in the side of the pipe aim a jet of oil at each rotating cam lobe. The surplus splashes over the valve assembly and then falls back into the sump.

On cars where a chain drives the cam, a small tapping from the main oil gallery sprays oil on the chain as it moves past, or the chain may simply dip in the sump oil.

Filters   Even new engines can contain very small particles of metal left over from the manufacturing process, or grains of sand which have not been removed from the crankcase after casting. Old engines continually deposit tiny bits of metal worn from highly loaded components such as the piston rings. To prevent any of these lodging in bearings or blocking oil ways, the oil is filtered.

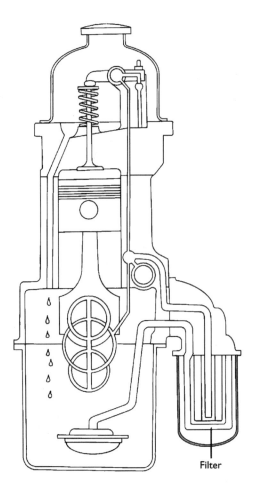

Filter

Figure 10.6 Full flow filter system

The primary filter is a wire mesh strainer that stops particles of dirt or swarf from entering the oil pump. This is normally on the end of the oil pickup pipe. An extra filter is also used to stop very fine particles. The most common type has a folded, resin impregnated paper element. Pumping oil through it removes all but the smallest solids from the oil.

Most engines use a full flow system to filter all of the oil after it leaves the pump. The most popular method is to pump the oil into a canister containing a cylindrical filter. From the inner walls of the canister the oil flows through the filter and out from the centre to the main oil gallery. Full flow filtration works well, provided the filter is renewed at regular intervals. If it is left in service too long, it may become blocked. When this happens the buildup of pressure inside the filter forces open a spring loaded relief valve in the housing, and the oil bypasses the filter. This valve prevents engine failure, but the engine will be lubricated with dirty oil until the filter is renewed. This is better than no oil!

A bypass filtration system was used on older vehicles. This system only filters a proportion of the oil pump output. The remainder is fed directly to the oil gallery. At first view this seems a strange idea, but all of the oil does eventually get filtered. The smaller amount through the filter allows a higher degree of filtration.

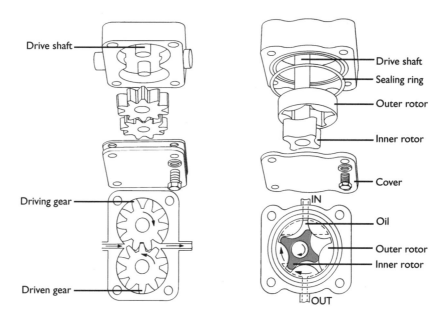

Figure 10.7 Gear type and rotary type oil pumps

Oil pumps

In its simplest form an oil pump consists of two gear wheels meshed together in a tight space so that oil cannot escape past the sides. One wheel is driven by the engine. As the gears rotate in opposite directions, the gap between each tooth in each wheel traps a small quantity of oil from an inlet port. The trapped oil is carried round by each wheel towards an outlet port on the opposite side. It is now forced out by the meshing teeth.

The principle of squeezing oil from an ever decreasing space is also used in the rotor type pump. An inner and outer rotor are mounted on different axes in the same cylinder. The inner rotor, which commonly has four lobes, is driven by the engine. It meshes with an outer rotor which has five lobes. As they rotate, the spaces between them change size. The inlet port is at a point where the space between the rotor lobes is increasing. This draws the oil in to the pump. The oil is then carried round the pump. As rotation continues, the space between the lobes gets smaller. This compresses the oil out of the outlet port.

Pressure relief valve

Oil pumps can produce more pressure than is required. A valve is used to limit this pressure to a set value. The pressure relief valve is a simple device which in most cases works on the ball and spring principle. This means that when the pressure on the ball is greater than on the spring, the ball moves. The pressure relief valve is placed in the main gallery so that excess pressure is prevented. When the ball moves, oil is simply returned to the sump.

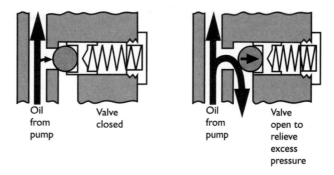

Figure 10.8 Oil pressure relief valve

Crankcase ventilation – engine breather systems

If we were unable to breathe, we would die! It is almost as important for an engine breathing system to work correctly. There are two main reasons for engine breathers:

1. Prevent pressure build up inside the engine crankcase due to combustion gases blowing past the pistons. The buildup of pressure will blow gaskets and seals, but there is also a high risk of explosion.

2. Prevent toxic emissions from the engine. Emission limits are now very strict, and for good reason; our health!

Crankcase breathing or ventilation of the engine was first achieved by what is known as an open system, but this has now been completely replaced by the closed system.

Open system

Air at atmospheric pressure entered at the top of the engine, in most cases through a combined oil filler and breather cap. The air was caused to circulate through the inside of the engine by a breather pipe. The lower end of this pipe was placed in the air stream under the car. Removal of the crankcase gases therefore depended upon the movement of the vehicle. The air circulation in the crankcase was assisted by the rotation of the crankshaft. A basic problem with this simple system was that ventilation was poor at low speeds and during idling – when it was most needed.

Closed system

The gases escaping from an engine with open crankcase ventilation as described above are very toxic. Legislation now demands a positive closed system of ventilation. This makes the pollution from cylinder blowby gases negligible. Positive crankcase ventilation is the solution to this problem.

In early types of closed system crankcase ventilation, the lower pressure at the carburettor air cleaner was used to cause an air flow through the inside of the engine. The breather outlet was simply connected by a pipe to the air cleaner. This caused the crankcase gases to be circulated and then burned in the engine cylinders. A flame trap was included in the system, to prevent a crankcase explosion if the engine backfired.

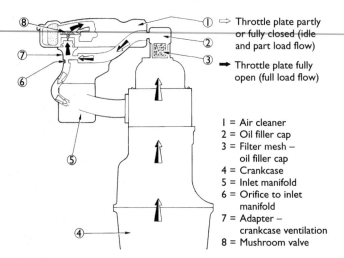

① ⇨ Throttle plate partly or fully closed (idle and part load flow)

➡ Throttle plate fully open (full load flow)

1 = Air cleaner
2 = Oil filler cap
3 = Filter mesh – oil filler cap
4 = Crankcase
5 = Inlet manifold
6 = Orifice to inlet manifold
7 = Adapter – crankcase ventilation
8 = Mushroom valve

Figure 10.9 Crankcase ventilation – closed system

In modern closed systems the much lower pressure within the inlet manifold is used to extract crankcase gases. This has to be controlled in most cases by a variable regulator valve or pressure conscious valve (PCV). The valve is fitted between the breather outlet and the inlet manifold. It consists of a spring loaded plunger, which opens as the inlet manifold pressure reduces. When the engine is stationary the valve is closed. Under normal running conditions the valve opens to allow crankcase gases to enter the inlet manifold with minimum restriction. At low manifold pressures during idling and overrun (pressure is less than atmospheric), further travel of the valve plunger against its spring closes it in the opposite direction. This reduces gas flow to the inlet manifold. This feature makes sure that the fuel control process is not interfered with under these conditions. The valve also acts as a safety device in case of a backfire. Any high pressure created in the inlet manifold will close the valve completely. This will isolate the crankcase and prevent the risk of explosion.

LEARNING TASKS

➡ Look back at the key words. Explain each one to a friend, and/or write out a short description to keep as evidence.

➡ Examine real lubrication system components. How would you decide if they were still serviceable?

➡ Examine a real system and make a simple sketch to show the breather system.

➡ Write a short explanation about why crankcase ventilation is important.

---

3 Diagnostics

Systematic testing

FAULT FINDING

1. Verify the fault
2. Collect further information
3. Evaluate the evidence
4. Carry out further tests in a logical sequence
5. Rectify the problem
6. Check all systems

For example, if the reported fault is that the oil pressure light comes on at low speed, you could proceed as follows:

1. Run the engine and see when the light goes off or comes on.
2. Is the problem worse when the engine is hot? Check the oil level! When was the vehicle last serviced?
3. If the oil level is correct, then you must investigate further.
4. Carry out an oil pressure test to measure the actual pressure.
5. If the pressure is correct, then renew the oil pressure switch. If this does not solve the problem, engine strip down is likely.
6. Run and test for leaks.

Test equipment   Always refer to the manufacturers' instructions appropriate to the equipment you are using.

Figure 10.10 Oil pressure gauge

Oil pressure test gauge

This is a simple pressure gauge that can be fitted with suitable adapters into the oil pressure switch hole. The engine is then run and the pressure readings compared to data.

Vacuum gauge or absolute pressure gauge

A simple 'U' tube full of water is often used. This is connected to the oil dip stick tube and the engine is run. The gauge should show a pressure less than atmospheric (a partial vacuum). This checks the operation of the crankcase ventilation system.

Test results   The following table shows some of the information you may have to get from other sources such as data books or a workshop manual.

Test carried out	Information required
Oil pressure	Oil pressure is measured in bars. A typical reading would be about 3 bar
Crankcase pressure	By tradition pressures less than atmosphere are given in strange ways, such as inches of mercury or inches of water! This is why I like to stick to absolute pressure and the bar! 0 bar is no pressure, 1 bar is atmospheric pressure and so on. 2 to 3 bar is more than atmospheric pressure, like in a tyre. Standards vary, so make sure you compare like with like! Crankcase pressure should be less than atmospheric – check data

Fault diagnosis

Symptom	Possible causes of faults	Suggested action
Low oil pressure	Lack of oil Blocked filter Defective oil pump Defective oil pressure relief valve	Top up Renew oil and filter Renew after further tests Adjust if possible or renew
High crankcase pressure	Blocked crankcase breather Blocked hose Pressure blowing by pistons	Clean or replace Clean or renew hose Engine overhaul may be required

Symptom	Possible causes of faults	Suggested action
Loss of oil	Worn piston rings	Engine overhaul may be required
	Leaks	Renew seals or gaskets

LEARNING TASKS

➡ Practise fault finding on real vehicles.

➡ Make a list of steps you would take to find some of the faults causing the symptoms listed in the table.

11 Transmission

1 Introduction

Start here! Transmission is a general term used to describe all the components required to transmit power from the engine to the wheels. The power needs to be converted from the relatively high velocity and low torque of the engine crankshaft to the variable, usually lower speed and higher torque needed at the wheels.

The two basic types of transmission use either a manual gearbox, in which the gears are selected by the driver, or an automatic gearbox, in which the gears are changed automatically.

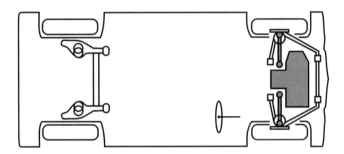

Figure 11.1 Layout of the front wheel drive transmission system

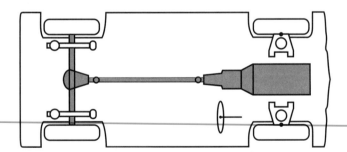

Figure 11.2 Layout of a rear wheel drive transmission system

The main components of a typical front wheel drive transmission system (working from the engine to the wheels) are as follows:

- clutch
- gearbox
- final drive
- differential
- drive shafts (then to the wheels).

Each of these main areas will be examined in more detail in this chapter.

KEY WORDS

- All words in the table
- Ratio
- Torque and speed

Terminology

Clutch	Fitted between engine and gearbox, the clutch allows the drive to be disconnected when the pedal is pushed down. It allows a smooth takeup of drive and allows gears to be changed
Manual gearbox	A box full of gears of varying ratios! The ratio most suitable for the current driving conditions can be selected by the gear stick. Most boxes contain about thirteen gear cogs which allow five forward gears and one reverse
Torque converter	This is sometimes called a fluid flywheel and is used in conjunction with an automatic gearbox. It is in two main parts: as the input section rotates, fluid pressure begins to act on the output section to make it rotate. As speed increases, a better drive is made. The drive therefore takes up automatically and smoothly
Automatic gearbox	As the name suggests, this is a gearbox which operates automatically. Most types contain special gear arrangements, known as epicyclic gear trains. Some now use very complicated electronic control, but the basic principle is that fluid pressure from a pump is used to change the gears. The fluid pressure changes with road speed
Final drive	To produce the required torque at the road wheels, a fixed gear reduction from the high engine speed is required. The final drive consists of just two gears with a ratio of about 4:1
Differential	A special combination of gears which allow the driven wheels of a vehicle to rotate at different speeds. Think of a car going round a roundabout: the outer wheel has to travel a greater distance, and hence must rotate at a faster speed than the inner wheel. If this was not allowed for, the drive would 'wind up' and something would break
Driveshafts	Two driveshafts are used to pass the drive from the outputs of the final drive to each wheel. Each driveshaft contains two CV joints
Propshaft	On rear wheel drive vehicles, the drive has to be passed from the gearbox output to the final drive and differential unit in the rear axle. The propshaft (short for propeller shaft) is a hollow tube with a universal joint (UJ) at each end. If removed, the UJs must be aligned correctly
UJ	Universal joint. The UJ is like a cross with a bearing on each leg. It allows drive to be transmitted through an angle. This is to allow for suspension movement
CV joint	Constant velocity joint. The CV joint is a bit like a UJ, but it is used on front wheel drive driveshafts. It allows smooth drive to be passed through, even when the suspension moves it up and down, and the steering moves it side to side

LEARNING TASKS

➡ Look back at the key words. Explain each one to a friend, and/or write out a short description to keep as evidence.

➡ Make a simple sketch to show the layout of a transmission system.

➡ Examine a real system and note how the main components are placed and make sure you can name and state the purpose of each main part.

➡ Write a short explanation about why a vehicle needs a gearbox of some kind.

2 Clutch and gearbox

Clutch

A clutch is a device for disconnecting and connecting rotating shafts. In a vehicle with a manual gearbox, the driver pushes down the clutch when changing gear, thus disconnecting the engine from the gearbox. It allows a temporary neutral position for gear changes and also a gradual way of taking up drive from rest.

The clutch is made of two main parts, a pressure plate and a driven plate. The driven plate, often termed the clutch disc, is fitted on the shaft which takes the drive into the gearbox. When the clutch is engaged, the pressure plate presses the driven plate against the engine flywheel. This allows drive to be passed to the gearbox. Pushing down the clutch springs the pressure plate away, which frees the driven plate.

Cars with automatic transmission do not have a clutch as described here.

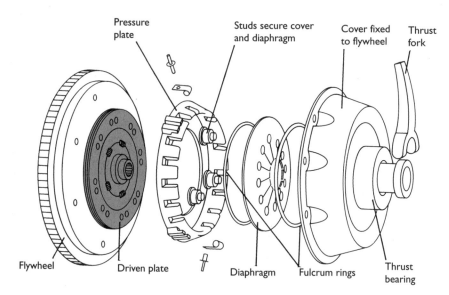

Figure 11.3 Diaphragm type clutch

Drive is transmitted from the flywheel to the automatic gearbox by a torque converter, sometimes called a fluid clutch.

The following table describes the main clutch and flywheel components.

Component	Purpose
Flywheel	Keeps the engine running smoothly between power strokes, but also acts as a surface for the driven plate to press against
Driven plate	Friction material plate which is clamped between the pressure plate and the flywheel. It is splined on to the gearbox input shaft. The small coil springs are to prevent the clutch snatching as drive is taken up
Pressure plate	The cover of the pressure plate is fixed to the flywheel with a ring of bolts. The fingers in the centre act as springs and levers to release the pressure. Drive is transmitted unless the fingers are pressed in towards the flywheel
Thrust bearing	This bearing pushes against the clutch fingers when the pedal is pushed down to release the drive

Component	Purpose
Thrust fork	Connects to the bearing
Release spring	A return spring so that when the clutch pedal is not pushed down, the bearing allows the fingers to return outwards
Clutch cable	Makes a secure connection to the clutch pedal. Strong steel wire is used. A few vehicles use hydraulics to operate the clutch
Bell housing	A general cover for the clutch assembly, but also to secure the clutch and gearbox to the engine

Manual gearbox   For most light vehicles a gearbox has five forward gears and one reverse gear. It is used to allow operation of the vehicle through a suitable range of speeds and torque. A manual gearbox needs a clutch to disconnect the engine crankshaft from the gearbox while changing gears. The driver changes gears by moving a gear lever, which is connected to the box by a mechanical linkage.

The gearbox converts the engine power by a system of gears, providing different ratios between the engine and the wheels. When the vehicle is moving off from rest, the gearbox is placed in first, or low gear. This produces a high torque at low wheel speed. As the car speeds up, the next higher gear is selected. With each higher gear, the output turns faster but with less torque.

Lets look at this idea of ratios in a little more detail. When the vehicle starts from rest in first gear, the gear ratio might be 3:1. This means that the crankshaft turns three times to turn the output shaft once. As the vehicle gains some speed, the gearbox is moved into second gear, with a gear ratio of, say, 2:1. After a further increase in wheel speed, a move is made into the next higher gear, and so on. Fourth gear on most *rear* wheel drive light vehicles is called direct drive, because there is no gear reduction in the gearbox. In other words, the gear ratio is 1:1 (the output of the gearbox turns at the same speed as the crankshaft). For front wheel drive vehicles, the ratio can be 1:1 or slightly different. Most modern light vehicles now have a fifth gear. This can be thought of as a kind of overdrive because the output turns faster than the engine crankshaft.

Older vehicles used sliding mesh gearboxes where the cogs moved in and out of contact with each other, but these have now been replaced by synchromesh. This means that the gear teeth are in constant mesh and can turn freely on the shaft. To make a gear selection, the required combination of gears is first synchronised (which means the teeth on the two dog clutches are brought to the same speed) and then locked together so that power is transmitted. Special mechanisms are used to prevent more than one gear being selected at any one time (interlocks).

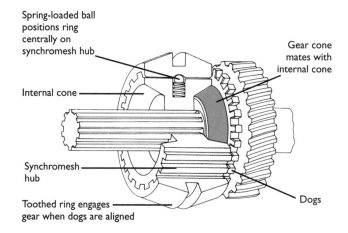

Spring-loaded ball positions ring centrally on synchromesh hub

Internal cone

Synchromesh hub

Toothed ring engages gear when dogs are aligned

Gear cone mates with internal cone

Dogs

Figure 11.4 Synchromesh assembly

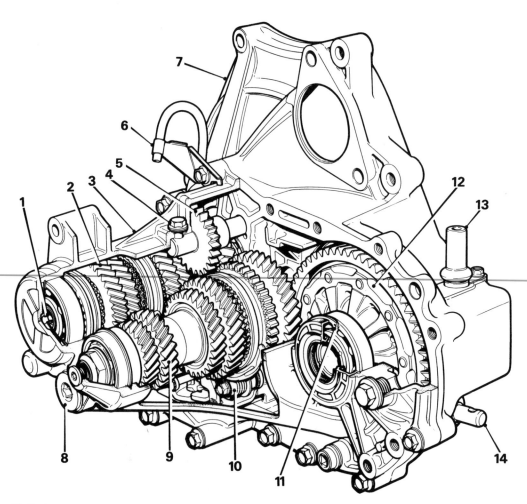

Figure 11.5 A typical manual gearbox showing all the main components

The following table describes the main components of a manual gearbox.

No.	Component	Purpose
1	Oil guide plate	Ensures suitable lubrication
2	Mainshaft assembly	This shaft carries all the main forward gears, and the selectors and clutches
3	Gear case	The box to hold it all together and act as a seal and reservoir for the lubrication oil
4	Reverse shaft bolt	A simple fixing for the reverse gear shaft
5	Reverse idler gear	An extra gear has to be engaged to reverse the direction of the drive. A low ratio is used for reverse, in many cases even lower than first gear
6	Breather pipe and bracket	A pipe to prevent pressure buildup, and a bracket to hold it!
7	Bell housing	For fixing to the engine and as a cover for the clutch
8	Access plug	For access to, say, a bearing circlip during repairs. Different gearboxes will vary quite a lot
9	Countershaft assembly	Sometimes called a layshaft, this is usually a solid shaft containing four or more gears. Drive is passed from here to the output shaft
10	Selector interlock	The interlock is to prevent more than one gear being selected at any one time. Otherwise the gearbox would lock as the gears would be trying to turn the output at two different speeds at the same time
11	Selective spacer	Just a spacer used on this type of box, selected to set up the correct thrust on the final drive assembly
12	Final drive assembly	Contains the final drive gears and also the differential
13	Speedometer drive	A connection for the speedometer cable or electronic sensor
14	Gearshift rod	This rod is connected to the selectors to allow gears to be engaged. A connection is also made to the gear stick with suitable linkages

Automatic transmission

Automatic transmissions use a torque converter to couple the engine and the gearbox. The torque converter is a fluid coupling, in which one rotating part causes the transmission fluid to rotate. This in turn imparts a rotation to another part, which is connected to the gearbox. The coupling of the torque converter allows slippage for when the car is starting from rest. As the car

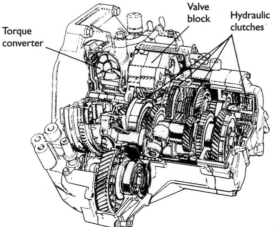

Figure 11.6 Automatic gearbox and torque converter

gains speed, the slippage is reduced; at cruising speeds the driven member turns almost as fast as the driving member. Some modern systems can actually lock the two together to eliminate slip completely. The gearbox contains epicyclic or planetary gears, with clutches and brake bands for engaging the desired gears.

LEARNING TASKS

➡ Look back at the key words. Explain each one to a friend, and/or write out a short description to keep as evidence.

➡ Make a simple list to outline the purposes of the clutch and gearbox. What are they for?

---

3 Driveshafts and wheel bearings

Introduction

Light vehicle driveshafts now fall into one of two main categories, the first being by far the most popular:

KEY WORDS

- CV joint gaiter
- Sliding joint
- Bearings

■ Driveshafts with constant velocity joints (FWD) – transmit drive from the output of the final drive to each front wheel. They must also allow for suspension and steering movements.

■ Propshaft with universal joints (RWD) – transmits drive from the gearbox output to the final drive in the rear axle. Drive then continues through the final drive and differential, via two half shafts to each rear wheel. The propshaft must also allow for suspension movements.

Wheel bearings allow smooth rotation of the wheel but must also be able to withstand high stresses such as from load in the vehicle and when cornering.

The following table describes the main propshaft components.

Component	Purpose
Main shaft	A hollow steel tube. This is quite light weight, but will still transfer considerable turning forces
Universal joints	Sometimes called 'Hooke' joints, the UJs are to allow a small movement of the rear axle with the suspension, while the gearbox remains fixed. Two joints are used on most systems and must always be aligned correctly
Sliding joint	As the suspension moves up and down, the length of the propshaft has to be able to change slightly. The splined sliding joint allows for this to happen

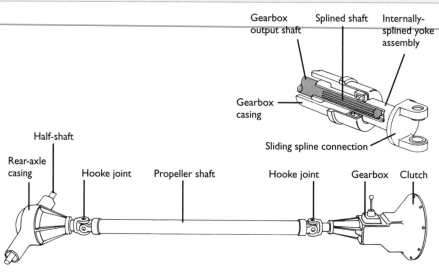

Figure 11.7 Propshaft

The next table explains the main driveshaft components.

Component	Purpose
Main shaft	Solid steel shaft to transmit the drive
Constant velocity joint	Allows constant speed rotation even as the suspension and steering move the joint
CV joint – cage	Positions the steel balls within the sockets. The cage is fixed to the main shaft
CV joint – steel balls	Carried in grooves to link the cage and the outer socket. The balls transmit the drive, but are also free to slide in the grooves to take up the suspension and steering movement
CV joint – outer socket	Fixed to the output shaft going into the wheel hub
Gaiter or rubber boot	Keeps out the dirt and water and keeps in the lubricant such as grease

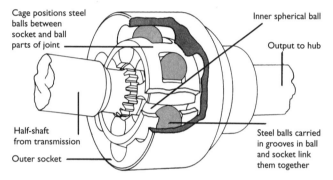

Figure 11.8 Driveshaft constant velocity joint

The following table describes the main components of the front wheel bearings (the components are shown in the diagram from left to right).

Component	Purpose
Seal	Keeps out dirt and water and keeps in the grease lubrication
Spacer	Ensures the correct positioning of the seal
Inner bearing	Supports the weight of the vehicle at the front, when still or moving. Ball bearings are used for most vehicles, with specially shaped tracks for the balls. This is so that the bearings can stand side loads when cornering
Swivel hub	Attachment for the suspension and steering as well as supporting the bearings
Outer bearing	As for inner bearing
Drive flange	Runs inside the centre race of the bearings. The wheel is bolted to this flange

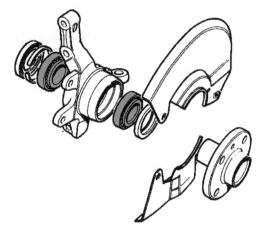

Figure 11.9 Front wheel bearing assembly

The next table describes the main components of the rear wheel bearings. The components are shown in the diagram from left to right.

Component	Purpose
Stub axle	Solid mounted to the suspension arm, the stub axle fits in the centre of the two bearings
Seal	Keeps out dirt and water and keeps in the grease lubrication
Inner bearing	Supports the weight of the vehicle at the rear, when still or moving. Ball bearings are used for most vehicles, with specially shaped tracks for the balls. This is so that the bearings can stand side loads when cornering
Spacer	To ensure the correct spacing and pressure between the two bearings
Drum	For the brakes and attachment of the wheel
Outer bearing	As for inner bearing
Washer	The heavy washer acts as a face for the nut to screw against.
Castle nut and split pin	Holds all parts in position securely. With this type of bearing, no adjustment is made because both bearings are clamped on to the spacer. Some older cars use tapered bearings, and adjustment is very important
Grease retainer cap	Retains grease, but should not be overpacked. Also keeps out the dirt and water

Figure 11.10 Rear wheel bearing assembly

LEARNING TASKS

➡ Look back at the key words. Explain each one to a friend, and/or write out a short description to keep as evidence.

➡ Examine a real system and note the layout of driveshafts and bearings.

4   Final drive and differential

Introduction

Because of the speed at which an engine runs, and in order to produce enough torque at the road wheels, a fixed gear reduction is required. This is known as the final drive and consists of just two gears. On front wheel drive vehicles these are fitted after the output of the gearbox; on rear wheel drive vehicles they are in the rear axle after the propshaft. The gears also turn the drive through 90° on rear wheel drive vehicles. The ratio is normally about 4:1; in other words: when the gearbox output is turning at 4 000 rev/min, the wheels will turn at 1 000 rev/min.

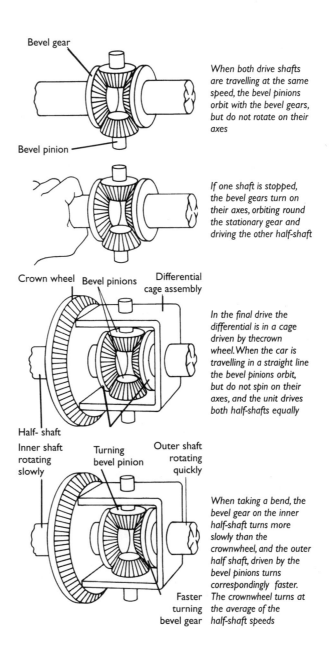

Bevel gear

When both drive shafts are travelling at the same speed, the bevel pinions orbit with the bevel gears, but do not rotate on their axes

Bevel pinion

If one shaft is stopped, the bevel gears turn on their axes, orbiting round the stationary gear and driving the other half-shaft

Crown wheel   Bevel pinions   Differential cage assembly

In the final drive the differential is in a cage driven by the crown wheel. When the car is travelling in a straight line the bevel pinions orbit, but do not spin on their axes, and the unit drives both half-shafts equally

Half- shaft

Inner shaft rotating slowly   Turning bevel pinion   Outer shaft rotating quickly

When taking a bend, the bevel gear on the inner half-shaft turns more slowly than the crownwheel, and the outer half shaft, driven by the bevel pinions turns correspondingly faster. The crownwheel turns at Faster turning the average of the bevel gear half-shaft speeds

Figure 11.11 Action of the differential

The differential is an arrangement of gears within the final drive of a vehicle's transmission system. Its purpose is to allow the driving wheels to turn at different speeds when cornering. The differential consists of sets of bevel gears and pinions within a cage attached to the large final drive gear. When cornering, the bevel pinions rotate on their shaft; this allows the outer wheel to turn faster than the inner.

The following table describes the main components of the final drive and differential.

No.	Component	Purpose
1	Final drive pinion	Brings the drive from the gearbox to the final drive gear
2 & 6	Bearing	Supports the differential casing, which in turn is bolted to the final drive gear
3	Final drive gear	Sets a fixed gear reduction in conjunction with the final drive pinion
4	Pin	For secure and correct location of the casing
5	Differential casing	Transmits the drive from the final drive gear to the planet gear pinion shaft
7	Circlip	Secures the whole gear train in position
8	Sun gear pinions	Splined to the drive shafts, the sun gears take their drive from the planet gears
9	Thrust washer	Sets basic clearances
10	Planet gear pinions	These gears are pushed round by their shaft
11	Planet gear pinion shaft	This shaft is secured in the differential casing so that it pushes the planet gears. If the sun gears (which are attached to the road wheels via the drive shafts) are moving at the same speed, the planet gears do not spin on their shaft. If the sun gears need to move at different speeds when the vehicle is cornering, then the planet gears spin on their shaft to make up for the difference

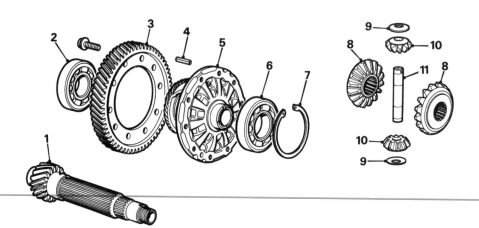

Figure 11.12 Final drive and differential assembly

5 Diagnostics

Systematic testing

For example, if the reported fault is a slipping clutch, you could proceed as follows:

1. Road test to confirm when the fault occurs.
2. Look for oil leaking from the bell housing or general area of the clutch. Check adjustment if possible.
3. If adjustment is correct, then the clutch must be examined.
4. In this example the clutch assembly must be removed for visual examination.
5. Replace parts as necessary; this is often done as a kit comprising the clutch plate and cover and in some cases a bearing.
6. Road test and check operation of the transmission.

Fault diagnosis

Symptom	Possible causes of faults	Suggested action
Clutch slipping	Clutch worn out	Renew
	Adjustment incorrect	Adjust or check auto-adjuster
	Oil contamination	Rectify oil leak – clutch may also need to be renewed
Jumps out of gear	Gearbox detent fault	Gearbox may require overhaul
Noisy when changing gear	Synchromesh worn	Gearbox may require overhaul
Rapid knocking noise when cornering	Driveshaft CV joints worn or without lubrication	Renew or lubricate joint. Ensure gaiter is in place and in good condition
Whining noise	Wheel bearing worn	Renew
	Other bearings	Investigate and renew if possible
Difficult to change gear	Clutch out of adjustment	Adjust or check auto-adjuster
	Clutch hydraulic fault	Check system for air and/or leaks
	Gearbox selectors worn	Gearbox may require overhaul

LEARNING TASKS

➡ Practise fault finding on real vehicles.

➡ Make a list of steps you would take to find some of the faults causing the symptoms listed in the table

12 Suspension

1 Introduction

Start here! The suspension system has the following main tasks:

- Cushion the car, passengers and load from road surface irregularities.
- Resist the effects of steering, braking and acceleration, even on hills and when loads are carried.
- Tyres must be kept in contact with the road at all times.
- Work in conjunction with the tyres and seat springs to give an acceptable ride at all speeds.

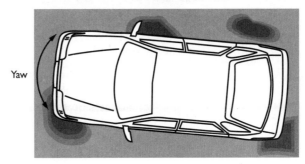

Figure 12.1 A car riding over rough ground

The above list is difficult to achieve completely, so some sort of compromise has to be reached. Because of this many different methods have been tried, and many are still in use. Keeping these four main requirements in mind will help you to understand why some systems are constructed in different ways.

Terminology

Spring	The part of the suspension system that takes up the movement or shock from the road or vehicle movement. The energy of the movement is stored in the spring. There are many different forms of spring, ranging from a steel coil to a pressurised chamber of nitrogen
Damper	The energy stored in the spring after a bump has to be got rid of, otherwise the spring would oscillate (bounce up and down). The damper reduces these oscillations by converting the energy from the spring into heat. If working correctly, the spring should stop moving after just one bounce and rebound
Shock absorber	This term describes the action of a spring. It is often used incorrectly to describe a damper
Strut	Often the combination of a coil spring with a damper inside it, between the wheel stub axle and the inner wing. This is a very popular type of suspension
Wishbone	A triangular shaped component with two corners hinged in a straight line on the vehicle body and the third corner hinged to the moving part of the suspension
Bump stop	When a vehicle hits a particularly large bump, or if it is carrying a heavy load, the suspension system may bottom out (reach the end of its travel). The bump stop, usually made of rubber, prevents metal to metal contact which would cause damage
IFS	Independent front suspension
IRS	Independent rear suspension
Independent suspension	This allows a wheel of the vehicle to move without affecting the one at the other side
Link	A very general term to describe a bar or similar component that holds or controls the position of another component. Other terms may be used such as tie bar
Beam axle	A solid axle from one wheel to the other. Not now used on the majority of light vehicles, but still common on heavy vehicles as it makes a very strong construction
Gas/fluid suspension	The most common types of spring are made from spring steel. However some vehicles use pressurised gas as the spring (think of a balloon or a football). On some vehicles a connection between wheels is made using fluid running through pipes from one suspension unit to another

Keeping you further in suspension

A vehicle needs a suspension system to cushion and damp out road shocks, so providing comfort to the passengers and preventing damage to the load and vehicle components. A spring between the wheel and the vehicle body allows the wheel to follow the road surface. The tyre plays an important role in absorbing small road shocks. It is often described as the primary form of suspension.

The vehicle body is supported by springs located between the body and the wheel axles. Together with the damper, these components are referred to as the suspension system.

Now remember that the main function of a suspension system is to stop road shocks from being transmitted to the vehicle body. The weight of the vehicle, including its load, acts on the springs. The springs and other components compress and expand as the wheels hit bumps or holes in the road. The function of the suspension components is to allow the wheels to move up and down without moving the vehicle body.

As a wheel hits a bump in the road, it is moved upwards with quite some force. An unsprung wheel is affected only by gravity, which will try to return the wheel to the road surface, but most of the energy will be transferred to the body. When a spring is used between the wheel and the vehicle body, most of the energy in the bouncing wheel is stored in the spring and not passed to the vehicle body. The vehicle body will now only move upwards through a very small distance compared to the movement of the wheel.

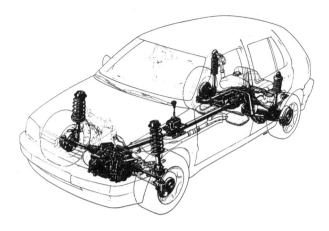

Figure 12.2 Vehicle showing main suspension components

Consideration must be given to the difference between 'sprung' and 'unsprung' mass of a suspension system. Sprung mass is that which is supported by the vehicle springs. Unsprung mass is that of the components between the springs and the road. For most vehicles, unsprung mass includes wheels, tyres, brake, steering and suspension components, as well as part of the drive shafts. But some of the suspension and drive components are sprung at one end and unsprung at the other! The less mass the road wheel and the other units attached to it have, the smaller is the total energy involved when they are moved. Vehicles are made with as little unsprung mass as possible as this reduces the effect of road shock on the vehicle body. Soft springs provide the best comfort, but stiff springs can be better for high performance. Vehicle springs and suspension therefore are made to provide a compromise between good handling and comfort.

LEARNING TASKS

➠ Look back at the key words. Explain each one to a friend, and/or write out a short description to keep as evidence.

➠ Examine a real system and make a simple sketch of how the suspension components are connected.

➠ Write a short explanation about what a suspension system must be able to do.

---

2   Types of spring

Coil springs

Although modern vehicles use a number of different types of spring medium, the most popular is the coil (or helical) spring. Coil or helical springs used in vehicle suspension systems are made from round spring steel bars. The heated bar is wound on a special former and then heat treated to obtain the correct elasticity (springiness). The spring can withstand any compression load, but not side thrust. It is also difficult for a coil spring to resist braking or driving thrust. Suspension arms are used to resist these loads.

Coil springs are used with independent suspension systems; the springs are usually fitted on each side of the vehicle, between the stub axle assembly and the body. The spring remains in the correct position because recesses are made in both the stub axle assembly and body. Due to the weight of the vehicle the spring is always under compression and hence holds itself in place.

Leaf springs   The leaf spring can provide all the control for the wheels during acceleration, braking, cornering and general movement caused by the road surface. They are used with fixed axles. There are two main types of leaf spring:

- laminated or multi leaf springs
- single leaf or mono leaf springs

A third type, known as the tapered leaf spring, is a combination of these two.

The multi leaf spring was widely used at the rear of cars and light vehicles and is still used in commercial vehicle suspension systems. It consists of a number of steel strips or leaves placed on top of each other and then clamped together. The length, cross section and number of leaves is determined by the loads carried.

The top leaf is called the main leaf, and each end of this leaf is rolled to form an eye. This is for attachment to the vehicle chassis or body. The leaves of the spring are clamped together by a bolt or pin known as the centre bolt. The spring eye allows movement about a shackle and pin at the rear, allowing the spring to flex. The vehicle is pushed along by the rear axle through the front section of the spring which is anchored firmly to the fixed shackle on the vehicle chassis or body. The curve of a leaf spring straightens out when a load is applied to it, and its length changes.

Because of this change in length, the rear end of the spring is fixed by a shackle bolt to a swinging shackle. As the road wheel passes over a bump, the spring is compressed and the leaves slide over each other. As it returns to its original shape, the spring forces the wheel back in contact with the road. The leaf spring is usually secured to the axle by means of U bolts. As the leaves of the spring move, they rub together. This is known as interleaf friction, which also has a damping effect.

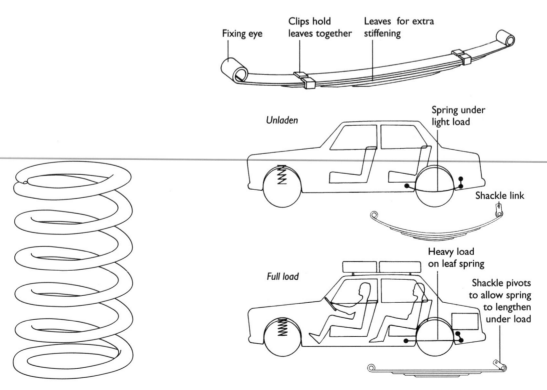

Figure 12.3 Coil spring   **Figure 12.4** Laminated leaf spring

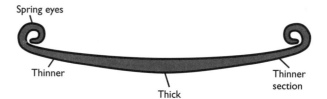

Figure 12.5 Single leaf spring

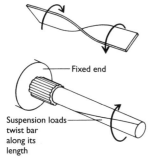

Figure 12.6 Torsion bar spring

A single leaf spring, as the name implies, consists of one uniformly stressed leaf. The spring varies in thickness from a maximum at the centre to a minimum at the spring eyes. This type of leaf spring is made to work in the same way as a multi leaf spring. Advantages of this type of spring are as follows:

- simplified construction
- constant performance over a period of time because interleaf friction is eliminated
- reduction in unsprung mass.

Leaf springs are now rarely found on light vehicles, but never say never!

Torsion bars   This type of suspension uses a metal bar which provides the springing effect as it is twisted. It has the advantage that the components do not take up too much room. Some vehicles that use torsion bars do not have dampers. This is because some layouts have a self damping effect.

Pneumatic suspension   Steel springs must be stiff enough to carry a vehicle's maximum load. This can result in the springs being too stiff to provide consistent ride control and comfort when the vehicle is empty. Pneumatic suspension can be made self compensating. It is fitted to many heavy goods vehicles and buses, but is also becoming more popular on some off road light vehicles.

The air spring is a reinforced rubber bellow fitted between the axle and the chassis, or vehicle body. An air compressor is used to increase or decrease the pressure depending on the load in the vehicle. This is done automatically, but some manual control can be retained for adjusting the height of the vehicle or stiffness of the suspension.

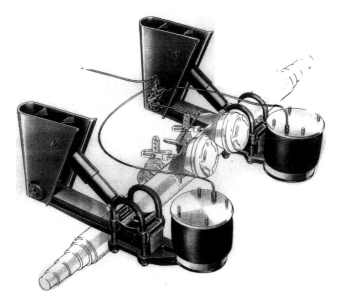

Figure 12.7 Air suspension (heavy vehicle)

Rubber springs   This is now a very old system, but often old ideas come back! The suspension medium, or spring, is simply a specially shaped piece of rubber. This technique was used on early Minis, for example. In most cases the rubber did not require damping.

Figure 12.8 Rubber spring suspension

Hydrolastic suspension   The suspension unit is supported by a rubber spring. Under the spring a chamber of fluid is connected by a pipe to the corresponding front or rear unit. This system was the forerunner to the hydragas system.

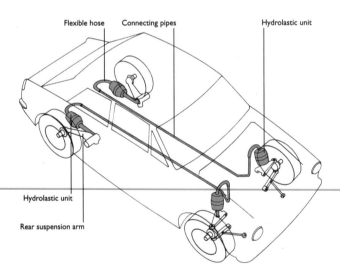

Figure 12.9 Hydrolastic suspension

Hydragas suspension   In the hydragas suspension system, each wheel has a sealed displacer unit with nitrogen gas under very high pressure. This works in much the same way as the steel spring in a conventional system. A damper is also incorporated within the displacer unit. The lower part of the displacer units is filled with a suspension fluid (usually a type of wood alcohol). The units can be joined by pipes or used individually.

Connecting suspension units by fluid in pipes is designed to improve the ride quality. Linking front to rear makes the rear unit rise as the front unit is compressed by a bump. This tends to keep the vehicle level.

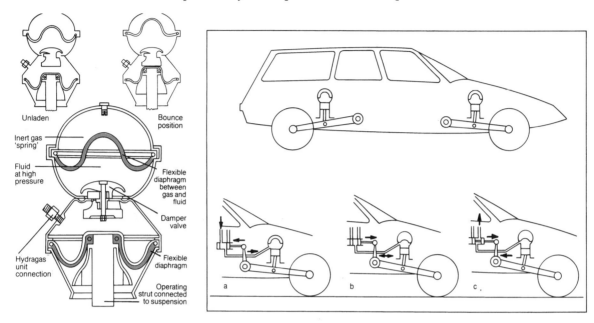

Figure 12.10 Hydragas suspension

3 Dampers

Introduction

KEY WORDS

- Bump
- Rebound
- Valve orifice

As a spring is deflected, energy is stored in it. If the spring is free to move, the energy is released in the form of oscillations for a short time, before coming to rest. This principle can be demonstrated by flicking the end of a ruler placed on the edge of a desk. The function of the damper is to absorb the stored energy which reduces the rebound oscillation. A spring without a damper would build up dangerous and uncomfortable bouncing of the vehicle.

Hydraulic dampers are the most common type used on modern vehicles. They work by forcing fluid through small holes. The energy in the spring is converted into heat as the fluid (a type of oil) is forced rapidly through the small holes (orifices). The oil temperature in a damper can reach over 150°C during normal operation. As an example think of using a hand oil pump and how hard it is to make the oil flow quickly.

The main type of hydraulic damper is known as the telescopic type. A lever arm type used on earlier vehicles works on the same principle. Hydrolastic and hydrogas suspension systems have the damper built in to the displacer units.

Telescopic dampers   This is the most common type of hydraulic damper used on modern vehicles. The damper is mounted between the body and the axle or wishbone. A piston, connected to a rod fixed via a rubber bush to the vehicle body, moves oil in a circuit around the damper through valves from one chamber to another. On some types oil passes through valves in the piston. The units are filled with a thin oil and are usually sealed for life. Most dampers contain rubber bushes in mounting eyes. A double acting damping action works on both the bump and rebound (up and down) strokes.

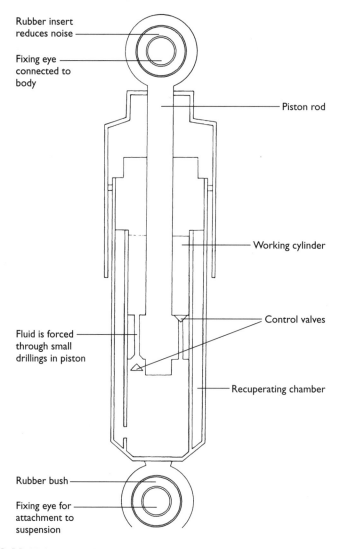

Rubber insert reduces noise

Fixing eye connected to body

Piston rod

Working cylinder

Control valves

Fluid is forced through small drillings in piston

Recuperating chamber

Rubber bush

Fixing eye for attachment to suspension

Figure 12.11 Telescopic damper

A typical double acting telescopic damper is made with a central pressure tube surrounded by a reservoir tube. Two valves are fitted in the base of the pressure tube to control the movement of fluid between the two tubes. The pressure and reservoir tubes are filled with fluid and are sealed. The pressure tube contains a sliding piston and valve assembly at the lower end of the piston rod. There is usually another tube over the rod and cylinder – this is simply a dirt shield.

On the compression stroke (bump stroke), the axle pushes the piston into the cylinder and oil pressure opens the piston compression valve. Oil passes via the port in the piston from the lower to the upper chamber. The oil also passes through the compression valve to the reservoir. On the rebound stroke, the piston and the base valves close and oil passes through the rebound valves to the lower chamber.

Resistance to movement is determined mostly by the size of the valve orifice (small hole). A difference between bump and rebound can be obtained simply with different sized valves. The damper can be designed to give a soft downwards movement when the vehicle first hits a bump, with a harder rebound movement on the return stroke. This type of damper is called a single acting. The only difference in operation is that larger orifices are used in the bump valves.

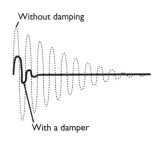

Figure 12.12 Action of a spring with and without a damper

LEARNING TASKS

➠ Look back at the key words. Explain each one to a friend, and/or write out a short description to keep as evidence.

➠ Make a simple sketch to show a *single acting* damper.

4 Suspension system layouts

Introduction

On most older types of vehicle a beam axle was used to support two stub axles. Beam axles are now rarely used in car suspension systems, although many commercial vehicles use beam axles because of their greater strength and constant ground clearance.

KEY WORDS

■ Strut

■ Wishbone

■ Swivel joint

The need for a better suspension system came from the demand for improved ride quality and improved handling. Independent front suspension (IFS) was developed to meet this need. The main advantages of independent front suspension are as follows:

■ When one wheel is lifted or drops, it does not affect the opposite wheel.

■ The unsprung mass is lower, therefore the road wheel stays in better contact with the road.

■ Problems with changing steering geometry are reduced.

■ More space for the engine at the front.

■ Softer springing with larger wheel movement is possible.

A number of basic suspension systems are in common use.

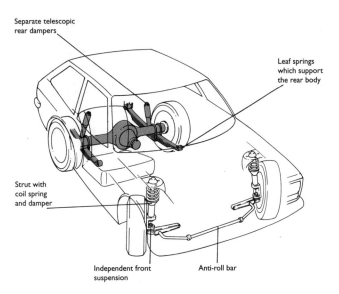

Figure 12.13 Rear beam axle suspension with front struts

Wishbone suspension

Twin unequal length wishbone suspension is widely used on light vehicles. A coil spring is used between two suspension arms. The suspension arms are 'wishbone' shaped, and the bottom end of the spring fits in a plate in the lower wishbone assembly. The top end of the spring is located in a section of the body. The top and bottom wishbones are attached to the chassis by rubber bushes. A damper is fitted inside the spring and, as the spring, is attached at the top to the body and at the bottom to the lower wishbone. The stub axle and swivel pins are connected to the outer ends of the upper and lower wishbones by ball or swivel joints.

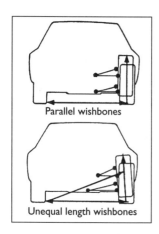

Parallel wishbones

Unequal length wishbones

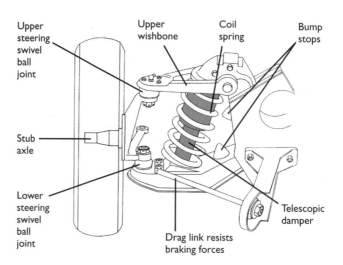

Figure 12.14 Wishbone suspension layout

Strut type suspension

This type of suspension system has been used for many years. It is often referred to as the MacPherson Strut system. With this system, the stub axle is combined with the bottom section of a telescopic tube which incorporates a damper. The bottom end of the strut is connected to the outer part of a

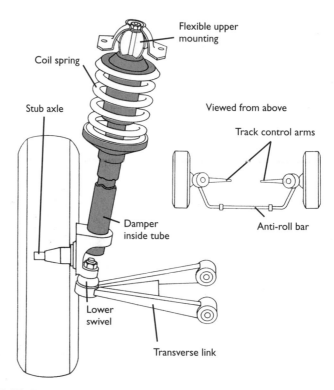

Figure 12.15 Strut type suspension

transverse link (like a wishbone again) by means of a ball joint. The inner part of the link is secured to the body by rubber bushes. The top of the strut is fixed to the vehicle body by a bearing which allows the complete strut to swivel. A coil spring is located between the upper and lower sections of the strut. This suspension system is quite simple in construction and is very effective in operation. However, when the suspension is moved, the steering angles do change a little.

Rear wheel suspensions

The systems used for the rear suspension of light vehicles vary, depending on the requirements of the vehicle and whether the vehicle is front or rear wheel drive. Old vehicles using leaf type springs were described briefly earlier. This leaves two main types using IRS:

■ strut type (front wheel drive)

■ trailing and semi-trailing arm with coil springs (rear wheel drive).

The strut type is very much the same as used at the front of the vehicle. The damper can be mounted separately or inside the coil spring. Note that suitable links are used to allow up and down movement but to prevent the wheel moving in any other direction. Some change in the wheel geometry is designed in to improve handling on corners.

Trailing arm suspension and semi-trailing arm suspension both use two wishbone shaped arms hinged on the body. Trailing arms are at right angles to the vehicle centre line and semi-trailing arms are at an angle. This changes the geometry of the wheels as the suspension moves. The final drive and differential unit is fixed with rubber mountings to the vehicle body. Drive shafts must therefore be used to allow drive to be passed from the fixed final drive to the moveable wheels. The coil springs and dampers are mounted between the trailing arms and the vehicle body. Because of the shape of the arms, the wheels are fixed so that they will only move up and down with the suspension.

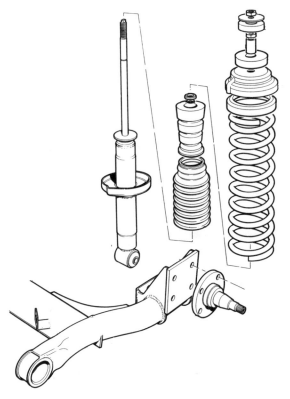

Figure 12.16 Rear wheel suspension – strut type

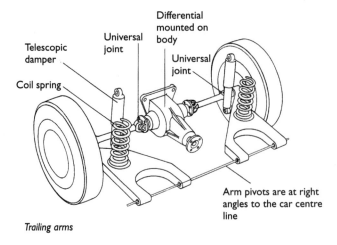

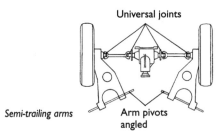

Figure 12.17 Rear wheel suspension – trailing arm method

Active suspension

Electronic control of suspension or active suspension, like many other innovations, was born in the Grand Prix world. It is now slowly becoming more popular on production vehicles. It is interesting to note that just as it was perfected by some Formula 1 teams, the rules changed (1993/4) to prevent its use! Conventional suspension systems are always a compromise between soft springs for comfort and harder springing for better cornering ability.

Active suspension allows the best of both worlds. This is achieved by replacing the conventional springs with double acting hydraulic units. These are controlled by an ECU which receives signals from various sensors. Oil

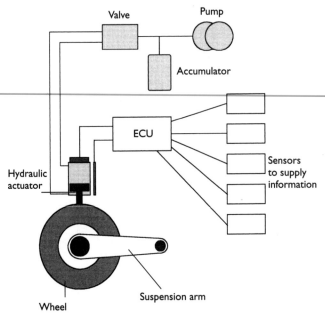

Figure 12.18 Active suspension block diagram

pressure in excess of 150 bar (that's 150 times atmospheric pressure) is supplied to the hydraulic units from a pump. The main benefits of active suspension are:

- improvements in ride comfort, handling and safety
- predictable control of the vehicle under different conditions
- no change in handling between laden and unladen.

The benefits are considerable, and as component prices fall the system will become available on more vehicles. Lotus Engineering have been one of the main companies involved in developing active suspension and deserve credit for advancing the system. It is expected that even off road vehicles may be fitted with active suspension in the near future.

LEARNING TASKS

➡ Look back at the key words. Explain each one to a friend, and/or write out a short description to keep as evidence.

➡ Examine a real system and make simple sketches to show three different suspension layouts.

---

5   Diagnostics

Systematic testing

KEY WORDS

1. Verify the fault
2. Collect further information
3. Evaluate the evidence
4. Carry out further tests in a logical sequence
5. Rectify the problem
6. Check all systems

For example, if the reported fault is poor handling, you could proceed as follows:

1. Road test to confirm the fault.
2. With the vehicle on a lift, inspect obvious items like tyres and dampers.
3. Consider if the problem is suspension related, for example, or in the steering. You may have decided this from road testing.
4. Inspect all the components of the system you suspect. For example, check dampers for correct operation and suspension bushes for condition and security. Let's assume the fault was one front damper not operating to the required standard.
5. Renew both of the dampers at the front to ensure balanced performance.
6. Road test again and check for correct operation of the suspension and other systems.

Test results

The following table shows some of the information you may have to get from other sources such as data books or a workshop manual.

Test carried out	Information required
Damper operation	The vehicle body should move down as you press on it, bounce back just past the start point and then return to the rest position
Suspension bush	Simple levering, if appropriate, should not show up excessive condition movement, cracks or separation of rubber bushes
Trim height	This is available from data books as a measurement from, say, the wheel centre to a point on the car wing above

Fault diagnosis

Symptom	Possible causes of faults	Suggested action
Excessive pitch or roll when driving	Dampers worn	Replace in pairs
Car sits lopsided	Broken spring Leak if hydraulic suspension	Replace in pairs Rectify by replacing unit or fitting new pipes
Knocking noises	Excessive free play in a suspension joint	Renew
Excessive tyre wear	Steering/suspension geometry incorrect (may be due to accident damage)	Check and adjust or replace any 'bent' or out of true components

LEARNING TASKS

➠ Practise fault finding on real vehicles.

➠ Make a list of steps you would take to find some of the faults causing the symptoms listed in the table.

13 Brakes

1 Introduction

The main purpose of the braking system is simple: to slow down or stop a vehicle. To do this, the energy in the vehicle movement must be taken away (or converted). Friction is used to do this. It is worth remembering that the brakes on a bicycle work by the same principle. In this case hard rubber blocks are pressed against the wheel rim. This friction causes heat, which takes energy away from the movement.

The main braking system of a car works by hydraulics. This means that when the driver presses the brake pedal, liquid pressure forces pistons to apply brakes on each wheel.

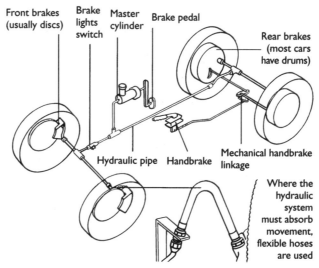

Figure 13.1 Braking system layout

Two types of light vehicle brakes are used. Disc brakes are used on the front wheels of some cars and on all wheels of sports and performance cars. Braking pressure forces brake pads against both sides of a steel disc. Drum brakes are fitted on the rear wheels of some cars and on all wheels of older vehicles. Braking pressure forces brake shoes to expand outwards into contact with a drum. The important part of brake pads and shoes is a friction lining that grips well and withstands wear.

Terminology	
Foot brake	The brake control pedal which operates the main braking system
Hand brake	Lever operates a mechanical linkage to lock the wheels for parking but can also act as an emergency brake
Brake pads	Steel backed blocks of friction material which are pressed to both sides of the disc. Older types were asbestos based, so you must not inhale the dust. Follow manufacturers' recommended procedures

Terminology

Brake shoes	Steel crescent shaped shoes with a friction material lining which is pressed inside the drum. Note the same precautions as above
Disc	Circular steel disc which rotates with the wheel. Some are solid, but some have ventilation holes
Drum	Steel drum shape which rotates with the wheel. The brake shoes work inside the drum
Brake fluid	A special fluid used in all hydraulic systems to transmit force or pressure through the pipes
Master cylinder	The master cylinder piston is moved by the brake pedal. It is basically like a syringe which forces brake fluid through the pipes
Wheel or slave cylinders	Pressure in the pipes causes a small movement to either operate brake shoes or pads. The cylinder works like the syringe above, only in reverse
Brake servo	This increases the force applied by the driver on the pedal. It makes the brakes more effective. Low air pressure from the engine inlet manifold is used to work many servos
Multi circuit systems	As a safety precaution (because brakes are quite important!), brake systems are split into two parts. If one fails (for example if a pipe breaks), the other part will operate at least some of the brakes
Metal pipes	Strong, high quality pipes which connect the master cylinder to the wheel cylinders
Flexible pipes	Fluid connection from the vehicle body to the wheels has to be through flexible pipes to allow suspension and steering movement
ABS	Antilock brake system. If brakes lock the wheels and makes them skid, steering is lost and the brakes do not stop the car as quickly. ABS uses electronic control to prevent this happening

LEARNING TASKS

➡ Look back at the key words. Explain each one to a friend, and/or write out a short description to keep as evidence.

➡ Examine a real system and note the layout of the braking system components.

2   Hydraulic braking systems

Principle of hydraulic braking

KEY WORDS

- Flexible pipes
- Hydraulics
- Force ratio
- Tandem master cylinder
- Wheel cylinders

Figure 13.2 shows the principle of hydraulic brakes. Note in particular how the force is increased. The lever action of the pedal gives about a 2:1 reduction in distance, so a 1:3 increase in force. The distance moved by the master cylinder piston is about three times the distance moved by the slave cylinder pistons. The overall increase in force is therefore about nine. This can be called a liquid lever.

A complete system includes a master cylinder operating several wheel cylinders. The system is designed to give the power amplification needed for braking the vehicle. When braking, a lot of the weight is transferred to the front wheels. Most braking effort is therefore designed to work on the front brakes. Some cars have special hydraulic valves to limit rear wheel braking. This reduces the chance of the rear wheels locking and skidding.

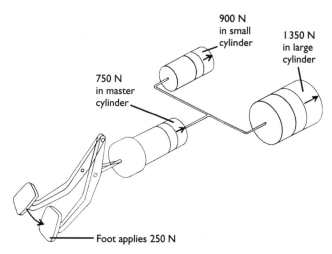

Figure13.2 Hydraulic braking principle

Notes on hydraulic brakes

The main merits of hydraulic brakes are as follows:

- almost immediate reaction to pedal pressure (no free play as with mechanical linkages)
- automatic even pressure distribution (fluid pressure effectively remains the same in all parts of the system)
- increase in force (liquid lever).

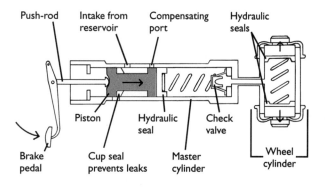

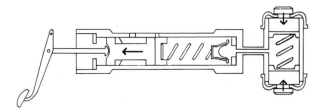

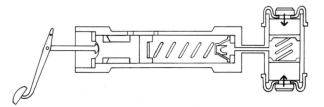

Figure 13.3 Master cylinder and slave cylinders

Caution and regular servicing is required to ensure the following:

- No air must be allowed in the hydraulic circuits (air compresses and would not transfer the force).

- Correct adjustment must be maintained between shoe linings and drums, and between pads and discs (otherwise the pedal movement would be too large).

- Lining materials must be free from contamination (such as oil, grease or brake fluid).

Layouts of brake circuits

Figure 13.4 shows the layout of a typical modern braking system. A separate mechanical system (not shown here) is a good safety feature. Most vehicles have the mechanical hand brake working on the rear wheels, but a few have it working on the front – take care.

Note the importance of flexible connections to allow for suspension and steering movement. These flexible pipes are made of high quality rubber and are covered in layers of strong mesh to prevent expansion when under pressure.

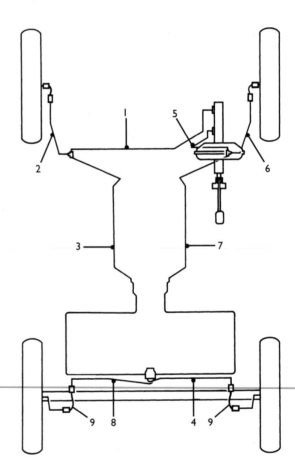

Secondary circuit
1. Master cylinder to tee-piece
2. Tee-piece to L.H. front hose and brake calliper
3. Tee-piece to load sensing valve
4. Load sensing valve to R.H. rear hose and brake cylinder

Primary circuit
5. Master cylinder to tee-piece
6. Tee-piece to R.H. front hose and brake calliper
7. Tee-piece to load sensing valve
8. Load sensing valve to L.H. rear hose and brake cylinder
9. Flexible pipes (both circuits)

Figure 13.4 Full modern braking system

Multi circuit systems

Extra safety is built into braking systems by using a double acting master cylinder (Figure 13.5). This is often described as 'tandem' and can be thought of as two cylinders in one housing. The pressure from the pedal acts on both cylinders, but fluid can't pass from one to the other. Each cylinder is then connected to a complete circuit by one of a number of methods, shown in Figure 13.6 (in each case, if a leak develops, half the brakes will still work):

- front and rear split
- diagonal split
- duplicated front.

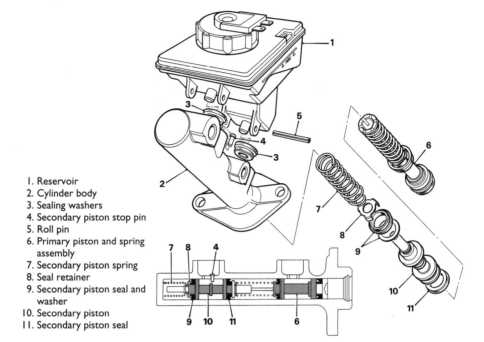

1. Reservoir
2. Cylinder body
3. Sealing washers
4. Secondary piston stop pin
5. Roll pin
6. Primary piston and spring assembly
7. Secondary piston spring
8. Seal retainer
9. Secondary piston seal and washer
10. Secondary piston
11. Secondary piston seal

Figure 13.5 Double acting master cylinder

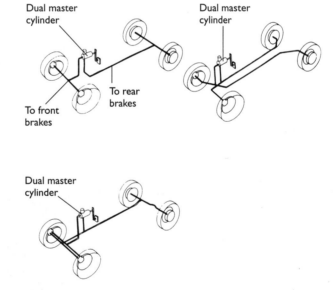

Figure 13.6 Multi circuit brake systems

LEARNING TASKS

➡ Look back at the key words. Explain each one to a friend, and/or write out a short description to keep as evidence.

➡ Make a simple sketch to show the operation of a wheel cylinder.

➡ Write a short explanation about why air must not be allowed in to a hydraulic system.

3 Disc and drum brake systems

Disc brakes

Figure 13.7 shows typical disc brake calliper pads and disc. The type shown is known as single acting sliding calliper. This is because only one cylinder is used, but the sliding action ensures that pads are still pressed equally on both sides of the disc. Disc brakes keep cooler because they are in the air stream and only part of the disc is heated as the brakes are applied. They also throw off water better than drum brakes. In most cases servicing is minimal. Disc brakes are self adjusting, and replacing pads is usually a simple task. In the type shown just one bolt has to be removed to hinge the calliper upwards. Figure 13.8 shows a slightly older disc brake calliper which uses two cylinders, but the principle is the same.

Disc brakes provide for good braking and are less prone to brake fade that drum brakes. This is because they are more exposed and can get rid of heat more easily. Brake fade occurs when the brakes become so hot they cannot transfer energy any more and stop working! This type of problem can happen, say, after keeping the car brakes on for a long time when travelling down a long steep hill. This is why a lower gear should be used to employ the engine as a brake. It is clearly important to use good quality pads and linings because inferior materials can fail if overheated.

Disc brakes make it difficult to fit a parking brake, which is one reason why many cars still use shoes and drums on the rear.

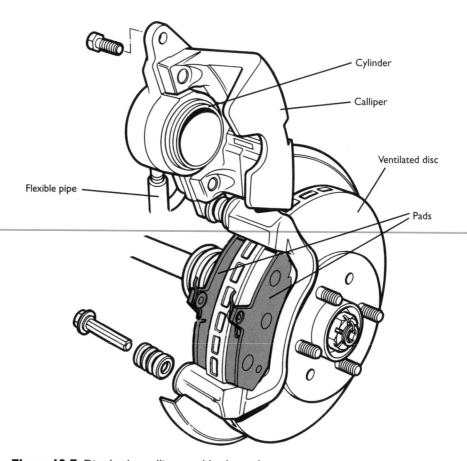

Figure 13.7 Disc brake, calliper and brake pads

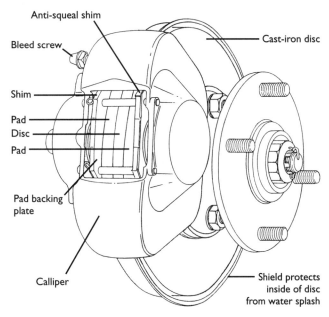

Anti-squeal shim

Bleed screw

Cast-iron disc

Shim

Pad

Disc

Pad

Pad backing
plate

Calliper

Shield protects
inside of disc
from water splash

Figure 13.8 Earlier type of disc brake

Drum brakes   Drum brakes operate by shoes being forced onto the inside of the drum. A common type with a ratchet for automatic adjustment is shown in Figure 13.9. Shoes can be moved by double or single acting cylinders. These two types together with a disc brake cylinder are shown in Figure 13.10. The most common layout is to use one double acting cylinder and brake shoes on each rear wheel of the vehicle and disc brakes on the front wheels. A double

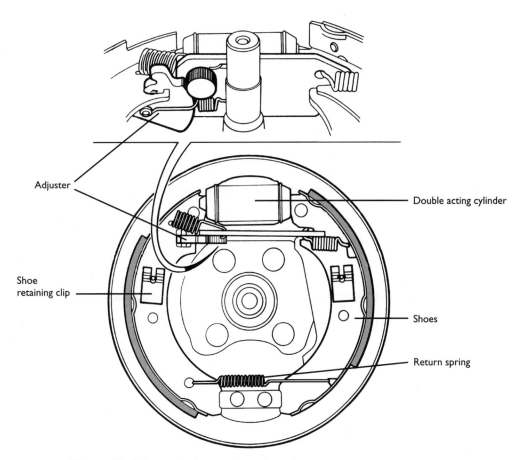

Adjuster

Double acting cylinder

Shoe
retaining clip

Shoes

Return spring

Figure 13.9 Drum brakes with ratchet adjustment

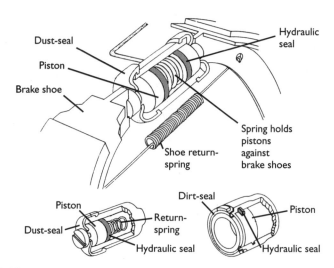

Figure 13.10 Single and double acting wheel cylinder and disc brake cylinder

acting cylinder simply means that, as fluid pressure acts through a centre inlet, pistons are forced out of both ends. Figure 13.11 shows a further drum brake layout.

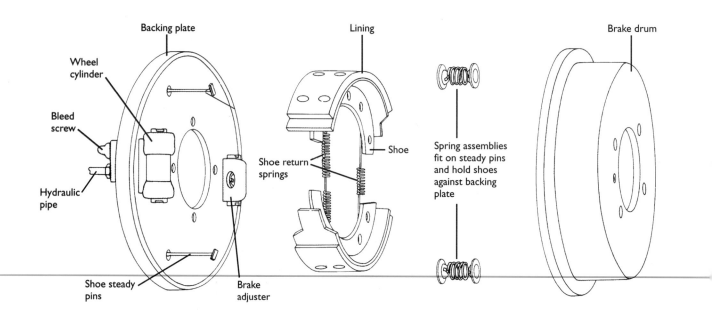

Figure 13.11 Earlier drum brake system

Drum brakes more affected by wet and heat than disc brakes because both water and heat are trapped inside the drum. However, they are easier to fit with a mechanical hand brake linkage.

Brake adjustments

Brakes must be adjusted so that minimum movement of the pedal starts to apply the brakes. The adjustment in question is the gap between the pads and disc and/or the shoes and drum.

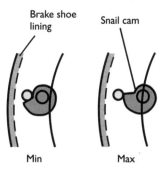

Figure 13.12 Old method of brake shoe adjustment

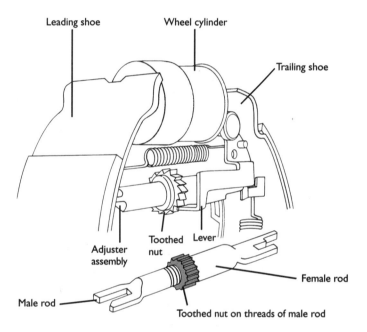

Figure 13.13 Drum brake adjuster – threaded rod

Disc brakes are self adjusting because, as pressure is released, it moves the pads just away from the disc. Drum brakes are different because the shoes are moved away from the drum to a set position by a pull-off spring. The set position is adjustable, and this can be done in a number of ways.

Self adjusting drum brakes are almost universal now on light vehicles. A common type uses an offset ratchet which clicks to a wider position if the shoes move beyond a certain amount when operated (see Figure 13.9). Modern cars frequently have a self adjusting hand brake.

Screwdriver adjustment through a hole in the wheel is also used. This is often a type of nut on a threaded bar which pushes the shoes out as it is screwed along the thread. This method can also have an automatic adjuster fitted.

An adjustment screw on the back plate is now quite an old method: a screw or square head protruding from the back plate moves the shoes by a snail cam.

The adjustment procedure stated by the manufacturer must be followed. As a guide, though, most recommend tightening the adjuster until the wheels lock and then moving it back until the wheel is just released. You must ensure that the brakes are not rubbing, as this would build up heat and wear the friction material very quickly.

The effects of incorrect adjustment are as follows:

- reduced braking efficiency
- unbalanced braking
- excessive pedal travel.

Hand brake linkages

At the drum the hand brake linkage is usually a simple lever mechanism as shown in Figure 13.14. This lever pushes the shoes against the drum and locks the wheel. The hand brake lever pulls on one or more cables and has a ratchet to allow it to be locked in the 'on' position. Figure 13.15 shows four ways in which the hand brake linkage can be laid out:

- splitter linkage connects main cable to two at the rear
- two cables, one to each rear wheel
- single cable to small linkage on the rear axle
- equaliser on a single cable pulls a 'U' section to balance effort through the rear cable.

Figure 13.14 Hand brake lever

Servo assisted braking

Brake servos are used to improve braking and make driving the vehicle easier. If the servo fails, normal braking is retained, albeit with heavier pedal pressure. Servo systems are designed to give little assistance for light braking but increase the assistance as pedal pressure is increased.

A common servo system uses low pressure from the manifold on one side and the higher atmospheric pressure on the other side of a diaphragm. The low pressure is taken via a non return safety valve from the engine inlet manifold. This pressure difference causes a force which is made to act on the master cylinder.

Brake fluid

Always use new and approved brake fluid when topping up or renewing the system. Manufacturers' recommendations must always be followed. Brake fluid is hygroscopic, which means that over a period of time it absorbs water.

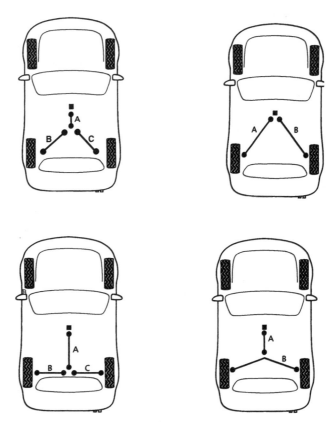

Figure 13.15 Hand brake linkages

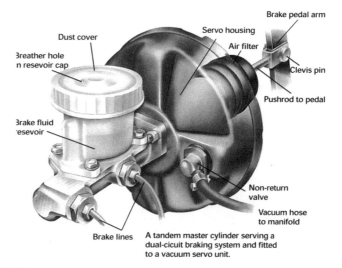

Figure 13.16 Brake servo

This increases the risk of the fluid boiling due to the heat from the brakes. Pockets of steam in the system would not allow full braking pressure to be applied. Many manufacturers recommend that the fluid is changed at regular intervals. In some cases once per year, or every 18 000 miles. Make sure the correct grade of fluid is used. Most are now given a DOT (Department of Transport) number. Note that brake fluid is toxic.

MOT test requirements   As with most other vehicle systems, all components of the braking system must be in good working order for the vehicle to pass an MOT test. However, the test includes additional requirements relating to braking efficiency, the braking force compared to the weight of the vehicle. For example, the brakes on a vehicle with a weight of 10 kN (1 000 kg × 10 [g]) could provide a braking force of 7 kN. This is said to be a 70% efficiency. During an MOT test this is measured on brake rollers. The current efficiency requirements are as follows:

- service brake efficiency – 50%
- second line brake efficiency – 25%
- parking brake efficiency – 16%.

On vehicles with split line brakes, the second line or emergency brake is half of the main system, that is two out of four brakes still working. If the vehicle has a single line system the hand brake is also the second line, and it must therefore work at 25%.

'Always check the latest MOT requirements.'

LEARNING TASKS

➧ Look back at the key words. Explain each one to a friend, and/or write out a short description to keep as evidence.

➧ Examine a real system and note the name and purpose of all the braking components.

➧ Look up in a data book or workshop manual the manufacturer's recommendations for brake fluid changes.

---

4 Diagnostics

Systematic testing

FAULT FINDING

1. Verify the fault
2. Collect further information
3. Evaluate the evidence
4. Carry out further tests in a logical sequence
5. Rectify the problem
6. Check all systems

For example, if the reported fault is the hand brake not holding, you could proceed as follows:

1. Confirm the fault by trying to pull away with the hand brake on.
2. Check the foot brake operation. If correct, this suggests the brake shoes and drums (or pads and discs) are likely to be in good order.
3. Do you need to remove the wheels and drums or could it be a cable fault?
4. Check cable operation by using an assistant in the car while you observe.
5. Renew the cable if seized.
6. Check hand brake operation and all associated systems.

Test equipment

Always refer to the manufacturers' instructions appropriate to the equipment you are using.

Brake fluid tester

Because brake fluid can absorb a small amount of water, it must be renewed or tested regularly. It becomes dangerous if the water turns into steam inside the cylinders or pipes, causing the brakes to become ineffective. The tester measures the moisture content of the fluid.

Brake roller test

This is carried out as part of the complete MOT test. The front or rear wheels are driven into a pair of two rollers. The rollers drive each wheel of the car and, as the brakes are applied, the braking force affects the rotation. A measure of braking efficiency can then be worked out.

Test results

The following table shows some of the information you may have to get from other sources such as data books or a workshop manual.

Test carried out	Information required
Brake roller test	Required braking efficiency: 50% for first line brakes, 25% for second line brakes and 16% for the parking brake. On modern vehicles half of the main system is the second line (dual line brakes). Old vehicles had to use the parking brake as the second line, therefore this had to work at 25%
Brake fluid condition	Manufacturers specify maximum moisture content

Fault diagnosis

Symptom	Possible causes of faults	Suggested action
Excessive pedal travel	Incorrect adjustment	Adjust it! But check condition as well
Poor performance when stopping	Pad and/or shoe linings worn	Renew (both sides)
	Seized calliper or wheel cylinders	Renew or free off if possible and safe
	Contaminated linings	Renew (both sides)
Car pulls to one side when braking	Seized calliper or wheel cylinder on one side	Overhaul or renew if piston or cylinder is worn
	Contaminated linings on one side	Renew (both sides)
Spongy pedal	Air in the hydraulic system	Bleed system and then check for leaks
	Master cylinder seals failing	Overhaul or renew
Pedal travels to the floor when pressed	Fluid reservoir empty	Refill, bleed system and check for leaks
	Failed seals in master cylinder	Overhaul or renew
	Leak from a pipe or union	Replace or repair as required
Brakes overheating	Shoe return springs broken	Renew (both sides)
	Callipers or wheel cylinders sticking	Free off or renew if in any doubt
Brake judder	Linings worn	Renew
	Drums out of round	Renew
	Discs have excessive runout	Renew
Squeaking	Badly worn linings	Renew
	Dirt in brake drums	Clean out with proper cleaner
	Antisqueal shims missing at rear of pads	Replace and smear with copper grease

LEARNING TASKS

➡ Practise fault finding on real vehicles.

➡ Make a list of steps you would take to find some of the faults causing the symptoms listed in the table.

14 Steering, wheels and tyres

1 Introduction

Start here! The three areas covered in this chapter are linked, but each has a particular purpose.

KEY WORDS

- Steering
- Wheels
- Tyres

- Steering – controls the direction of the vehicle under a variety of operating conditions.
- Wheels – support the vehicle as well as transferring braking and driving force through the tyres to the road.
- Tyres – allow transfer of braking and driving force but also allow the vehicle to be controlled by the steering system. The tyres also provide the primary suspension.

Some very complex design and development work has gone into the way modern vehicles perform. The steering, wheels and tyre systems are no exception. Our job as technicians is to understand the main issues to help diagnose faults and make repairs.

> **LEARNING TASK**
>
> ➟ Examine a real system or pictures to become familiar with the main components.

2 Steering

Introduction When the driver turns the steering wheel, the front wheels move and the car turns the corner! From the driver's point of view it is that simple, but many more things have to be taken into consideration. For example:

- the effect of road surface irregularities
- tyre behaviour under cornering stresses
- an efficient mechanical system to give easy turning of the steering wheel
- driver feel must be maintained
- no (or very little) difference between empty and fully loaded
- the effect of accelerating or braking when the wheels are turned
- the front wheels should have a natural tendency to return to the straight ahead position.

Imagine a car driving round a roundabout, as in Figure 14.1: the outer wheels have to travel a greater distance than the inner wheels. This is why a differential, as described in Chapter 11, is needed in the transmission system. Also notice that the inner steered wheel has to travel round a sharper corner than the outer one.

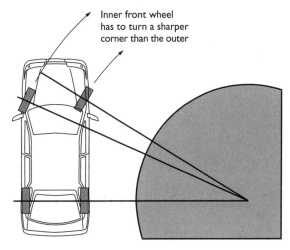

Figure 14.1 Car going round a roundabout – note wheel position

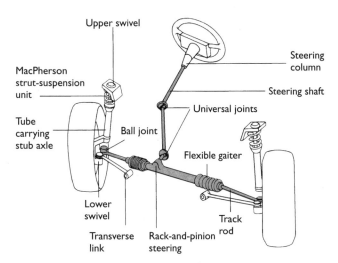

Figure 14.2 Steering system

This requirement has to be met by a car steering system. A special linkage between the two front wheels is made so that each is turned a slightly different amount to keep them rolling 'true', however sharp or gentle the corner is. Running or rolling true means that the wheels must always be turning exactly end over end, much like a coin rolling across a desk. If this was not the case, there would be a 'scrubbing' action. This would result in considerable tyre wear. The linkage set up to allow this slight difference in turning of each front wheel is known as the 'Ackerman Linkage', named after the person who invented the technique. The slight change in angle between the wheels as they are steered is often known as toe out on turns.

Terminology

Steering wheel	The bit that the driver holds on to!
Steering column	The shaft connecting the steering wheel to the steering rack or steering box
Steering rack	A combination of a small gear and a toothed rack. This changes the rotation of the steering wheel into a back and forth movement of the rack which in turn moves the road wheels
Steering box	This does a similar job to the rack but needs extra linkages and rods to connect it to the road wheels. Mostly used on old cars, but still in use on larger vehicles

Terminology

Track rod	A rod to connect the left and right steered wheels. The steering rack is also the track rod
Track rod end	A ball joint to allow steering and suspension movement
Swivel joint	Part of the suspension system, but these are the joints which allow the steered wheels to turn left and right
PAS	Power assisted steering. An engine driven pump or an electric motor (on very new systems) provides extra force to help move the steering. The driver has to apply less effort
Steering geometry	A term used to describe the different angles which are used to set up the steering and suspension systems
Tracking	Often known as toe in or toe out, the tracking is set so the front wheels, when looked at from above, point in or out very slightly
Camber	This is the angle between the centre line of the wheel and a vertical line, when viewed from the front or rear of the vehicle
Castor	When looked at from the side, this is the angle between the vertical and a line through the swivel joints
Swivel axis or king pin inclination	When looked at from the front or rear, this is the angle between the vertical and a line through the swivel joints
Rear wheel steering	Some sophisticated cars have complex linkages or electronics to allow the rear wheels to steer slightly to improve handling

Positioning the wheels – steering geometry

Tracking

As a front wheel drive car moves, the tyres pull on the road surface, taking up the small amount of free play in the mountings and joints. For this reason the tracking is often set toe out, so that the wheels point straight ahead when the vehicle is moving. Rear wheel drive tends to make the opposite happen because it pushes against the front wheels. The front wheels are therefore set toe in. When the car moves, the front wheels are pushed out, taking up the slack in the joints; the wheels again end up straight ahead. The amount of toe in or toe out is very small, normally not exceeding 5 mm (the difference in the distance between the front and rear of the front wheels). Correctly set tracking ensures true rolling of the wheels.

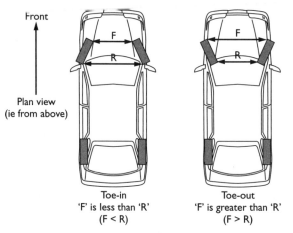

Toe-in
'F' is less than 'R'
(F < R)

Toe-out
'F' is greater than 'R'
(F > R)

Note: the difference is usually only a few millimetres

Figure 14.3 Tracking

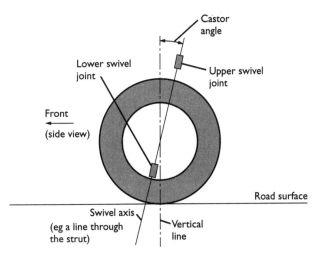

Figure 14.4 Castor angle

Castor angle

The front wheels tend to straighten themselves out after cornering. This is due to a castor action. Supermarket trolley wheels automatically run straight when pushed; this is because the axle on which they rotate is behind the swivel mounting. Vehicle wheels get the same result by leaning the swivel mounting back, so that the wheel axle is moved slightly behind the line of the swivel. The further the axle is behind the swivel, the stronger will be the straightening effect. The main reason for the castor angle is the self centering action it produces.

Camber angle

On many cars the front wheels are not mounted vertical to the road surface. Often they are further apart at the top than at the bottom. This is called positive camber and is done for many reasons, such as:

- easier steering, less turning effort required
- less wear on the steering linkages
- less stress on main components.

Some cars have rear wheels with negative camber. With independent suspension systems, wheels can change their camber from positive to neutral to negative. This varies, though, with the design and position of the suspension hinge points.

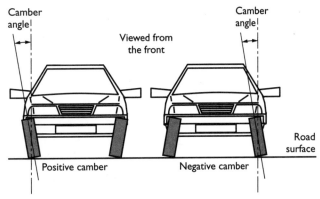

(Note: the angles are exaggerated to help you see more clearly)

Figure 14.5 Camber angle

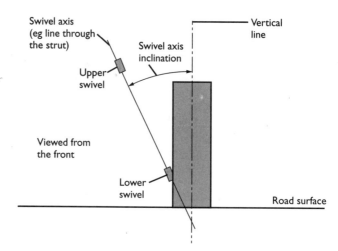

Figure 14.6 Swivel axis inclination

Swivel axis inclination

The final setting that affects the angle of the steered wheels is the swivel axis inclination: the angle compared to vertical made by the two swivel joints when viewed from the front or rear. On a strut type suspension system the angle is that made by the strut. This angle always leans in towards the middle of the vehicle. The swivel axis inclination (also called king pin inclination) is mainly for:

- producing a self centre action
- improved steering control on corners
- lighter steering action.

Steering box Steering boxes contain a spiral gear, known as a worm gear, which rotates with the steering column. One form of design has a nut wrapped round the spiral and is therefore known as a worm and nut steering box. The grooves can be filled with recirculating ball bearings which reduce backlash or slack in the system; they also reduce friction, making steering lighter. On vehicles with independent front suspension, an idler unit is needed, together with a number of links and several joints.

The basic weakness of the steering box system is in the number of swivelling joints and connections. If there is just slight wear at a number of points, the steering will not feel or be positive.

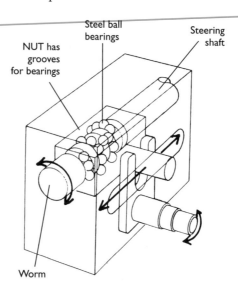

Figure 14.7
Recirculating ball steering box

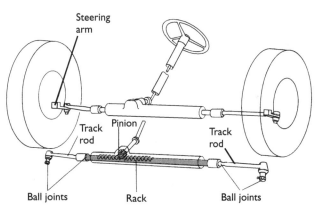

Figure 14.8 Rack and pinion steering

Rack and pinion steering

The steering rack is now used almost without exception on light vehicles. This is because it is simple in design and very long lasting. The wheels turn on two large swivel joints. Another ball joint (often called a track rod end) is fitted on each swivel arm. The track rods are connected by a further ball joint to the ends of the rack. The rack is inside a lubricated tube, and gaiters protect the inner ball joints. The pinion meshes with the teeth of the rack; as it is turned by the steering wheel, the rack is made to move back and forth, swivelling the front wheels on their swivel joints.

Power assisted steering

Rack and pinion steering requires more turning effort than a steering box, although this is not too noticeable with smaller vehicles. However, heavier cars with larger engines or with wider tyres (which scrub more) often benefit from power steering.

Most vehicles use a belt driven hydraulic pump to supply fluid under pressure for use in the system. Inside the rack and pinion housing is a hydraulic valve which is operated as the pinion is turned for steering. The valve controls the flow of oil into a cylinder which has a piston connected to the rack. This assists with the steering effort quite considerably.

A well designed system will retain the 'feel' of road conditions for the driver to control the car. Steering a slow moving heavier vehicle when there is little room can be tiring, even impossible for some drivers. This is where power steering comes into its own. Many modern systems are able to make the power steering progressive. This means that, as the speed of the vehicle increases, the assistance provided by the power steering reduces. This maintains better driver feel.

Very modern systems are starting to use electric power steering. This employs a very powerful electric motor as part of the steering linkage.

LEARNING TASKS

➠   Look back at the key words. Explain each one to a friend, and/or write out a short description to keep as evidence.

➠   Make simple sketches to illustrate castor angle, camber angle, track and swivel axis inclination.

➠   Examine a real system and note the layout of the steering components.

➠   Write a short explanation about how to check the tracking of a vehicle using only a good tape measure.

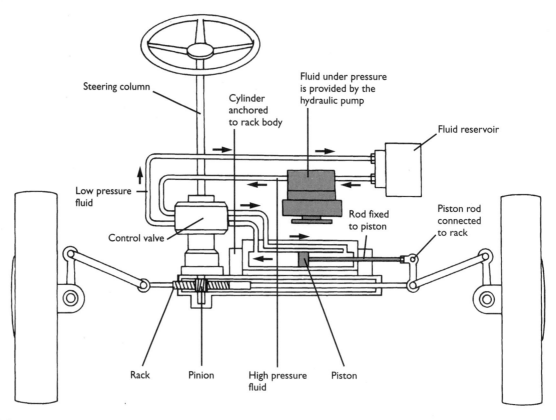

Figure 14.9 Power assisted steering

3 Wheels

Introduction

Together with the tyre, a road wheel must support the weight of the vehicle and be capable of withstanding a number of side thrusts when cornering and torsional forces when driving. Road wheels must be strong, but light in weight. They must be cheap to produce, easy to clean, and simple to remove and refit.

KEY WORDS

■ All words in the table
■ Torque
■ Rim

Figure 14.10 Modern road wheels

Terminology	
Steel wheels	A very popular design of wheel. Usually covered with plastic wheel trims. Very strong and cheap to produce
Alloy wheels	Good, attractive looking wheels generally fitted to higher specification vehicles. Many designs are used; they are lightweight but can be difficult to keep clean
Spoked wheels	Attractive wheels, but only used on older type sports cars. A smaller diameter but stronger version of a cycle wheel
Split rims	Many commercial vehicles use split rims, either of a two or three piece construction. The tyre is held in place by what could be thought of as a very large circlip. Do not remove or fit tyres on this type of wheel unless you have received proper instruction
Divided rims	On a very few specialist vehicles, the rims are made in two halves which are bolted together. The nuts and bolts holding them together should be specially marked because undoing them when the tyre is inflated would be very dangerous
Temporary or 'space saver' wheels	In order to save space in the boot and to save on costs, some cars with large and expensive alloy wheels use a small, thin steel wheel as the spare. The speed of the vehicle is restricted when this type of wheel is used. It is only intended for emergency use

Types of road wheels

Two main types of road wheels are in service on modern light vehicles:

- pressed steel
- cast alloy.

The centre of pressed steel wheels is made by pressing a disc into a dish shape to give it greater strength. The rim is a rolled section which is circled and welded. The rim is normally welded to the flange of the centre disc. The centre disc has a number of slots under the rim. This is for ventilation to the brakes as well as the wheel itself. This type of wheel is cheap to produce and strong.

The bead of a tyre is made from wire, which cannot be stretched for fitting or removal. The wheel rim must therefore be designed to hold the tyre in place, but also to allow for easy removal. This is done by using a 'well base' in the rim. For tyre removal one bead must be forced into the well. The other bead can then be levered over the edge of the rim. The bead seats are made with a taper so that, as the tyre is inflated, the bead is forced up the taper by the air pressure. This locks the tyre on to the rim, making a good seal.

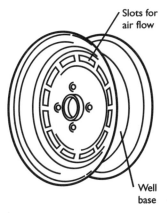

Slots for air flow

Well base

Figure 14.11 Features of a pressed steel wheel

Figure 14.12 Alloy wheel

A large number of vehicles are fitted with wheels made from light alloy. Wheels of this type are generally produced from aluminium alloy castings, which are then machine finished. The main advantage of cast alloy road wheels is their light weight, and of course they look good. The disadvantages are their lower resistance to corrosion, and that they are more prone to accidental damage. The general shape of the wheel, as far as tyre fitting is concerned, is much the same as the pressed steel type.

Fixing the road wheels on to the car

Light vehicle road wheels are usually held in place by four or five nuts or bolts. The fixing holes in the wheels are stamped or machined to form a cone shaped seat. The wheel nut, or bolt head, fits into this seat. This ensures that the wheel fits in exactly the right position. In the case of steel pressed wheels it also strengthens the wheel centre round the stud holes.

When fitting a wheel, the nuts or bolts must be tightened evenly in a diagonal sequence. It is also vital that they are set to the correct torque.

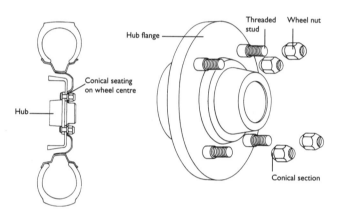

Figure 14.13 Road wheel fixings

LEARNING TASKS

➡ Look back at the key words. Explain each one to a friend, and/or write out a short description to keep as evidence.

➡ Make a simple sketch to show how a wheel is correctly positioned and secured to a hub using bolts.

---

4 Tyres

Introduction

The tyre performs two basic functions:

■ It acts as the primary suspension, cushioning the vehicle from the effects of a rough surface.

■ It provides frictional contact with the road surface. This allows the driving wheels to move the vehicle. The tyres also allow the front wheels to steer and the brakes to slow or stop the vehicle.

The tyre is a flexible casing which contains air. Tyres are manufactured from reinforced synthetic rubber. The tyre is made of an inner layer of fabric plies

Figure 14.14 High performance tyres

which are wrapped around bead wires at the inner edges. The bead wires hold the tyre in position on the wheel rim. The fabric plies are coated with rubber, which is moulded to form the side walls and the tread of the tyre. Behind the tread is a reinforcing band, usually made of steel, rayon, or glass fibre. Modern tyres are mostly tubeless, so they have a thin layer of rubber coating the inside to act as a seal.

Terminology

Radial	The modern construction technique for tyres. It simply means that the main plies of the tyre are constructed radially
Cross ply	An earlier form of tyre construction. The plies are made in a type of crisscross pattern around the circumference of the tyre
Bead	This is a continuous loop of thin steel wire which is an anchorage for the plies. For a tubeless tyre the bead must also provide an air tight seal with the wheel rim
Tread	This provides the traction or grip with the road surface. Grooves in the tyre tread pattern assist in clearing away any water to prevent aquaplaning
Plies	Layers of strong fabric cords, to build up the shape and strength of the tyre
Valve	A simple one way valve to allow the tyre to be inflated and the pressure to be checked
Side walls	This is the part of the tyre between the tread and the beads. However, the air supports the tread, not the side wall. The main function of the side walls is to allow the tyre to flex
Inner tube	The inner tube is a soft rubber tube fitted inside the tyre. Its purpose is to maintain the air pressure. Tubed tyres are now generally used only for special rims, like the older spoked type

Construction of a tubeless radial tyre

The wheel is made with a leak proof rim, and the valve is rubber mounted into a hole formed in the well of the rim. The tyre is made with an accurate bead which fits tightly on to the rim. A thin rubber layer in the interior of the tyre makes an air tight seal.

The plies of a radial tyre pass from bead to bead at 90° to the circumference, or radially. A rigid belt band, consisting of several layers of textile or metallic threads, runs round the tyre under the tread. Steel wire is often used in the construction of radial tyres. The radial tyre is flexible but retains high strength. It has good road holding and cornering power. In addition, radial tyres are economical due to their low 'rolling resistance'.

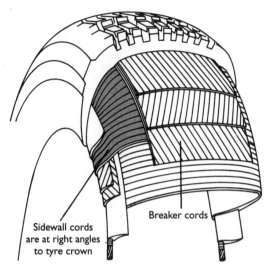

Sidewall cords
are at right angles
to tyre crown

Breaker cords

Figure 14.15 Radial tyre construction

A major advantage of a radial tyre is its greatly improved grip even on wet roads. This is because the rigid belt band holds the tread flat on the road surface when cornering. The rigid belt band also helps with the escape of water from under the tyre.

The legal bit about tyres

It is dangerous to mix cross ply and radial ply tyres on a vehicle. Only very old vehicle use cross ply tyres, so this is not a problem you are likely to come across. The safest and best method is often to fit radial tyres all round. However, you must refer to manufacturers' recommendations if in any doubt.

It is an offence to use a light vehicle on the road if any of its tyres have any of the following faults:

- A tread pattern depth of less than 1.5 mm throughout at least 75% of the tread width and no visible tread on the rest.
- A cut deep enough to reach the fabric and measuring in excess of 25 mm or 10% of the section width of the tyre, whichever is the greater.
- A lump or bulge caused by separation or other structural fault.
- Any portion of the ply or cord body is exposed.
- It has been re-cut or re-grooved.
- It is not suitable for the use to which the vehicle is being put, or to the type of tyres fitted to its other wheels.
- It is incorrectly inflated.
- Tyres of different types of construction are fitted to the same axle.

Tyre sizes and markings

Markings on the sides of tyres are quite considerable and can be a little confusing. The following is a list of the information given on modern tyres. I will just examine the size, speed and load headings in a little more detail.

- size (e.g. 195/55–15)
- speed rating (eg. H, V, Z)
- load index (e.g. 84, 89, 92)
- UTQG ratings (Temperature, Traction, Tread wear)

- M&S designation

- max. load

- max. press

- type of construction

- EU approval mark

- US approval mark

- manufacture date.

A tyre's size is expressed in the format WWW/AA–DD (Eg. 195/55–15):

- WWW is the tyre's sidewall to sidewall *width* in millimetres (195).

- AA is the *aspect ratio* or profile. This gives the tyre's height as a percentage of its width (55% of 195 = 107 mm).

- DD is the *diameter* of the wheel in inches (15 inches). Some tyres now also give this in millimetres.

If the size is shown as P205/60R15, the 'P' stands for 'Passenger' and the 'R' is for 'Radial ply' construction.

For an older tyre without an aspect ratio (e.g. 175R13), it is assumed to be about an 80 series tyre (e.g. 175/80R13). The practice of listing the aspect ratio is becoming more common.

The speed rating was traditionally shown as a part of the tyre's size (e.g. 195/55VR15). Since the inclusion of load ratings, many manufacturers now show the speed rating after the size, in combination with the load rating (e.g. 195/55R15 84V).

Commonly used speed ratings include:

Rating	Certified Maximum Speed (km/h)	Certified Maximum Speed (mph)
N	140	88
Q	160	100
S	180	112
T	190	118
U	200	124
H	210	130
V	240	150*
Z	over 240	over 150
W	270	169
Y	300	188

* (Originally, V was 'over 130 mph'. As W and Y ratings are quite new, Z is redundant and will probably be dropped at some time in the future.)

The load index indicates the maximum weight the tyre can carry at the maximum speed indicated by its speed rating. Some 'load rating indices' are listed in the following table.

Rating	Capacity (kg)	Capacity (lb)
75	387	853
82	475	1 047
84	500	1 102
85	515	1 135
87	545	1 201
88	560	1 235
91	615	1 356
92	630	1 389
93	650	1 433
105	925	2 039

Tyre valves   The valve is to allow the tyre to be inflated with air under pressure, prevent air from escaping after inflation and to allow the release of air for adjustment of pressure. The valve assembly is contained in a brass tube which is bonded into a rubber sleeve and mounting section.

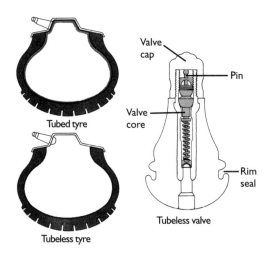

Figure 14.16 Tubed and tubeless tyre with a typical tubeless valve

The valve core consists of a centre pin with metal and rubber disc valves. When the tyre is inflated, the centre pin is depressed, the disc valve moves away from the bottom of the seal tube and allows air to enter the tyre. To release air or for pressure checking, the centre pin is depressed. During normal operation, the disc valve is held in place by its spring and by the pressure of air. If all the air needs to be released, the valve core assembly can be removed. The upper part of the valve tube is threaded to accept a valve cap. This prevents dirt and grit from entering the valve and acts as a secondary seal.

Tyre inflation pressures   The pressure at which the tyres should be set is determined by a number of factors such as:

- load to be carried
- number of plies
- operating conditions
- section of the tyre.

Tyre pressures must be set at the manufacturer's recommended values. Pressure will vary according to the temperature of the tyre – this is affected by operating conditions. Tyre pressure should always be adjusted when the tyre is cold and be checked at regular intervals.

Tyre faults   The following table lists some of the faults which can occur if tyres and/or the vehicle are not maintained correctly.

Fault	Possible cause
Wear on both outer edges of the tread	Underinflation
Wear in the centre of the tread all round the tyre	Overinflation
Wear just on one side of the tread	Incorrect camber
Feathering	Tracking not set correctly
Bald patches	Unbalanced wheels or unusual driving technique!

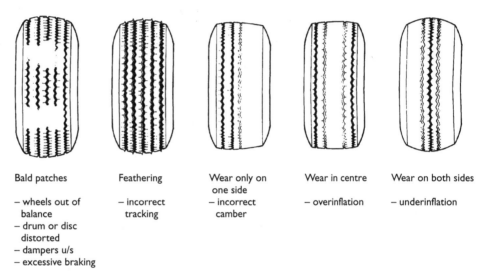

Bald patches	Feathering	Wear only on one side	Wear in centre	Wear on both sides
– wheels out of balance – drum or disc distorted – dampers u/s – excessive braking	– incorrect tracking	– incorrect camber	– overinflation	– underinflation

Figure 14.17 Tyre faults

LEARNING TASKS

➥ Look back at the key words. Explain each one to a friend, and/or write out a short description to keep as evidence.

➥ Make a simple sketch by copying a tyre, showing the information given on the side.

➥ Write a short explanation about how various tyre faults could be caused, in addition to the above list.

5 Diagnostics

Systematic testing

FAULT FINDING

1. Verify the fault
2. Collect further information
3. Evaluate the evidence
4. Carry out further tests in a logical sequence
5. Rectify the problem
6. Check all systems

For example, if the reported fault is heavy steering, you could proceed as follows:

1. Ask if the problem has just developed. Road test to confirm.
2. Check the obvious, such as tyre pressures. Is the vehicle loaded to excess? Check geometry.
3. Assuming tyre pressure and condition is as it should be, move on to further tests.
4. For example, jack up and support the front of the car. Operate the steering lock to lock. Disconnect one track rod end and move the wheel on that side, and so on.
5. If the fault is in the steering rack, then this should be replaced and the racking should be set.
6. Test the operation with a road test and inspect all other related components for security and safety.

Test equipment

Always refer to the manufacturers' instructions appropriate to the equipment you are using.

Tyre pressure gauge and tread depth gauge

These pieces of test equipment are often underated. Correctly inflated tyres make the vehicle handle better, stop better and use less fuel. The correct depth of tread means the vehicle will be significantly safer to drive, particularly in wet conditions.

Tracking gauges

The toe in and toe out of a vehicle's front wheels is very important. Many types of tracking gauges are available. One of the most common kind uses a frame placed against each wheel, with a mirror on one side and a moveable viewer on the other. The viewer is moved until marks are lined up and the tracking can then be measured.

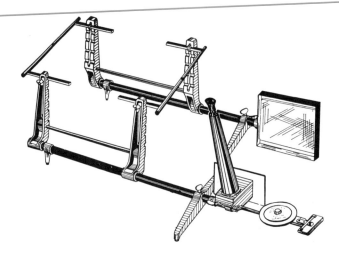

Figure 14.18 Tracking gauges

Wheel balancer

This is usually a large fixed piece of equipment. The wheel is removed from the car, fixed on to the machine and spun at high speed. Sensors in the tester measure the balance of the wheel. The tester then indicates the amount of weight which should be added to a certain position. The weight is added by fitting small lead weights.

Test results

The following table shows some of the information you may have to get from other sources such as data books or a workshop manual.

Test carried out	Information required
Tracking	The data for tracking will be given as either an angle or a distance measurement. Ensure you use the appropriate data for your type of test equipment. The distance will be a figure, such as 3 mm toe in, an angle could be 50′ toe in: 50′ means 50 minutes – one degree is split into 60 minutes, so in this case the angle is 50/60, or 5/6 of a degree
Pressures	A simple measurement, which should be in bar. Many places still use psi, or pounds per square inch! As in all other cases, only compare like with like
Tread depth	A measurement of a few millimetres. Remember the legal requirements

Fault diagnosis

Symptom	Possible causes of faults	Suggested action
Excessive free play at steering wheel	Play between the rack and pinion or in the steering box	Renew in most cases but adjustment may be possible
	Ball joints or tie rod joints worn	Renew
	Column coupling loose or bushes worn	Secure or renew
Vehicle wanders, hard to keep in a straight line	As above	As above
	Alignment incorrect	Adjust to recommended setting
	Incorrect tyre pressure or mix of tyre types is not suitable	Adjust pressures or replace tyres as required
	Worn wheel bearings	Renew
Stiff steering	Wheel alignment incorrect	Adjust to recommended setting
	Tyre pressures too low	Adjust pressures
	Ball joints or rack seizing	Renew
Wheel wobble	Wheels out of balance	Balance or renew
	Wear in suspension linkages	Renew
	Alignment incorrect	Adjust to recommended setting
Understeer or oversteer	Tyre pressures incorrect	Adjust pressures
	Dangerous mix of tyre types	Replace tyres as required
	Excessive free play in suspension or steering system	Renew components as required

LEARNING TASKS

➡ Practise fault finding on real vehicles.

➡ Make a list of steps you would take to find some of the faults causing the symptoms listed in the table.

15 Electrical and electronic systems

I Introduction

Start here! Electrical and electronic systems are becoming increasingly important in motor vehicle engineering. Often electronics form the main part of systems like fuel injection, traction control or turbo chargers. The idea of this book, as you will realise by now, is to introduce you to the main things you need to know about motor vehicles and the industry. This chapter will give you a good grounding in the subject of electrics and electronics.

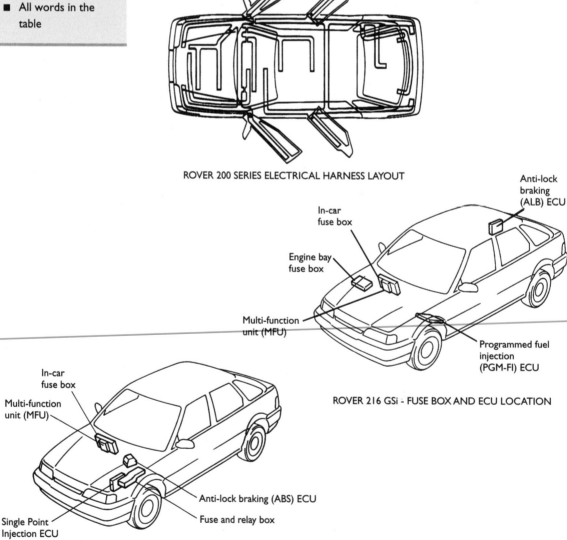

ROVER 200 SERIES ELECTRICAL HARNESS LAYOUT

In-car fuse box

Engine bay fuse box

Multi-function unit (MFU)

Anti-lock braking (ALB) ECU

Programmed fuel injection (PGM-FI) ECU

ROVER 216 GSi - FUSE BOX AND ECU LOCATION

In-car fuse box

Multi-function unit (MFU)

Anti-lock braking (ABS) ECU

Fuse and relay box

Single Point Injection ECU

ROVER 214 MODELS - FUSE BOX AND ECU LOCATION

Figure 15.1 Car shown with just some of its electrics

Terminology

Battery	Stores electricity in a chemical form, for the vehicle to use when the engine is not running
Starter motor	A very powerful electric motor which uses electricity from the battery to crank the engine which should then run on its own
Alternator	The alternator generates electricity when the engine is running: to charge the battery and to run all the electrical things on the vehicle
Lighting	Lights controlled by switches so the driver can see, be seen or signal that he or she is going to turn or stop
Auxiliaries	This heading covers most other standard electrical systems on the car, such as wipers, heater blower and heated rear window
Instruments	The instruments provide information for the driver about the operation of the vehicle. The most common are the speedometer, rev counter, fuel and temperature gauges
Wires	Made from strands of copper insulated with PVC, the wires simply carry electricity from one point to another – but only if a complete circuit is made
Terminals	Connections to join wires to components. They are often made waterproof and also latch together so they don't fall off
Wiring harness	Many modern cars have well over one thousand separate wiring circuits! A wiring harness is made by bundling different wires together for neatness and safety
Voltage	The pressure which pushes electricity through a circuit
Current	The flow rate of electricity through a circuit
Resistance	Opposition to flow of electricity. Resistance is often supplied by a bulb or motor, but a dirty connection can cause resistance which will prevent the circuit working properly
Power or wattage	A measure of how much energy is being converted, in this case electrical energy to, say, heat energy. Consider the difference between a headlight bulb and a panel light bulb
Chassis or negative earth return	To save wires and simplify the circuits, the body and chassis of most vehicles are used as a common connection; this is usually described as 'earth'. All modern vehicles have the chassis, or earth, connected to battery negative
Insulated earth	A very few vehicles use earth wires instead of the chassis. This is often for safety reasons, for example to reduce the risk of a spark on a petrol tanker!
Open circuit	A broken wire or connection
Short circuit	Part of a circuit, such as a wire or terminal, is touching something it shouldn't – e.g. a live wire touching to earth
High resistance	A dirty or loose connection can cause a high resistance in the circuit. This restricts the flow of electricity and could, for example, cause a dim headlight
Bad earth or bad connection	'Bad' is often used to describe one of the last three terms! The problem is that 'bad' could mean open circuit, short circuit or high resistance. It is good to learn the correct way of describing a fault

LEARNING TASKS

➡ Look back at the key words. Explain each one to a friend, and/or write out a short description to keep as evidence.

➡ Examine a real system and note the extensive use of electrical components. Make a note of the main systems.

2   Basic electrical things

Bulbs

A bulb is a thin strand of metal in a glass envelope used to make light. The number, shape and size of bulbs on vehicles is increasing all the time. The bulbs for vehicle lighting are generally either normal tungsten filament bulbs or tungsten halogen. In the glass bulb, the tungsten filament is heated by the electric current until it is white hot. The filament is usually wound into a 'spiralled spiral' to allow a length of thin wire in a small space. The glass bulb is filled with a gas such as argon. This allows the filament to work at a high temperature without burning, and it produces a whiter light. A few common bulbs are described below.

KEY WORDS

- Colour codes
- Cable sizes
- Terminal numbers
- Fuses
- Halogen bulb
- Wiring diagrams

Tungsten halogen headlight bulb

Almost all vehicles now use tungsten halogen bulbs for the headlights. This bulb has a long life and, unlike other bulbs, will not blacken over a period of time. The glass envelope used for the tungsten halogen bulb is made from quartz. The bulb has two filaments and three terminals, one for main beam, one for dip beam and the other for an earth connection. Figure 15.2 shows a typical tungsten halogen headlight bulb, together with some examples of bulbs in common use (briefly described below).

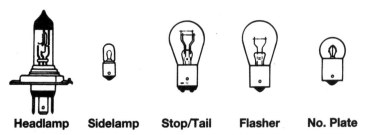

Headlamp   Sidelamp   Stop/Tail   Flasher   No. Plate

Figure 15.2 Halogen headlight bulb and other types used on light vehicles

Miniature centre contact

This bulb has a bayonet cap consisting of two pins projecting from either side of the cylindrical cap. It has a single central contact, with the metal cap body forming the second or earth connection. It is made with various power ratings, ranging from 1 to 5 watts. It is typically used for panel lights or side lights.

Double contact, small bayonet cap

These bulbs have a bayonet cap with a glass envelope enclosing two filaments. One end of each filament is connected to an end contact; both of the other ends are joined to the body, which is the earth. These caps have offset bayonet pins, so that the two filaments (which have different wattages) cannot be fitted the wrong way round. One filament is used for the stop light, the other for the tail light. They are rated at 21 and 5 watts (21/5W).

Single contact, small bayonet cap

These bulbs have a bayonet cap with a glass envelope enclosing a single filament. The filament is connected to a single central contact and uses the metal cap body to form the second contact. The size or wattage of the bulb is normally 5 W or 21 W.

The larger 21 W bulb is used for indicators, reversing and rear fog lights, the small 5 W bulb for number plate lights or side tail lamps.

Two other types of bulbs, not shown in the diagram, are the festoon and the capless type.

Festoon

The glass envelope has a tubular shape, with the filament stretched between brass caps cemented to the tube ends. It is often used for interior lighting.

Capless bulb

These bulbs have a tubular glass envelope with a flattened end which provides the support for the terminal wires; these wires are bent over to form the two contacts. Capless bulbs have power ratings up to 5 W and are used for panel lights, side lights and parking lights. They are now very popular due to the low cost of manufacture.

Fuses Some form of circuit protection is required for the electrical wiring of a vehicle and also for the electrical and electronic components. It is now common practice to protect almost all electrical circuits with a fuse. A fuse is the weak link in a circuit. If an overload of current occurs, the fuse will melt and disconnect the circuit before any serious damage is caused. Automobile fuses are available in three types: glass cartridge, ceramic and blade type. The blade type is now the most popular choice due to its simple construction and reliability. Figure 15.3 shows these three types of fuses.

Fuses are available in a number of rated values, as listed in the following table together with their colour code. Only the fuse recommended by the manufacturer should be used.

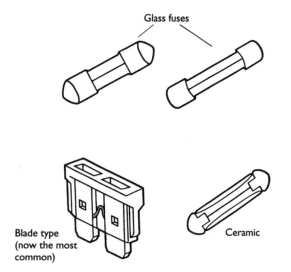

Glass fuses

Blade type
(now the most
common)

Ceramic

Figure 15.3 A selection of vehicle fuses

Type	Current rating	Colour code
Blade type	3	Violet
	4	Pink
	5	Clear/Beige
	7.5	Brown
	10	Red
	15	Blue
	20	Yellow
	25	Neutral/White
	30	Green
Ceramic type	5	Yellow
	8	White
	16	Red
	25	Blue

A fuse protects the device as well as the wiring, so the fuse rating needs to be considered. If you used a fuse with a much higher than stated rating in a wiper motor circuit, the fuse would probably still protect against a severe short circuit. However, if the wiper blades froze to the screen, a large value fuse might not protect the motor from overheating.

Fusible links in the main output feeds from the battery protect against major short circuits in the event of an accident or error in wiring connections. These links are simply heavy duty fuses and are rated in values such as 50, 100 or 150 A.

Occasionally circuit breakers are used in place of fuses, this being more common on heavy vehicles. A circuit breaker has the same rating and function as a fuse, but with the advantage that it can be reset.

Terminals and connectors

Many types of terminals are available and have developed from early bullet type connectors into the high quality waterproof systems now in use. A popular choice for many years was the spade or 'Lucar' type terminal. This is still a standard choice for connection to relays, for example, but is now losing ground to the smaller blade terminals. A selection of terminals is shown in Figure 15.4. Circular multipin connectors are used in many cases; the pins vary in size from 1 mm to 5 mm. With any type of multipin connector, an offset slot or similar is used to prevent incorrect connection.

Protection against corrosion of the connector is provided in a number of ways. Earlier methods included applying a suitable grease to the pins to repel water. It is now more usual to use rubber seals to protect the terminals, although a small amount of contact lubricant can still be used. Many multiway connectors use some kind of latch to prevent individual pins working loose; they also ensure that the complete plug and socket is held securely. Figure 15.4 shows several types of connector.

Wires

Cables used for motor vehicle applications are now almost always copper strands insulated with PVC. Copper, beside its very low resistance, has ideal properties such as ductility and malleability (see Chapter 20 for more details). This makes it the natural choice for most electrical conductors. PVC

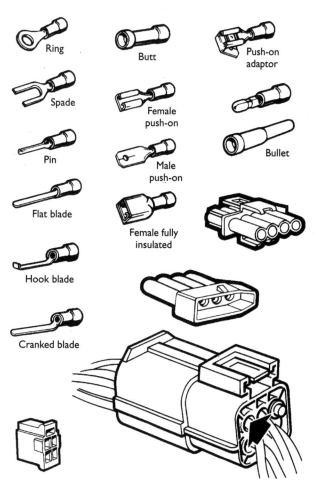

Figure 15.4 Wiring terminals and connector blocks

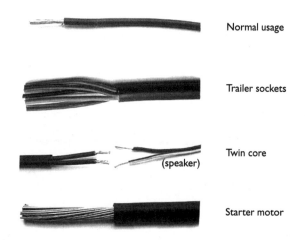

Figure 15.5 Wires

is an ideal insulator: it has very high electrical resistance, but is also very resistant to petrol, oil, water and other contaminants.

The choice of cable size depends on the current it will have to carry. The larger the cable used, the better it will be able to carry the current and supply all of the available voltage. But if it is too large, the wiring becomes cumbersome and heavy! In general, the voltage supply to a component must not be less than 90% of the system supply. Cable is available in stock sizes, and the next table lists some typical sizes and uses. A good 'rule of thumb' is that one strand of 0.3 mm diameter wire will carry 0.5 amps safely.

Cable size Strands/diameter (mm)	Cross sectional area (mm²)	Rating (amps)	Example uses
9/0.30	0.6	5.75	Side lights etc
14/0.25	0.7	6	Clock, radio
14/0.30	1.0	8.75	Ignition
28/0.30	2.0	17.5	Headlights, heated rear window
65/0.30	4.6	35.0	Main supply
97/0.30	6.9	50.0	Charging wires
120/0.30	8.5	60.0	Main supply
37/0.90 to 61/0.90	23.5 to 39.0	350.0 to 700.0	Starter supply

Terminal numbers and colour codes

Three main methods are mentioned here to help with tracing circuits: British colour code system, European system and DIN terminal numbers. Please note that some manufacturers will not use colours or numbers exactly as listed here!

The British Standard system uses twelve colours to determine the main purpose of the cable, and tracer colours to further define its use. The main colour uses and some other examples are given in the following table.

Colour	Symbol	Destination
Brown	N	Main battery feed
Blue	U	Headlight switch to dip switch
Blue/White	UW	Headlight main beam
Blue/Red	UR	Headlight dip beam
Red	R	Side light main feed
Red/Black	RB	Left side lights and number plate
Red/White	RW	Right side and panel lights
Purple	P	Constant but fused supply
Green	G	Ignition controlled fused supply
Green/Red	GR	Left side indicators
Green/White	GW	Right side indicators
Light Green	LG	Instruments
White	W	Ignition to ballast resistor
White/Black	WB	Coil negative
Yellow	Y	Overdrive and fuel injection
Black	B	All earth connections
Slate	S	Electric windows

Colour	Symbol	Destination
Pink/White	KW	Ballast resistor wire
Green/Brown	GN	Reverse
Green/Purple	GP	Stop lights
Blue/Yellow	UY	Rear fog light

A European system used by Ford, VAG, BMW and other manufacturers is based *broadly* on the following table. Please note that there is no connection between the European system and the British standard colour codes. In particular, note the use of the colour brown in each system!

Colour	Symbol	Destination
Red	Rt	Main battery feed
White/Black	Ws/Sw	Headlight switch to dip switch
White	Ws	Headlight main beam
Yellow	Ge	Headlight dip beam
Grey	Gr	Side light main feed
Grey/Black	Gr/Sw	Left side lights
Grey/Red	Gr/Rt	Right side lights
Black/Green	Sw/Gn	Ignition controlled supply
Black/White/Green	Sw/Ws/Gn	Indicator switch
Black/White	Sw/Ws	Left side indicators
Black/Green	Sw/Gn	Right side indicators
Light Green	LGn	Coil negative
Brown	Br	Earth connections
Pink/White	KW	Ballast resistor wire
Black	Sw	Reverse
Black/Red	Sw/Rt	Stop lights
Green/Black	Gn/Sw	Rear fog light

Once you've practised and familiarised yourself with these colour code systems, you will find fault finding an electrical circuit a little easier!

A popular system is the terminal designation. This helps to ensure correct connections are made on the vehicle, particularly in after sales repairs. Note that the designations do not identify individual wires but define the terminals of a device. Listed below are some of the most popular numbers.

No.	Designation
1	Ignition coil negative
4	Ignition coil high tension
15	Switched positive (ignition switch output)
30	Input from battery positive
31	Earth connection

No.	Designation
49	Input to flasher unit
49a	Output from flasher unit
50	Starter control (solenoid terminal)
53	Wiper motor input
54	Stop lamps
55	Fog lamps
56	Headlamps
56a	Main beam
56b	Dip beam
58L	Left side lights
58R	Right side lights
61	Charge warning light
85	Relay winding output
86	Relay winding input
87	Relay contact input (change over relay)
87a	Relay contact output (break)
87b	Relay contact output (make)
L	Left side indicators
R	Right side indicators
C	Indicator warning light (vehicle)

Symbols and circuit diagrams

Figure 15.6 is a guide to some commonly used symbols, but note that some manufacturers use their own variation. The idea of a symbol is to represent a component in a very simple, but easily recognisable form.

A conventional wiring diagram shows the electrical connections of a circuit but makes no attempt to show the various parts in any particular order or position. Figure 15.7 shows an example of this type of diagram.

A layout circuit diagram makes an attempt to show the main electrical components in a position similar to those on the actual vehicle. Due to the complex circuits and the number of individual wires, some manufacturers now use two diagrams: one to show electrical connections and the other to show the actual layout of the wiring harness and components, see Figure 15.8.

A terminal diagram shows only the connections of the devices, not any of the wiring. The terminal of each device, which can be represented pictorially, is marked with a code. This code indicates the device terminal designation, the destination device code and its terminal designation and in some cases the wire colour code. Figure 15.9 shows an example of this technique.

A current flow system, see Figure 15.10, is laid out to show current flow from the top of the page to the bottom. These diagrams often have two supply lines at the top of the page, marked 30 (main battery positive supply) and 15 (ignition controlled supply). At the bottom of the page is a line marked 31 (earth or chassis connection).

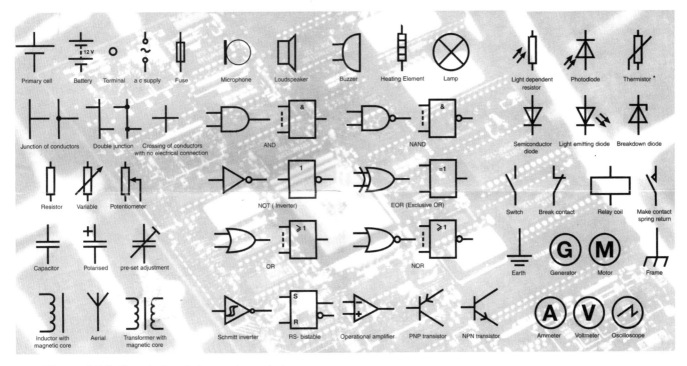

Figure 15.6 Electrical and electronic symbols

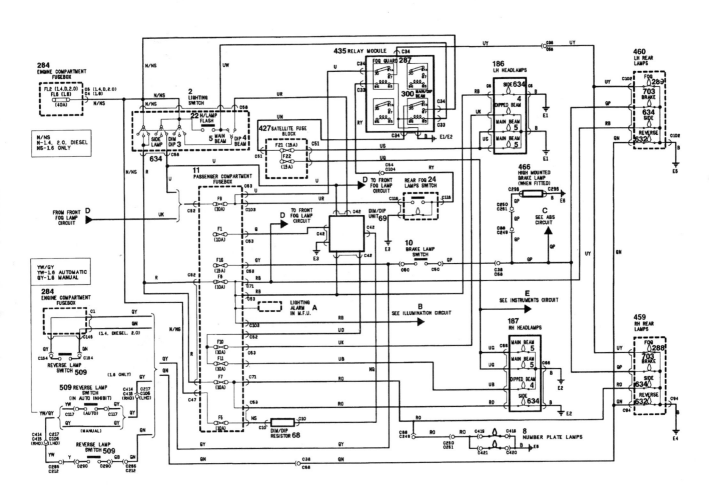

Figure 15.7 Conventional wiring diagram

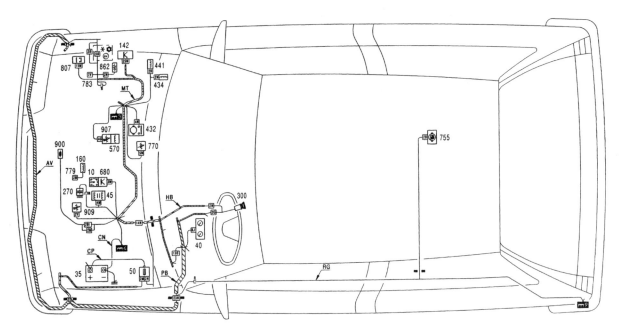

Figure 15.8 Layout wiring diagram

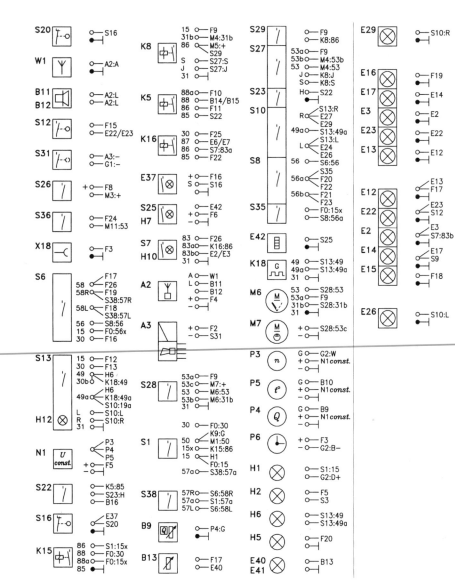

Figure 15.9 Terminal diagram

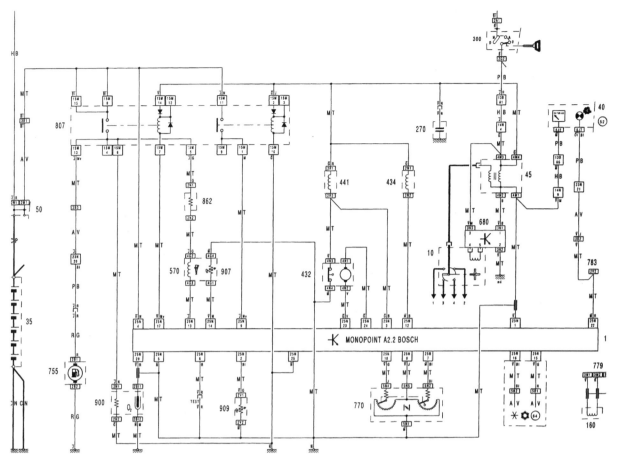

Figure 15.10 Current flow diagram

Relays

A relay is a very simple device. It can be thought of as a remote controlled switch. A very small electric current is used to magnetise a small winding. The magnetism then causes some contacts to close, which in turn can control a much heavier current. This allows small, delicate switches to be used to control large current users such as the headlights or the heated rear window. Figure 15.11 shows a typical relay.

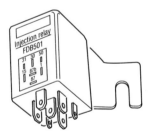

Figure 15.11 Common type of relay

LEARNING TASKS

➡ Look back at the key words. Explain each one to a friend, and/or write out a short description to keep as evidence.

➡ Look at some wiring diagrams relating to vehicles in your workshop. Can you follow any simple circuits?

3 Electrical systems

Battery

A lead acid cell is made of lead electrodes in a dilute solution of sulphuric acid. It is a means of converting chemical energy to electrical energy; when the electrical energy has been partly used, the cell can be re-energised or recharged. The voltage of a single lead acid cell is about 2 V. Cells are connected in series to form a battery of a set voltage, generally 12 V for

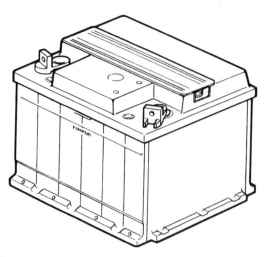

Figure 15.12 Modern vehicle battery

vehicle use. We say 12 V for convenience, but if you measure a good battery with a good voltmeter, you will find it is about 12.6 V!

Vehicle batteries are made up in plastic containers; these are acid resistant and strong, but still liable to damage if mishandled. A chemical action takes place when the cell gives out electrical energy, changing the chemicals of the plates and the electrolyte. To recharge the cell, the chemical action is reversed by passing a current through the cell in the opposite direction to the discharge current.

The chemical action during recharging releases hydrogen and oxygen. This is mainly absorbed by the electrolyte, but as the battery nears full charge, the gases are given off at the vents. The hydrogen gas is highly inflammable – take care!

The capacity of a battery is the amount of electrical energy which can be obtained from it. It is usually given in ampere/hours (Ah), reserve capacity (RC) and cold cranking amps (CCA).

Maintenance-free starter battery.
1 Cover
2 Terminal-post cover
3 Intercell connector
4 Post
5 Frit
6 Plate strap
7 Battery case
8 Bottom rail
9 Positive plates jacketed in plastic separators
10 Negative plates

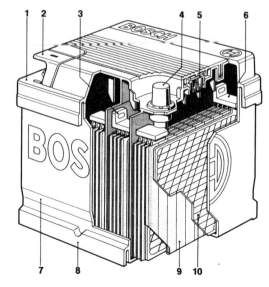

Figure 15.13 Battery construction

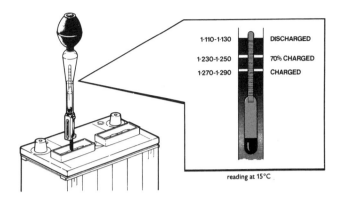

Figure 15.14 Hydrometer test of a battery

■ A 40 Ah battery should give 2 amps for 20 hours.

■ The reserve capacity indicates the time in minutes for which the battery will supply 25 A at 25°C.

■ Cold cranking current indicates the maximum battery current at –18°C for a set time, but standards vary:

Standard	Time
BS	60 seconds
DIN	30 seconds
SAE	30 seconds

A battery for normal light vehicle use may be rated at 40 Ah/65 minutes reserve capacity/160A cold cranking (BS).

For testing the state of charge of a non sealed type of battery, a hydrometer can be used. This is a syringe which draws electrolyte from a cell, and a float which will float at a particular depth in the electrolyte according to its density. The density or specific gravity is then read from the graduated scale on the float. A fully charged cell should show 1.280, when half charged 1.200 and if discharged 1.150.

Most vehicles are now fitted with maintenance free batteries and a hydrometer cannot be used to find the state of charge. This can only be determined by the voltage of the battery as given in the following table. An accurate voltmeter is required for this test.

Battery volts at 20°C	State of charge
12.2 V and under	Discharged
12.4 V	Half charged
12.6 V and over	Charged

A heavy duty discharge (HD) tester consists of a low value resistor and a voltmeter connected to a pair of heavy test prods. The test prods are firmly pressed on to the battery terminals. A heavily discharged battery will produce a voltmeter reading of 200–300 A.

A fully charged serviceable battery should read about 10 volts for a period of about 10 seconds. A sharply falling battery voltage to below 3 V indicates an unserviceable cell. Note also if any cells are gassing, as this indicates a short circuit. This will be indicated by a zero or extremely low reading. When using the HD tester the following precautions must be observed:

Figure 15.15 Heavy duty discharge test

Figure 15.16 Battery charger

■ Blow gently across the top of the battery to remove flammable gases.

■ The test prods must be positively and firmly pressed into the lead terminals of the battery to minimise sparking.

■ It should not be used while a battery is on charge.

Charging a battery is sometimes necessary. The charge rate (the amount of current to put back in a battery) is calculated from the Ah capacity, the reserve capacity or the cold cranking amps of the battery.

For example, the ideal rate for a 40 Ah battery is 4 A:

■ 1/10 of the ampere hour capacity, or

■ 1/16 of the reserve capacity, or

■ 1/40 of the cold cranking amps.

Normal charging – charge for 10 hours at the rate (as above). Boost charging – this may be carried out at five times the above rate and should bring the battery to about 80% of its full charge state in about one hour. It is best only to boost charge in an emergency as it can damage the battery.

The following points must be observed when working with batteries:

■ good ventilation

■ protective clothing

■ supply of water available (running water preferable)

■ first aid equipment available and to include eyewash

■ no smoking or naked lights permitted.

In use a battery requires very little attention other than the following:

■ Clean corrosion from terminals using hot water. Terminals should be smeared with petroleum jelly or Vaseline *not* ordinary grease.

■ Battery tops should be clean and dry.

■ If not sealed, cells should be topped up with distilled water 3 mm above the plates.

■ Battery should be securely clamped in position.

Alternator and charging system

The electrical requirements of modern vehicles are very high. The charging system must be able to meet these demands. In simple terms the vehicle charging system must, under all operating conditions, be able to supply all the consumers on the vehicle and still charge the battery.

Figure 15.17 shows a typical modern alternator; the name and purpose of each main component is as follows:

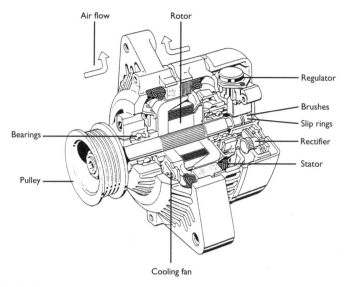

Figure 15.17 Alternator

Component	Purpose
Brushes	Made from soft carbon, the brushes allow a small electric current to pass through the slip rings to the field windings
Slip rings	Copper rings which, in conjunction with carbon brushes, allow electricity to pass through to a rotating component
Rotor and windings	The cast iron rotor contains the windings and is made magnetic
Pulley	The pulley transfers drive and hence energy from the engine. It is usually via a vee or poly vee belt and rotates the rotor
Stator	The stator has electricity induced in to it by the rotating magnetism of the rotor. It produces a three phase ac output
Rectifier	The three phase ac is rectified (converted) to dc by the action of diodes (one way valves for electricity)
Output terminals	The main positive output from the rectifier is connected here
Regulator	A small output from the rectifier is sent back to the field windings via the brushes. The regulator controls this output, thereby controlling the output voltage of the alternator
Warning light terminal	The same small output as for the field windings is also used to put out the warning light via this terminal
Bearings	As the alternator runs at a very high speed, good ball bearings are used at each end of the rotor to reduce friction
Cooling fan	The fan prevents the whole machine becoming too hot

Figure 15.18 shows the most basic principles of a single and three phase alternator and their outputs. Basic electromagnetic induction is caused by a rotating magnet inside a stationary loop or loops of wire. In a practical alternator the rotating magnet is an electromagnet which is supplied via two slip rings. Figure 15.19 shows the most common design, known as a claw pole rotor. Each end of the rotor will become a north or a south pole and hence each claw will be alternately north and south.

The stationary loops of wire are known as the stator and consist of three separate phases, each with a number of windings. The windings are mechanically spaced on a laminated iron core. Figure 15.19 shows a typical example. The three phase windings of the stator can be connected in two ways, known as star or delta.

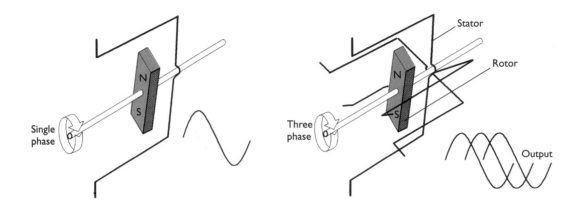

Figure 15.18 Alternator principle

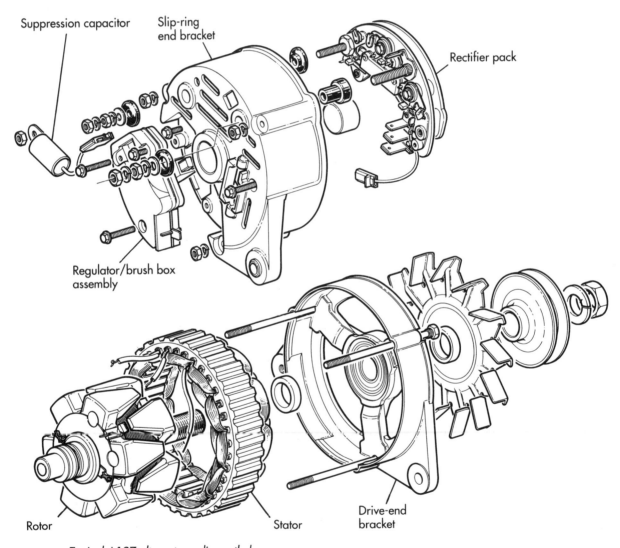

Typical A127 alternator – dismantled

Figure 15.19 Alternator shown with its main components

In order for the output of the alternator to be used to charge the battery and run other vehicle components it must be rectified, that is converted from alternating current (ac) to direct current (dc). The components most suitable for this task are diodes.

Six diodes are needed to rectify the output of a three phase machine. An extra three positive diodes are often included in a rectifier pack. These are usually smaller than the main diodes and are only used to supply a small current back to the field windings in the rotor. They are known as the field or excitation diodes. Due to the large currents flowing through the main diodes, a heat sink (which removes the heat from the diodes) is required to prevent damage.

To prevent the vehicle battery from being overcharged, the voltage should be kept at a set level. A figure of 14 V is typical of many, if not all, 12 V charging systems. Voltage regulation is a difficult task on a vehicle alternator because of the constantly changing engine speed. The output of an alternator without regulation would rise with engine speed. Alternator output is controlled by magnetic field strength of the rotor. It is the task of the regulator to control this field strength in response to alternator output voltage. Regulators can be mechanical or electronic.

In many cases the charging circuit is one of the simplest on the vehicle. The main output is connected directly to the battery via suitable size cable. The warning light is connected to an ignition supply on one side, to the alternator terminal at the other.

Figure 15.20 shows the meter connections required for testing an alternator charging system. Two common tests can be carried out:

■   maximum output current
■   regulated voltage.

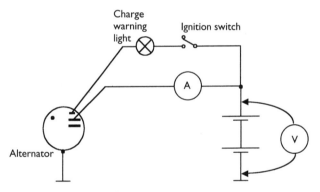

Figure 15.20 Testing an alternator

Starter   An internal combustion engine needs to be turned over at about 100 rev/min to then fire and run on its own. This is where the electric starter comes in. Assuming average mileage, the starter system is used about two thousand times a year in city traffic!

Figure 15.21 shows a typical starter motor, the name and purpose of each main component is as follows:

Component	Purpose
Solenoid	A winding which is magnetised when electricity is supplied
Engaging mechanism	The magnetism attracts the plunger, which levers the pinion into mesh with the ring gear on the engine flywheel. When the solenoid is switched off, a spring moves the pinion out of mesh

Component	Purpose
Main contacts	When the pinion is fully in mesh, these strong copper contacts close to make a good electrical connection from the battery to the main starter terminal and the brushes
Brushes	The copper carbon mix brushes pass the electricity to the commutator
Commutator	The many segments of the copper commutator pass electricity through the appropriate windings on the armature
Armature	The armature windings become magnetic and cause the motor to turn because the magnetism of the armature is repelled by the main field magnetism
Fields	The main magnetic field is caused by permanent magnets on this motor, but many use heavy duty windings instead
Pinion	The pinion is simply a small gear with a ratio of about 10:1 compared to the ring gear. A one way clutch behind the pinion prevents the motor being driven by the engine when it starts

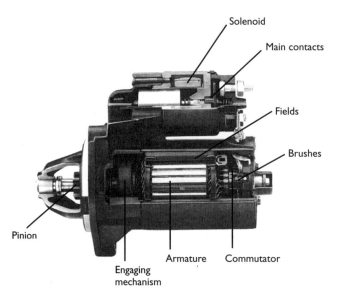

Figure 15.21 Permanent magnet starter motor

In comparison with most other circuits on the modern vehicle, the starter circuit is very simple. The problem to overcome, however, is that of voltage drop or loss in the main supply wires. The starter is usually operated by a spring loaded key switch, which also controls the ignition and accessories. The supply from the key switch, in many cases via a relay, causes the starter solenoid to operate and this in turn, by a set of heavy contacts, controls the heavy current. Figure 15.22 shows a basic starting circuit.

Put simply, a motor is a machine to convert electrical energy into mechanical energy. The starter motor is no exception. A current flowing through a conductor placed in a magnetic field creates a force which acts on the conductor. The main field is created by windings or permanent magnets. In any dc motor the conductor is shaped into a loop or many loops to form the armature. A commutator allows contact via brushes to the supply current.

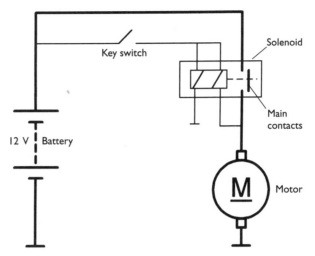

Figure 15.22 Basic starter circuit

In most cases four brushes are used to carry the heavy current. The brushes are made of a mixture of copper and carbon, like most motor or generator brushes. The armature consists of a segmented copper commutator and heavy duty copper windings.

A starter must also have some method of engaging with, and releasing from, the vehicle's flywheel ring gear on the back of the engine. In light vehicle starters this is by either the inertia type engagement or pre-engagement. In all standard motor vehicle applications the starter must be connected to the engine ring gear only during starting. If the connection remained permanent, the excessive speed at which the starter would be driven by the engine would destroy the motor almost immediately.

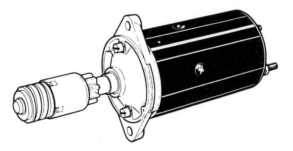

Figure 15.23 Lucas inertia starter motor

The inertia type of starter motor has been used for over eighty years, but it is now becoming redundant. The starter shown in Figure 15.23 is the Lucas M35J type. It was used on small to medium petrol engined vehicles. The starter engages a small pinion with the flywheel ring gear. The toothed pinion and a sleeve splined on to the armature shaft are threaded so that, when the starter is operated, the spinning armature will cause the sleeve to rotate inside the pinion. The pinion remains still due to its inertia and, because of the screwed sleeve rotating inside it, is moved into mesh with the ring gear.

When the engine fires and runs under its own power, the pinion is driven faster than the armature shaft. This causes the pinion to be screwed back along the sleeve and out of engagement with the flywheel. The main spring acts as a buffer when the pinion first takes up the driving torque; it also acts as a buffer when the engine throws the pinion back out of mesh.

One of the main problems with this type of starter was the aggressive nature of the engagement. This tended to cause the pinion and ring gear to wear. The pinion was also prone to seizure, often due to contamination by dust from the clutch. This was often made worse by application of oil to the pinion mechanism, which tended to attract even more dust. These problems have largely been overcome by the pre-engaged starter motor.

Pre-engaged starters are fitted to the majority of vehicles in use today. As full power is not applied until the pinion is fully in mesh, or pre-engaged, this type of starter provides a positive engagement with the ring gear. It prevents premature ejection as the pinion is held into mesh by the action of a solenoid. A one way clutch is incorporated into the pinion to prevent the starter motor being driven by the engine. Some starters now have a small gearbox built in to increase the torque. On vehicles with automatic transmission this starter circuit is interrupted by an inhibitor switch to prevent the engine being started in gear.

Diesel engined vehicles may have a connection between the starter circuit and a circuit to control the glow plugs. This may also use a timer relay.

Lighting All main exterior lights on the vehicle use a simple bulb, a reflector and a lens. The object of the reflector is to direct the random light rays produced by the light bulb into a beam or pattern. A reflector is basically a layer of silver, chrome or aluminium deposited on a smooth surface such as glass or plastic. The beam is improved by passing the reflected light rays through a transparent block of lenses. The lenses partially redistribute the reflected light beam and stray rays so that a better overall result is achieved. The lenses are coloured red, amber or white as appropriate. The headlights use the same technique on a larger scale.

A good headlight has a powerful far reaching main beam, around which the light is distributed to illuminate a good area of the road surface. The dip beam still provides good lighting, but it must not dazzle drivers coming in the opposite direction. Figure 15.24 shows how this is done by using a double filament bulb. The adjustment of headlight beams is done using a beam setter. Figure 15.25 shows a simplified vehicle lighting circuit.

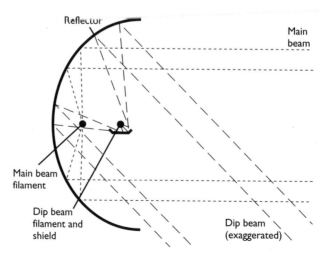

Figure 15.24 Creating a dip beam with a twin filament bulb

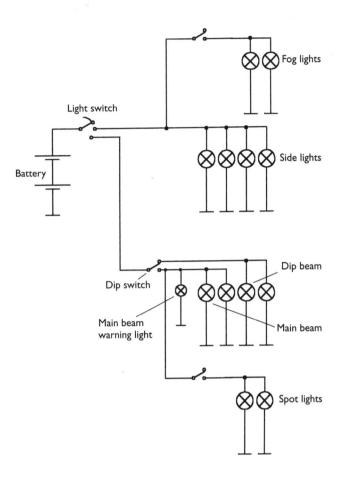

Figure 15.25 Simplified lighting circuit

Auxiliaries   The requirements of the wiper system are simple. The windscreen must be clean enough to provide suitable visibility at all times. The wiper blades are made of a rubber compound and are held on to the screen by a spring in the wiper arm. In modern vehicle design, as different air currents flow on and around the screen area, the aerodynamic properties of the wiper blades have become increasingly important.

Most wiper motors are permanent magnet. Drive is by a worm gear to increase torque and reduce speed. Three brushes allow two speed operation: because the third brush is closer to the common connection, more current will flow. Figure 15.26 shows a typical wiper motor.

The windscreen washer system consists of a permanent magnet motor driving a water pump. The water, preferably with a cleaning additive, is directed onto part of the screen by two or more jets. A non return valve is fitted in the line to the jets to prevent water running back to the reservoir. This also allows 'instant' operation when the washer button is pressed. The washer circuit is normally linked in to the wiper circuit so that, when the washers are operated, the wipers start automatically and will continue for several more sweeps after the washers have stopped.

Direction indicators have a number of statutory requirements. The colour must be amber, but they may be grouped with other lamps. The flashing rate must be between one and two per second. If a fault develops, this must be apparent to the driver by a pilot light on the dashboard. Figure 15.27 shows

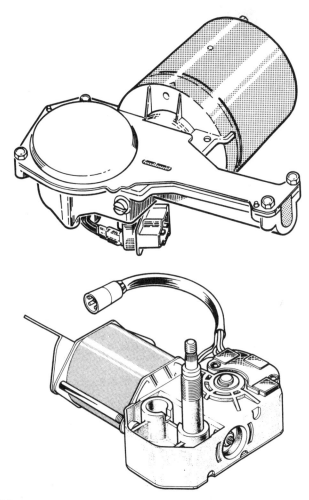

Figure 15.26 Typical wiper motors

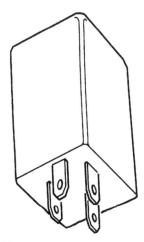

Figure 15.27 Electronic flasher unit

an electronic flasher unit. The type shown can operate up to four 21 W bulbs and two 5 W side repeaters when operating in hazard mode. This will continue for several hours if required. Flasher units capable of operating more bulbs (e.g. when towing a trailer or caravan) are available. In simple terms a flasher unit makes the supply to the bulbs switch on and off!

EU regulations state that the horn (or audible warning device) should produce a uniform sound. This makes sirens and melody or fanfare horns illegal! Most horns draw a large current, so are generally switched by a suitable relay. The standard horn operates by electromagnetism. As current flows, an armature attached a tone disc is attracted to a stop. A set of contacts opens, disconnecting the current and allowing the armature and disc to return under spring tension. The whole process repeats rapidly when the horn switch is on. This vibration produces the sound.

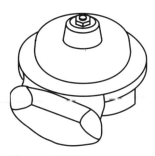

Figure 15.28 Vehicle horn

Engine cooling fan motors (radiator cooling) are permanent magnet types. Figure 15.29 shows an example. The fans often used to have the blades placed asymmetrically (balanced, but not regular) to reduce operating noise.

Headlight cleaning is a good contribution to road safety. There are two ways in which headlights are cleaned (other than by a damp cloth!): by high pressure jets or by small wiper blades with low pressure water supply. The second method is the same as windscreen cleaning but on a smaller scale. The high pressure system is popular, but can suffer in very cold conditions due to the fluid freezing. Headlight cleaners are often made so that they operate when the windscreen washers are activated if the headlights are also switched on.

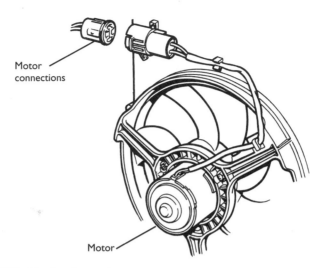

Figure 15.29 Cooling fan and motor

Figure 15.30 Headlight washers in action

Instruments Driver information is essential to ensure safe and trouble free operation of a modern vehicle. Most instruments are located in or around the vehicle dashboard. Instrumentation is not always associated with a gauge or a readout type display. In many cases the whole system can be used just to operate a warning light. The system must still work to certain standards: for example, if a low outside temperature warning light did not illuminate at the correct time, a dangerous situation could develop.

Thermal (or bi-metal) gauges are often used for fuel and engine temperature indication. The gauge works by using the heating effect of electricity. As a current flows through a simple heating coil wound on a bimetal strip, the heat causes the strip to bend. The bimetal strip is connected to a pointer on a scale. The amount of bend is proportional to the heat, which in turn is proportional to the current flowing. Providing the sensor can vary its resistance in proportion to the thing being measured (e.g. fuel level), the gauge will indicate a suitable representation.

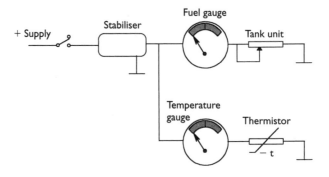

Figure 15.31 Fuel and temperature gauge circuit

Thermal type gauges are used with a variable resistor and float in a fuel tank or with a thermistor in the engine water jacket. Figure 15.31 shows the circuit of these two together. Note that a constant voltage supply is required to prevent changes in the vehicle system voltage affecting the reading. If system voltage increased, the current flowing would increase and the gauges would read higher.

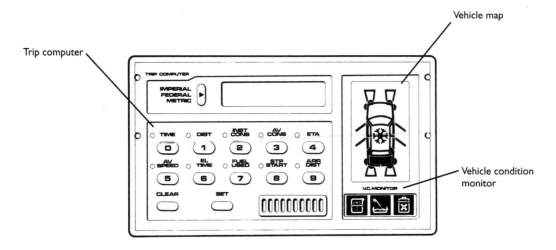

Figure 15.32 VCM and vehicle map display unit

VCM or vehicle condition monitoring is a form of instrumentation. Figure 15.32 shows a typical display unit used by Rover, which also incorporates the vehicle map. Systems which can be monitored:

■ high engine temperature

Figure 15.33 Modern dashboard layout

- low fuel
- low brake fluid
- worn brake pads
- low coolant level
- low oil level
- low screen washer fluid
- low outside temperature
- bulb failure
- doors, bonnet or boot open warning.

The oil level can be monitored by measuring the resistance of a heated wire on the end of the dip stick. A small current is passed through the wire to heat it. How much of the wire is covered by oil will determine its temperature and therefore its resistance.

The display is often a collection of light emitting diodes (LEDs), or a backlit liquid crystal display (LCD). These are arranged into suitable patterns and shapes to represent the circuit or system being monitored. An open door will illuminate a symbol which looks like the door on the vehicle map (plan view of the car) is open. Low outside temperature or ice warning is often a large snowflake!

Alarm systems   Stolen cars and theft from cars account for about a quarter of all reported crime. Up to 500 000 cars are reported missing each year in the UK, and about 100 000 are never recovered! Even when returned, many are found to be damaged. Most car thieves are opportunists, so even a basic alarm system serves as a deterrent.

Car and alarm manufacturers are constantly trying to improve security. The alarm system is now often a part of the vehicle electronic system as a whole. Even so, 'retro' fit systems can still be very effective. Three main types of intruder alarm are used, together with a number of ways to disable the vehicle:

- switch operated on all entry points
- battery voltage sensed
- volumetric sensing (movement in the vehicle)
- ignition and/or starter circuit cut off
- engine ECU code lock.

Alarms can be set by a separate switch or an infrared (IR) transmitter. More common now, they are set automatically when the doors are locked.

The following is an overview of the good alarm systems now available either as a 'retro' fit or factory fitted. They have electronic sirens and give an audible signal when arming and disarming. They are all triggered when the car door opens and will automatically reset after a period of time, often 1 or 2 minutes. The alarms are triggered instantly when any entry point is breached. Most systems are two piece, with separate control unit and siren, and most will have the control unit in the passenger compartment and the siren under the bonnet (out of reach).

Most systems now come with two infrared remote 'keys' that use small button type batteries and have a light emitting diode (LED) that shows when the signal is being sent. They operate with one vehicle only. The sirens produce a sound level of about 95 dB, when measured 2 m in front of the vehicle (95 decibels is very loud!). Figure 15.34 shows a block diagram of a complex alarm system.

Some factory fitted alarms are combined with the central door locking system. This allows the facility known as lazy lock. One press of the remote unit sets the alarm, closes the windows and sunroof and locks the doors.

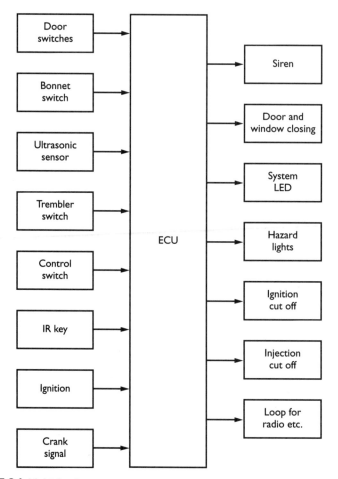

Figure 15.34 Vehicle alarm system

One of the latest ideas is to put a security code in the engine electronic control unit. A coded signal is needed to 'unlock' the code and allow the engine to start. Ford are using a special ignition key which is programmed with the required information. Even the correct 'cut' key will not start the engine. Citroën use a similar idea in their top range models, but the code has to be entered via a numerical keypad. Of course nothing will stop the car being lifted on to a lorry and driven away, but then a new engine control ECU will be needed. The cost will be high and also questions may be asked as to why a new ECU is required.

Infrared receiver

Transmitter

Professional car thieves will always find ways round the latest alarm systems, but the vehicle manufacturers are working to stay one step ahead. Legislation is being considered so that tracking devices can be built into an unknown part of the vehicle's chassis. This can be activated in the event of the car being stolen, allowing the police to trace the vehicle.

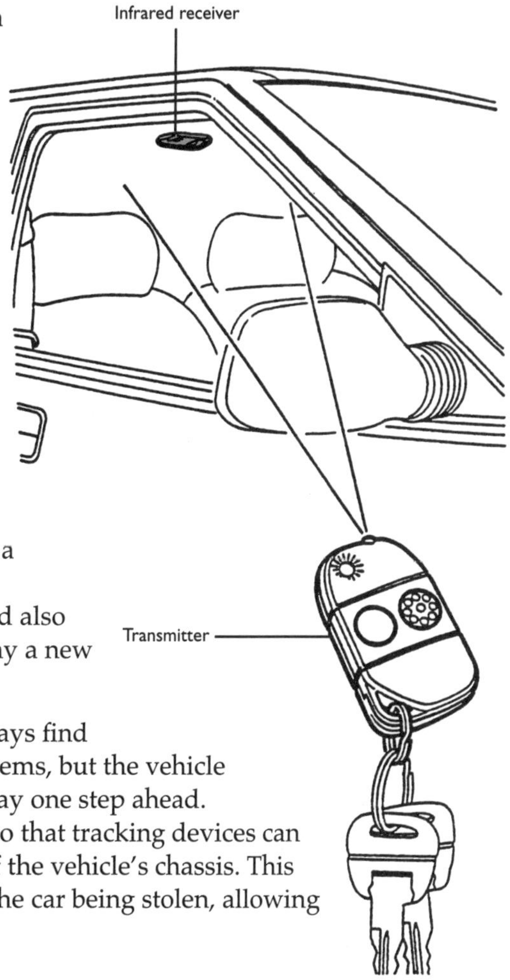

Figure 15.35 Alarm system operation

LEARNING TASKS

➡ Look back at the key words. Explain each one to a friend, and/or write out a short description to keep as evidence.

➡ Examine a real system and note all the electrical components you can see! Name and state the purpose of the main parts.

➡ Write a short explanation about how to check a battery.

---

4 Electronics

Basic electronic components

Figure 15.36 shows the symbols for some common electronic components. A brief description follows for several of the components shown. There is no particular symbol for integrated circuits.

Resistors are probably the most widely used component in electronic circuits. They are used to limit current flow and provide fixed voltage drops. Two factors must be considered when choosing a suitable resistor: ohms value (resistance) and power rating. Most resistors used in electronic circuits are made from small carbon rods; the size of the rod determines the resistance.

Capacitors consist of two plates separated by an insulator. The value is determined mostly by the area of the plates and the distance between them.

KEY WORDS

■ Electronic components

■ Electronic systems

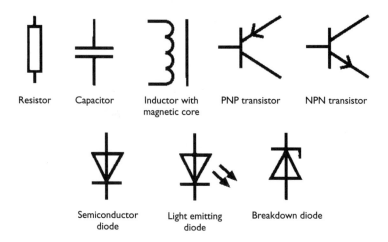

Resistor   Capacitor   Inductor with magnetic core   PNP transistor   NPN transistor

Semiconductor diode   Light emitting diode   Breakdown diode

Figure 15.36 Electrical and electronic component symbols

Capacitors are often constructed by metal foil sheets insulated by a type of paper and rolled up together inside a tin can.

Diodes are often described as one way valves, and for most uses this is a good description. They are usually constructed from two types of silicon. Zenner diodes are very similar in operation, except that they are designed to conduct in the reverse direction at a pre-set voltage. They can be thought of as a type of pressure relief valve.

Transistors are the device which has allowed the development of today's complex and small electronic systems. The transistor is used as either a solid state switch or as an amplifier. They are constructed from the same materials as diodes.

Inductors are most often used as part of an oscillator or amplifier circuit. In these applications it is essential for the inductor to be stable and of reasonable size. An inductor is basically a coil of wire wound on a former. The magnetic effect of the changes in current flow gives this device the properties of inductance.

Integrated circuits, or ICs, are constructed on a single slice of silicon. Combinations of some of the components mentioned previously can be combined to carry out various tasks. These tasks can range from simple switching to the microprocessor of a computer. The components required for these circuits can be made directly on to one slice of silicon. The great advantage of this is not just the size of the ICs (which can be very small) but the speed at which they can be made to work.

Electronic systems With most electronic systems on the car we don't need to know what the electronics do in great detail. You can think of electronic systems as having inputs and outputs. The 'brain' of the system will be the electronic control unit or ECU for short. Figure 15.37 shows, as an example, an antilock brake system. The inputs supply information to the ECU about how the car is operating. The ECU 'decides' what to do and then controls the output of the system – in this case the brakes.

When fault finding on a system of this type, we can consider just one part at a time until the fault is found. This type of work is very interesting, but you will need to understand the operation of all the basic principles first!

Figure 15.37 Antilock brake system electronics

5 Diagnostics

Systematic testing

For example, if the reported fault is that the engine will not crank over on the starter, you could proceed as follows:

FAULT FINDING
1. Verify the fault
2. Collect further information
3. Evaluate the evidence
4. Carry out further tests in a logical sequence
5. Rectify the problem
6. Check all systems

1. Try the operation to confirm the fault.

2. Does it crank at all, or slowly? Do the lights on the vehicle seem to work at full brightness. Can you turn the engine by hand?

3. If it cranks slowly, this could be because the battery is discharged or unserviceable, the starter is worn out or a high resistance connection exists in the starter circuit.

4. For example, check the battery condition. Let's assume it is discharged. Now check the charging system to make sure the alternator is working. Recharge the battery and start the engine. Measure the battery volts. Has it increased to 14 V? If not, the alternator may be defective.

5. Replace or repair the alternator.

6. Check all electrical systems for correct operation.

With this example fault the problem seemed at first related to the starter, but in fact was to do with the alternator. Watch out for this type of problem – the customer would not have been happy buying a battery, starter and an alternator, if you had guessed instead of following a logical test sequence.

Test equipment

Always refer to the manufacturers' instructions appropriate to the equipment you are using.

Multimeter

This is an essential tool for fault finding electrical circuits and systems. A good meter will have many functions, voltage, current and resistance measurement being the most common. Always read the instructions and ensure the meter is set to the correct range for what you are measuring.

Oscilloscope

This is a device which displays voltages in the form of patterns on a screen. It allows us to examine output signals from all types of electrical components. More details will be covered at NVQ level 3.

Dedicated test equipment

Many manufacturers provide this type of test equipment. It is often designed to work only with one range of vehicles. In some cases the instrument is plugged in to the vehicle in place of an electronic control unit and a series of automatic tests are carried out. You should take particular care to refer to the manufacturers' instructions with this type of equipment.

Test results

The following table shows some of the information you may have to get from other sources such as data books or a workshop manual.

Test carried out	Information required
Alternator charging voltage	A good voltmeter connected across the battery. For a 12 V vehicle the alternator should produce 14 V when running at a mid range speed
Component resistance test	When measuring the resistance of a component such as a temperature sensor, it must be disconnected from the vehicle wiring. Resistance figures are given in ohms (Ω); values vary too much to give an example
Battery electrolyte density	This data is often available on the side of the hydrometer. A reading of 1.28 means the electrolyte is 1.28 times heavier than water. If all cells read about the same, the battery is fully charged
Component voltage supply	In most cases all the major electrical devices (lights for example) should be supplied with battery voltage – when switched on. A small loss in the wires is acceptable (5 to 10%)

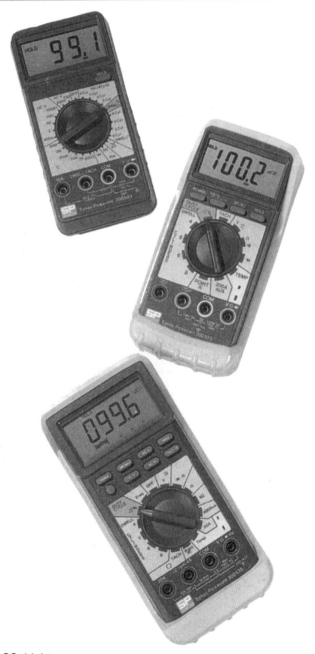

Figure 15.38 Multimeters

Fault diagnosis

Symptom	Possible causes of faults	Suggested action
Starter will not crank engine or cranks slowly	Battery discharged Starter has worn brushes or other fault High resistance connection	Recharge and test Renew or repair Repair
Battery is discharged	Battery has internal fault Alternator not charging Current drain on the vehicle	Renew Replace or repair Check with ammeter; boot light may be staying on
Light or lights do not work	Open circuit	Trace the fault in a logical manner. For example, a voltage one side of a connector but not the other means the connector is open circuit
Fuse keeps blowing	Short circuit	Check for wire rubbing to earth. This causes too much current to flow, which blows the fuse. Do *not* fit a larger fuse; a fuse is a weak link to prevent damage to other components and wires
Lights are too bright	Alternator is overcharging	Renew or replace regulator if possible
Wipers do not work	Open circuit Motor fault	Trace the fault in a logical manner If you have voltage supplies to the motor but it does not operate, then the fault must be internal

LEARNING TASKS

➡ Practise fault finding on real vehicles.

➡ Make a list of steps you would take to find some of the faults causing the symptoms listed in the table.

16 Body, chassis and fittings

1 Introduction

Start here!

Light vehicle bodies are usually made of pressed steel or, in a few cases, fibreglass. Body styles include two door, four door, hatchback, convertible and car derived vans. Designers try to produce models that are appealing to the eye, are similar to other products from the same manufacturer and are aerodynamic. Low wind resistance makes for good fuel economy and reduces turbulence, making it quieter inside for passengers. Ergonomics also plays a part in the design. This relates to the comfort and ease of operation for the driver and passengers.

As vehicle mechanical technicians we do not need to be expert in body repair. We must, however, be able to remove and refit major components as well as carry out work on security systems such as the door locks.

KEY WORDS

- All words in the table
- Aerodynamics
- Ergonomics

Figure 16.1 Modern vehicle body styles are very attractive

Terminology	
Chassis	The basic frame for a motor vehicle
A post	The post on which normal opening front doors hinge
Body mounting	Fittings for mounting the body to the chassis for older type cars or heavier vehicles
Composite construction	The chassis and body of the vehicle are built as two separate units
Integral construction	Most modern light vehicles use this method, also called mono or unity construction. The body and chassis are combined
Car derived van	A van which is based on a similar car, for example the Ford Escort van or Rover Maestro van
Body panels	Wings, bonnet and door for example
BC post	The centre post: the 'B' has the front door striker plate and the 'C' has the hinges for the rear doors. Only appropriate to four/five door vehicles
D post	The rear post on which the rear door striker is fitted. Front door striker if a two/three door vehicle

Terminology

Off side	In the UK – the right hand side when in the driver's seat
Near side	In the UK – the left hand side when in the driver's seat
Track	The width of a vehicle between its wheels (think of railway track)
Wheelbase	The distance from the front to the rear axles

LEARNING TASKS

➡ Look back at the key words. Explain each one to a friend, and/or write out a short description to keep as evidence.

➡ Make a simple sketch to show the wheel base, track, length and height of a vehicle.

➡ Examine a real system and note the position or construction of the terms in the table.

2 Body construction

Vehicle types

KEY WORDS

- Chassis
- Active safety
- Passive safety
- Security systems
- VIN

The development of the vehicle since the end of the nineteenth century has been quite fascinating and is worth further reading if you, too, find it interesting.

Convertible

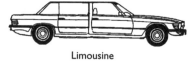
Limousine

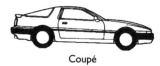
Coupé

Saloon

Estate

Sports

Hatchback

Light van

Figure 16.2 Different light vehicle types

Modern light vehicle types, referred to as light passenger cars and derivatives, mostly fall into the following categories:

- saloon
- hatchback
- estate
- coupé
- convertible
- sports
- limousine
- light van.

Body parts The detailed design and construction of the vehicle body is beyond the scope of this book. But a basic understanding of at least the name and purpose of the major parts is important. Figure 16.3 shows the main external components with the following parts:

1. bonnet panel
2. boot lid
3. centre pillar
4. front bumper
5. front door
6. front wing
7. headlights

8. radiator grill
9. rear bumper
10. rear door
11. rear quarter panel
12. roof panel
13. sidelights
14. sill panel.

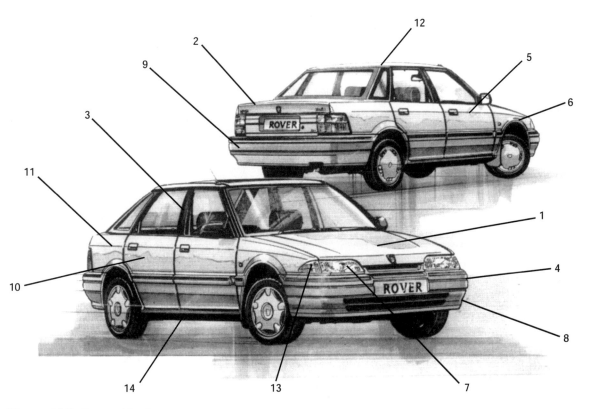

Figure 16.3 External body components

Figure 16.4 shows some of the main body shell components. The complete list is as follows:

1. back window upper rail
2. body side frame
3. bulkhead
4. centre pillar (BC post)
5. dash panel
6. D post
7. floor assembly
8. front body hinge pillar (A post)
9. front side member
10. front valance
11. radiator panel
12. rear quarter
13. rear wheel arch
14. roof bow
15. roof panel
16. sill panel
17. underbody
18. windscreen upper rail.

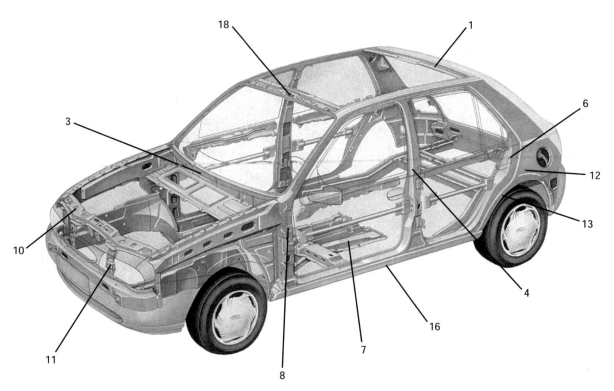

Figure 16.4 Body shell components

Chassis   Earlier cars had full, ladder type frames on which the body was mounted in separate pieces. Modern cars are made from a steel body that combines the function of the frame with the central cabin of the body. The subframe, front or rear, is a small steel brace that supports the engine or suspension and is welded to the car's body structure. The body forms the centre and connecting supports. A vehicle chassis includes and supports the car's frame, power train, suspension, wheels, steering and brake systems. Figure 16.5 shows an early type chassis. Some vehicles have a bolt on subframe which is used to support the front and/or rear running gear. In some cases this also supports the engine. It is in effect a small chassis.

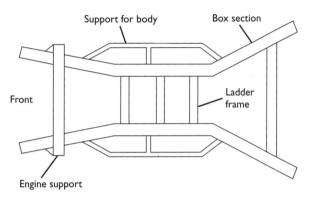

Figure 16.5 Early vehicle chassis

Safety features   Safety features on a vehicle can be thought of as active or passive. 'Active' means they are acting all the time, 'passive' that they wait until an accident occurs! The following two tables list some of the features incorporated into modern vehicles.

Passive systems	Notes
Air bags	In the event of an accident these bags 'explode' into position to cushion the driver and passenger
Antiburst door locks	It is better to be inside a car in the event of an accident than to be thrown out. These door locks prevent the doors from flying open
Collapsible steering column	To try and prevent chest injuries to the driver, the steering column collapses and is pulled down away from the driver in the event of a front end collision
Crumple zones	When an impact occurs, the movement energy has to be dispersed. If this is through the passengers, then serious injury will result. Crumple zones absorb as much of the impact energy as possible, reducing the risk to the occupants
Head restraints	These help to prevent whiplash injuries to the neck
Padded steering wheels	Helps to prevent injury to the driver's chest
Rollover cage	In the event of the vehicle rolling over, a cage prevents the cabin from collapsing
Seat belt tensioners	At the instant of impact the seat belts are pulled tighter to hold the passengers more securely
Side impact bars	Bars in the door strengthen the side of the vehicle to protect the occupants

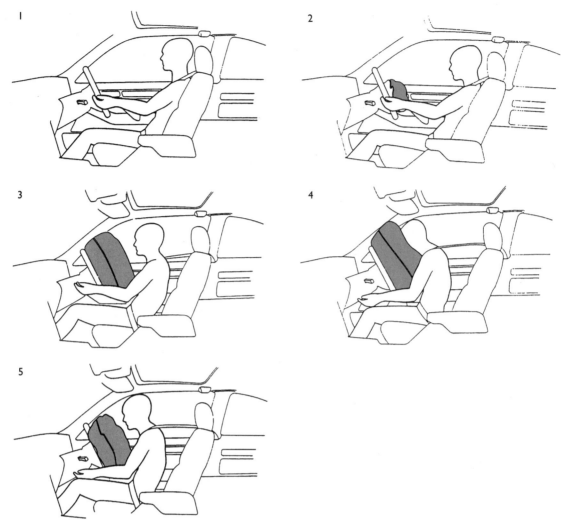

Figure 16.6 Air bag in action

Active systems	Notes
Antilock brakes	Electronically controlled system to prevent the wheels from locking and skidding when the brakes are applied. This helps the driver maintain control when braking
Aerodynamic stability	A stable car is less likely to go out of control
Dual circuit brakes	Standard on all modern cars; even if one brake pipe bursts, the brakes will still work on at least two wheels
Comfortable driving position	The driver is more likely to be able to react to potential trouble and therefore stay out of it!
Good ventilation	Helps to keep the driver awake and alert
Efficient bad weather equipment	Good lights and good windscreen wipers, to name just two parts, ensure the driver can see and be seen

Paintwork   The subject of vehicle painting is beyond the scope of this book. But you need to know how to protect the paintwork. Follow the guidelines listed below and use your common sense.

■ Always use covers when working on a vehicle. Wing covers are the most important.

- Do not allow any fluids, particularly solvents or brake fluid, to come into contact with the paintwork.
- Protect body panels when removing and storing; cloth and masking tape are often all that is required.
- Tools and parts should not be placed on the vehicle body.

Figure 16.7 The high quality finish of a modern vehicle

Security – door locks and alarms

Two main types of job are likely on a vehicle's door locks. The first of these is adjustments of the striker and/or the hinges to make the door close properly. The second will involve replacing parts or all of the door lock components. Figure 16.8 shows the components of a boot lock.

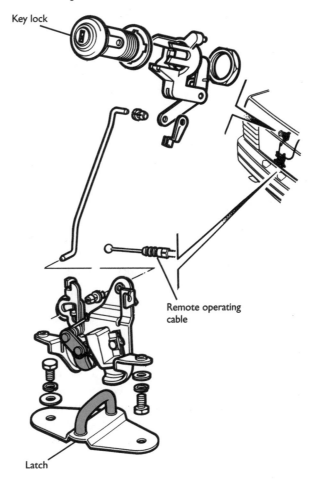

Figure 16.8 Boot lock components

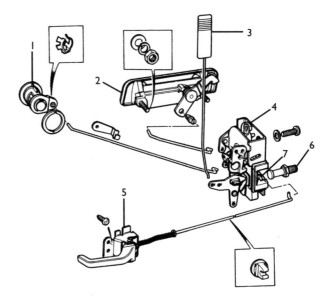

Figure 16.9 Front door lock components

Figure 16.9 shows an example of front door lock components from an earlier type of vehicle, but many of the methods are still current. The main parts shown are:

1. key locking assembly
2. exterior release lever
3. locking button
4. lock assembly
5. interior release lever
6. striker pin
7. latch.

Here is an example of how door lock adjustment is carried out:

- Ensure that the latch is in the open position.
- Slacken the striker pin or plate and adjust it until the door can be closed easily without rattling, lifting or dropping.
- Tighten the plate or pin, close the door and check by pressing on the door. You should feel slight movement as the door seals compress.

The following levels of vehicle security may be fitted to modern vehicles:

- central locking only
- central locking with double locking
- central locking with perimeter alarm
- central locking with double locking and perimeter alarm.

The following description, based on a Ford system, is typical of many modern security systems.

Some models have the option of an infrared remote control in conjunction with central locking, double locking and perimeter alarm. The central locking system enables the driver to lock or unlock all the doors simultaneously. The doors are automatically locked or unlocked when one of the front doors is locked or unlocked using the key or the interior door handle.

When double locking is fitted, a crash sensor in the control module unlocks central locking in case of an accident. On vehicles without double locking or

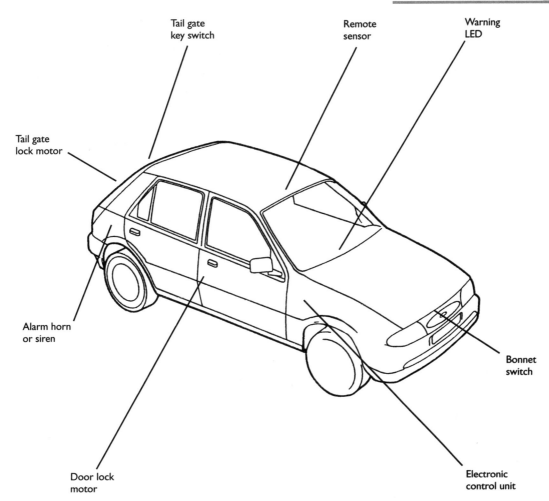

Tail gate
key switch

Remote
sensor

Warning
LED

Tail gate
lock motor

Alarm horn
or siren

Door lock
motor

Bonnet
switch

Electronic
control unit

Figure 16.10 Location of components in a security system

an alarm, a separate control module causes the lock control motors to operate a mechanical overload clutch. This makes it possible to unlock the doors mechanically in the event of a defect or accident. The tailgate/luggage compartment can be operated by a lock control motor with a separate button on the central console or externally, using the key.

When the double locking theft protection feature is fitted, the doors cannot be opened by use of the interior or exterior door handles, nor can the luggage compartment be opened with the remote electrical push button release. The feature is activated by turning the key in the driver's or front passenger's door to the unlock position and then to the lock position within three seconds. It is deactivated when one of the front doors is opened with the key. It can also be activated and deactivated using the remote control, when fitted.

A fuel shutoff crash sensor is utilised to deactivate the double and central locking in the event of an accident if the vehicle is being driven with the doors locked at the time. When the alarm system is fitted in conjunction with central and double locking, it will be automatically activated as the vehicle is central or double locked.

The alarm system is triggered when someone breaks into the vehicle via the doors, bonnet or luggage compartment door. This anti-theft alarm system can be activated only by locking the driver's or front passenger's door with the key, or with the remote control. It cannot be activated from the interior door handles or luggage compartment lock.

The alarm system is activated after a 20 second delay time, which is indicated by an LED flashing at a high frequency. The delay time starts when all doors, including the bonnet and luggage compartment door, are fully closed and the set switches are activated. The 20 second delay time is interrupted if a door is opened; it starts from the beginning when the door is closed again. After the 20 second delay, the system is armed.

Once the activation time delay has elapsed, the alarm is triggered if any of the doors, the bonnet or the luggage compartment are opened. The alarm is also activated if the ignition is turned on or the radio is disconnected. The alarm can be switched off only by unlocking the driver's or front passenger's door with the key or the remote control.

When the alarm is triggered (operating), its horn emits a intermittent signal for a maximum of 30 seconds (in order to comply with certain legislation). The hazard flashers may also operate for 5 minutes. The ignition circuit is also immobilised to prevent the car being driven when the alarm is operating.

Vehicle Identification Number (VIN)

The VIN number contains detailed information about the vehicle. You should always use it when ordering parts or making enquiries. On older vehicles the number was referred to as the chassis number. The VIN number should usually be recorded on the job card. It is normally located under the bonnet, in easy view. As an example, the VIN number
S A X XE Y L U 7 B M 531290 contains the following information:

S	geographic area
A	country
X	manufacturer
XE	model
Y	class
L	body
U	engine
7	transmission and steering
B	model change
M	assembly plant
531290	serial number.

LEARNING TASKS

➠ Look back at the key words. Explain each one to a friend, and/or write out a short description to keep as evidence.

➠ Make a simple sketch of a car and label the main body parts.

➠ Examine a real system and make notes about all its safety and security features.

➠ Write a short explanation of precautions you must take when working on the vehicle body.

3   Diagnostics

Systematic testing

For example, if the reported fault is the driver's door not closing correctly, you could proceed as follows:

FAULT FINDING

1. Verify the fault
2. Collect further information
3. Evaluate the evidence
4. Carry out further tests in a logical sequence
5. Rectify the problem
6. Check all systems

1. Try it and see what happens!
2. Does the lock work? Does the door close if pushed harder or lifted?
3. Is the problem the striker plate position or internal to the door?
4. Check to see if the door is hitting the striker correctly.
5. Adjust the striker position or repair/renew lock components.
6. Check operation again, check other doors for correct operation.

Fault diagnosis

Symptom	Possible causes of faults	Suggested action
Door will not close	Striker adjustment	Adjust
	Worn lock components	Renew
	Door hinge worn	Adjust or replace as required
Lock will not operate	Key worn	Try the spare!
	Lock components need lubrication	A spray lubricant is good for locks
	Lock components worn to excess	Renew
Central locking does not work	Electrical fault	Trace fault with voltmeter
	IR transmitter battery flat	Replace

LEARNING TASKS

➡ Practise fault finding on real vehicles.

➡ Make a list of steps you would take to find some of the faults causing the symptoms listed in the table.

17 Preparing vehicles

1 Introduction

Much of the required underpinning knowledge about the subject of vehicle preparation is covered in other sections about specific vehicle systems. For this reason I have not covered too much technology in this chapter. Also note that a large part of this chapter is related to servicing vehicles. More details about the service tasks are given in the next chapter.

So what does 'Prepare new, used or repaired vehicles for customer use' really mean? When a car is handed over to a customer, it must be safe, clean and in good working order. In some cases you will make recommendations about work required to bring the car up to standard. This means you must understand and be able to carry out two main tasks:

- Operate the full range of vehicle systems to make sure they work correctly.
- Examine the vehicle and make a report containing your findings and recommendations.

Inspecting a vehicle is a very practical task. It is also a very responsible task. If you say the brakes work, then they should work! In this chapter you will learn important background information about inspecting and testing vehicles.

Figure 17.1 A vehicle undergoing inspection

Terminology

Pre-delivery inspection or PDI	This normally relates to a new vehicle which must be checked and prepared before handing over to the customer. The inspection is to ensure the vehicle is fully operational
Used vehicle inspection or UVI	Similar to a PDI but relating to second hand (pre-owned!) vehicles. The inspection is as above but also will include checks for wear and tear as well as damage
Road test	After checking over a vehicle in the workshop, a road test helps to identify further problems, for example steering wobble. If you have not passed your driving test, you can still road test, a vehicle by telling a qualified driver what to do
Roller test	Some garages have rollers set into the workshop floor on which the wheels of the car can be run. A particular type of rollers is used to test brakes as part of an MOT test. Note the problems of four wheel drive vehicles if only one pair of rollers is available!
Recording system	Records must always be kept for both the customer and for use by the garage. When carrying out an inspection, you must record faults as they are found to ensure none are forgotten
Inspection procedure	A logical sequence in which to carry out an inspection to ensure all areas are covered
Vehicle specifications	Information from the vehicle manufacturers setting out the exact way in which a vehicle should operate. Also contain all the data such as tyre pressures, filling capacities and adjustment information

LEARNING TASKS

➡ Look back at the key words. Explain each one to a friend, and/or write out a short description to keep as evidence.

➡ Write a short explanation about why recording systems are important.

2   Inspections

Operation of vehicle systems

When a vehicle is presented to you for inspection, you must be able to operate all of its systems. So you need a working knowledge about the layout and operation of the following.

KEY WORDS

- Records
- Job card
- Road test

Controls or driver information displays	What you need to know
Steering wheel	The wheel should be secure and in good condition. It operates the steered wheels with little or no free play. Check workshop manuals; often 2 to 3 cm is the maximum free movement
Pedals	The security and 'feel' of the pedals. This means the accelerator pedal should move against a constant spring tension; the clutch pedal (if fitted) should fully disengage the clutch; the brake pedal must be firm after a small travel – it should not creep, feel spongy or 'pump up'
Hand brake lever	It must pull the brakes tight and still have reserve movement. The number of ratchet clicks can be used as a guide but will not be the same on all vehicles. The warning light must work
Gear lever	All gears must engage easily. You should feel for the 'gate' which prevents accidental movement into reverse gear
Lighting switches	All light switches should work in a positive manner. Include, in particular, dipping of the main headlights. Switches should be secure

Controls or driver information displays	What you need to know
Washers and wipers	These must clean the screen to allow the driver a clear view. Both or all washer jets must be clear and the wiper blades in good condition. Remember that wipers often operate at slow speed, fast speed, intermittent and when the washers are operated. The blades should also park at the bottom of the screen when switched off
Bonnet and boot release	Simple pull levers: one should open the bonnet to its first position; the other, if fitted, should allow the boot to be opened
Heating, ventilation and air conditioning controls	The engine will need to be warm to test all options. Check all possible modes of operation, such as: hot/cold, up/down/vent, fresh/recirculate and various speeds of booster fan. To check the air conditioning, the engine needs to be running. All the previous tests are the same, but to a better level of control. Many cars have automatic temperature control (ATC)
Speedometer and tachometer	These instruments should be smooth in operation; on road test the speedo mileage indicator should work correctly.
Fuel and temperature gauges	Readings on these gauges should be as you would expect depending on the current vehicle condition. For example, the temperature gauge should go up as the engine temperature increases; the fuel gauge should show a stable reading of fuel quantity
Warning lights	Almost too many to mention! The most common are oil pressure, indicators, main beam and the charge warning light. You should refer to manufacturers' data if necessary. Figure 17.2 shows some of the common symbols you should know. Note that a warning light tells of a problem by working in a different way to normal, not just by lighting up to warn of a fault. For example, the charge warning light comes on with ignition and goes out when the engine starts and the alternator is charging the battery. A fault in the alternator can stop the light working, but you would not know that when the engine is running

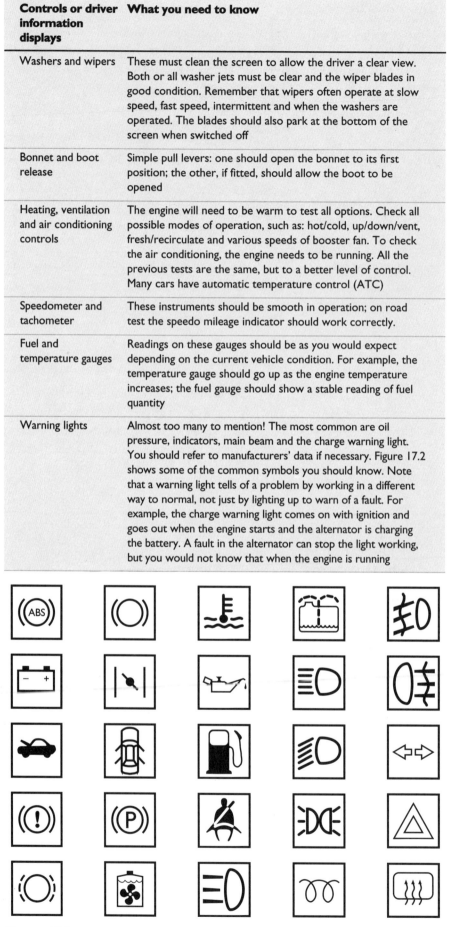

Figure 17.2 Warning light symbols

Controls or driver information displays	What you need to know
Interior lights	Most interior lights have their own switches but should also work when doors are opened. Check for delay operation – this means they can stay lit for a few seconds after the door is closed
Electric seats, windows and sunroof	Operation should be smooth and quiet. Many electric windows have 'one shot' operation: they open or close fully at one press of the switch. If appropriate, a switch near the driver should stop rear electric windows from being operated from the rear switches. This is for child safety
Alarm system	Too many different types are used to be specific. So the alarm system should operate as stated in the handbook. Check remote operation if appropriate

Vehicle specifications

Vehicle specifications give us the information we need to carry out all types of work. The specifications or information can be given in a number of ways:

- workshop manuals
- data books or sheets
- charts and tables

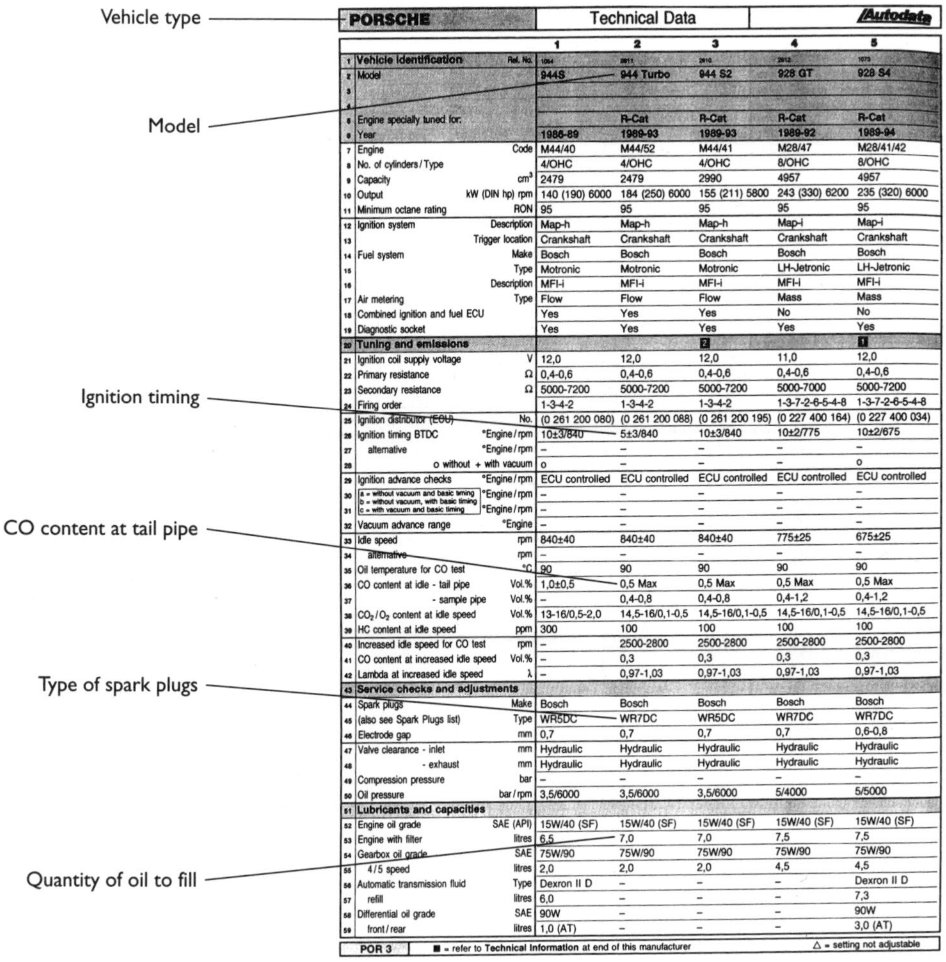

PORSCHE		Technical Data				Autodata
		1	**2**	**3**	**4**	**5**
1 Vehicle identification	Ref. No.	1064	4911	2610	2612	1075
2 Model		944S	944 Turbo	944 S2	928 GT	928 S4
3						
4						
5 Engine specialty tuned for:			R-Cat	R-Cat	R-Cat	R-Cat
6 Year		1986-89	1989-93	1989-93	1989-92	1989-94
7 Engine	Code	M44/40	M44/52	M44/41	M28/47	M28/41/42
8 No. of cylinders / Type		4/OHC	4/OHC	4/OHC	8/OHC	8/OHC
9 Capacity	cm³	2479	2479	2990	4957	4957
10 Output	kW (DIN hp) rpm	140 (190) 6000	184 (250) 6000	155 (211) 5800	243 (330) 6200	235 (320) 6000
11 Minimum octane rating	RON	95	95	95	95	95
12 Ignition system	Description	Map-h	Map-h	Map-h	Map-i	Map-i
13	Trigger location	Crankshaft	Crankshaft	Crankshaft	Crankshaft	Crankshaft
14 Fuel system	Make	Bosch	Bosch	Bosch	Bosch	Bosch
15	Type	Motronic	Motronic	Motronic	LH-Jetronic	LH-Jetronic
16	Description	MFI-i	MFI-i	MFI-i	MFI-i	MFI-i
17 Air metering	Type	Flow	Flow	Flow	Mass	Mass
18 Combined ignition and fuel ECU		Yes	Yes	Yes	No	No
19 Diagnostic socket		Yes	Yes	Yes	Yes	Yes
20 Tuning and emissions				■		■
21 Ignition coil supply voltage	V	12,0	12,0	12,0	11,0	12,0
22 Primary resistance	Ω	0,4-0,6	0,4-0,6	0,4-0,6	0,4-0,6	0,4-0,6
23 Secondary resistance	Ω	5000-7200	5000-7200	5000-7200	5000-7000	5000-7200
24 Firing order		1-3-4-2	1-3-4-2	1-3-4-2	1-3-7-2-6-5-4-8	1-3-7-2-6-5-4-8
25 Ignition distributor (ECU)	No.	(0 261 200 080)	(0 261 200 088)	(0 261 200 195)	(0 227 400 164)	(0 227 400 034)
26 Ignition timing BTDC	*Engine/rpm	10±3/840	5±3/840	10±3/840	10±2/775	10±2/675
27 alternative	*Engine/rpm	–	–	–	–	–
28 o without + with vacuum		o	–	–	–	o
29 Ignition advance checks	*Engine/rpm	ECU controlled	ECU controlled	ECU controlled	ECU controlled	ECU controlled
30 a = without vacuum and basic timing / b = without vacuum, with basic timing	*Engine/rpm	–	–	–	–	–
31 c = with vacuum and basic timing	*Engine/rpm	–	–	–	–	–
32 Vacuum advance range	*Engine	–	–	–	–	–
33 Idle speed	rpm	840±40	840±40	840±40	775±25	675±25
34 alternative	rpm	–	–	–	–	–
35 Oil temperature for CO test	°C	90	90	90	90	90
36 CO content at idle - tail pipe	Vol.%	1,0±0,5	0,5 Max	0,5 Max	0,5 Max	0,5 Max
37 - sample pipe	Vol.%	–	0,4-0,8	0,4-0,8	0,4-1,2	0,4-1,2
38 CO₂/O₂ content at idle speed	Vol.%	13-16/0,5-2,0	14,5-16/0,1-0,5	14,5-16/0,1-0,5	14,5-16/0,1-0,5	14,5-16/0,1-0,5
39 HC content at idle speed	ppm	300	100	100	100	100
40 Increased idle speed for CO test	rpm	–	2500-2800	2500-2800	2500-2800	2500-2800
41 CO content at increased idle speed	Vol.%	–	0,3	0,3	0,3	0,3
42 Lambda at increased idle speed	λ	–	0,97-1,03	0,97-1,03	0,97-1,03	0,97-1,03
43 Service checks and adjustments						
44 Spark plugs	Make	Bosch	Bosch	Bosch	Bosch	Bosch
45 (also see Spark Plugs list)	Type	WR5DC	WR7DC	WR5DC	WR7DC	WR7DC
46 Electrode gap	mm	0,7	0,7	0,7	0,7	0,6-0,8
47 Valve clearance - inlet	mm	Hydraulic	Hydraulic	Hydraulic	Hydraulic	Hydraulic
48 - exhaust	mm	Hydraulic	Hydraulic	Hydraulic	Hydraulic	Hydraulic
49 Compression pressure	bar	–	–	–	–	–
50 Oil pressure	bar/rpm	3,5/6000	3,5/6000	3,5/6000	5/4000	5/5000
51 Lubricants and capacities						
52 Engine oil grade	SAE (API)	15W/40 (SF)	15W/40 (SF)	15W/40 (SF)	15W/40 (SF)	15W/40 (SF)
53 Engine with filter	litres	6,5	7,0	7,0	7,5	7,5
54 Gearbox oil grade	SAE	75W/90	75W/90	75W/90	75W/90	75W/90
55 4/5 speed	litres	2,0	2,0	2,0	4,5	4,5
56 Automatic transmission fluid	Type	Dexron II D	–	–	–	Dexron II D
57 refill	litres	6,0	–	–	–	7,3
58 Differential oil grade	SAE	90W	–	–	–	90W
59 front/rear	litres	1,0 (AT)	–	–	–	3,0 (AT)
POR 3		■ = refer to Technical Information at end of this manufacturer				△ = setting not adjustable

Labels pointing to the table: Vehicle type · Model · Ignition timing · CO content at tail pipe · Type of spark plugs · Quantity of oil to fill

Figure 17.3 Vehicle specification

- drawings
- wiring diagrams
- computers
- microfiche.

Once you have found the correct information, you need to compare it to the vehicle. Tyre pressure is one example. The learning tasks at the end of this section will give you some practice in finding information.

Test and inspection procedures

A logical routine is very important when carrying out inspections. This is for two reasons:

- to ensure nothing is missed
- to keep time to a minimum.

Manufacturers often recommend a set procedure, which is in line with their record sheets. The MOT test even has a set routine to be followed. If there is no recommended routine for the test or inspection you are carrying out, follow this simplified guide:

1. Set the vehicle in the workshop on a vehicle hoist or ramp.
2. Sit in the driver's seat and operate all the controls (see above), noting correct operation. An assistant or a mirror may be needed for some tests, lights for example. (An assistant must be used for an MOT test.)
3. Check seats and seat belts.

No.	Defect corrected	Check
1.		
2.		
3.		
4.		
5.		
6.		
7.		
8.		
9.		
10.		
11.		
12.		
13.		
14.		
15.		

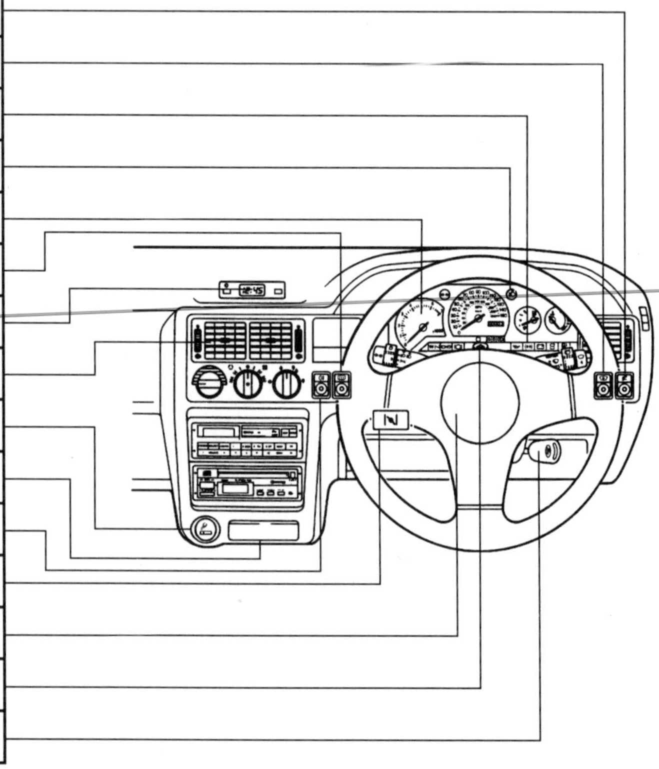

Figure 17.4 Inspection sheet example for just some of the required tests

4. Starting from the driver's door, work round the outside of the car checking door security, glass and body condition. Include the boot and bonnet as well as security of body components such as bumpers, trim and mirrors. And don't forget the dampers and spare wheel!

5. Raise the car to about waist height (wheels chocked and bonnet open). Work round each wheel, checking the tyres in particular.

6. With an assistant inside so you can ask for brakes, steering etc. to be operated, raise the car to head height.

7. Check all appropriate under car systems, first round under the engine and then round the rear of the car.

8. Lower the car to the floor and check all the under bonnet systems such as levels, drive belts and hoses. Run the engine and listen for noises.

9. Road test the vehicle under all normal operating conditions.

10. On return to the workshop, test exhaust gases.

Please remember that this list is a guide to the method of inspection, not a full check list. Throughout the inspection use the appropriate inspection sheets to make notes and tick off items as they are completed. This will ensure you do not forget anything. As well as helping you to cover all aspects of the vehicle, the sheets form part of the overall recording system.

Recording systems

The inspection sheets as used in the previous section form part of a recording system. This is for a number of reasons:

■ a check that all the required work has been done

■ a standard way of reporting your findings

■ a record of the time spent and materials used, allowing an invoice to be prepared if necessary

■ a record for the garage or workshop in case further queries arise at a later time

■ the sales department, for example, may need to know when the vehicle is ready

■ the customer can be given a copy of the inspection sheet so they know what has been checked.

Different workshops will use different systems, but all will be based on some or all of the following types of records:

Record	Details
Manufacturers' records	Records relating to specific vehicles, provided by the manufacturers. Particularly PDI check sheets
Fleet records	When operating a large fleet, the fleet manager needs to know details of all servicing and repairs carried out on the vehicles. This may be kept on computer and allows common problems to be identified
Company records	The company can have its own system so that when a vehicle returns to the workshop, details of previous work is available. Computer systems are being used more and more as they can, for example, automatically issue a reminder to a customer when an MOT test is due
Customer records	These can be interpreted in two ways: The customer's record may be a simple service book which is stamped by the garage. It provides 'service history' and is a good selling point for a used vehicle. The customer records held by the company are the personal and vehicle details: name, address, type of vehicle etc

Record	Details
Job cards	The job card is very important in a workshop. It allows a record to be kept of all work done and, in particular, the time spent and parts used. An invoice can then be generated, which in the end pays your wages!

Road safety

Road safety is covered by the highway code and therefore the driving test, but some further precautions are necessary when road testing vehicles. For example, when testing brakes you may have to stop very quickly; extra care should be taken to ensure it is safe. It may be necessary to drive at a set speed to check for vibration or wheel wobble. You must ensure a suitable road is used. In many cases it is better and safer for two people to carry out the road test. One can then sit in the back to listen for a rattle or noise, for example.

Many workshops have a specified road tester who is also an experienced technician. In this case you must explain clearly the work you have done, or what in particular you would like him or her to test. The key points follow:

- Under no circumstances must the highway code be broken when road testing.
- Consideration should be give to other road users at all times.
- Respect the customer's vehicle – no wheel spins out of the workshop, for example!

Figure 17.5 Vehicle on road test

Final notes

The best source of information about preparing a particular vehicle is the vehicle manufacturer. The MOT testers' manual provides useful information, and motoring organisations provide test sheets. Testing and preparing vehicles is a very responsible job, so:

'If you have any doubts or do not understand anything, you must ask your supervisor for help.'

LEARNING TASKS

➡ Look back at the key words. Explain each one to a friend, and/or write out a short description to keep as evidence.

➡ Choose five different cars and find the correct data for ignition timing, CO content, oil quantity and type of spark plug.

➡ Write a short explanation about why regular inspections are important.

18 Servicing

1 Introduction

Start here! This chapter has many things in common with the previous chapter about preparing vehicles. This is because a major part of servicing is to inspect the vehicle.

So, why is it important to carry out regular servicing and inspections of vehicles? I suggest there are several answers, most of which are quite obvious when you think about it:

- Ensure the vehicle stays in a safe condition.
- Keep the vehicle operating within tolerances specified by the manufacturer and by regulations.
- Ensure the vehicle is reliable and reduce down time.
- Maintain efficiency.
- Extend the life of individual components and the vehicle as a whole.
- Reduce running costs.
- Keep the vehicle looking good and limit damage from corrosion.

In order to carry out servicing and inspections, you need to understand how the vehicle systems operate. These are covered in other chapters in this book, and you can always refer back if you need to refresh your memory.

It is also important to keep suitable records, often known as the vehicle's service history. Vehicle service and inspection procedures vary a little from one manufacturer to another. As well as the original manufacturer's information, servicing data and servicing requirement books are also available. Always refer to whatever documentation is available to ensure that all the required tasks are completed.

KEY WORDS

- All words in the tables
- Road Vehicle Construction and Use Regulations

Figure 18.1 Vehicle being serviced

Terminology

First service	This service is becoming less common, but some manufacturers like new vehicles to be returned to the dealers after about a thousand miles or so. Certain parts are checked for safe operation, and in some cases oil is changed
Distance based services	Six thousand mile intervals are common, but manufacturers' recommendations vary. Most have different requirements at set distances. This is covered further later in this chapter
Time based services	For most light vehicles, distance based services are best. But some vehicles run for long periods of time and do not cover great distances. In this case the servicing is carried out at set time intervals. This could be every six months, six weeks or after a set number of hours run
Inspection	The MOT test, which must be carried out each year after a light vehicle is older than three years, is a good example of an inspection. However, an inspection can be carried out at any time and should form part of most services
Records	A vital part of a service. To ensure all aspects are covered and to keep information available for future use
Customer contracts	When you make an offer to do a service and the customer accepts the terms and agrees to pay, you have made a contract. This contract is legally enforceable by both parties

Rules and regulations

The Road Vehicle Construction and Use Regulations 1986 specify acceptable conditions for a vehicle. They are in effect summarised by the MOT test. This is the standard to which you should work at all times. Some of the main vehicle systems relating to safety are listed in the following table, together with examples of the requirements. Note that these are *just examples*; always refer to specific data relating to specific vehicles. The MOT testers' manual, for example, gives many more details.

Figure 18.2 MOT test station symbol

System	Requirements
Brakes	The foot brake must produce 50% of the vehicle weight braking force and the parking brake 16% (this assumes a modern dual line braking system). The brakes must work evenly and show no signs of leaks
Exhaust	Should not leak, which could allow fumes into the vehicle, and it should not be noisy!
Horn	It should be noisy!
Lights	All lights should work, and the headlights must be correctly adjusted
Number plates	Only the correct style and size must be fitted. The numbers and letters should also be correctly spaced and not altered (DAN 15H is right, DANISH is wrong)!

System	Requirements
Seat belts	All belts must be in good condition and work correctly
Speedometer	Should be accurate and illuminate when dark
Steering	All components must be secure and serviceable
Tyres	Correct tread depth is just one example
Windscreens and other glass	You should be able to see right through this one! No cracks allowed in the screen within the driver's vision

LEARNING TASKS

➡ Look back at the key words. Explain each one to a friend, and/or write out a short description to keep as evidence.

➡ Without just looking back and copying, see if you can list why regular servicing is important.

➡ Look at a copy of the MOT testers' manual and make notes about some of the important areas for inspection.

2 Servicing requirements

Service sheets and service records

KEY WORDS

- All words in the table
- Road test
- Service sheets

Service sheets are used and records must be kept because they:

- define the work to be carried out
- record the work carried out
- record the time spent
- record materials consumed
- allow invoices to be prepared
- record stock which may need replacing
- form evidence in the event of accident or customer complaint.

The following table is an *example* of a service sheet showing tasks carried out and at what service intervals (mileage). Please note once again that, whilst quite comprehensive, this list is not appropriate for all vehicles, and that manufacturers' recommendations must be followed. Some of the tasks are only appropriate to certain types of vehicle. The table here also lists the work in a recommended order, including the use of a lift.

Operation	1 000	6 000	12 000	24 000	48 000
Fit car protection kit	✓	✓	✓	✓	✓
Check condition and security of seats and seat belts		✓	✓	✓	✓
Drive on lift: stop engine	✓	✓	✓	✓	✓
Check operation of all lamps	✓	✓	✓	✓	✓ .
Check operation of horns	✓	✓	✓	✓	✓
Check operation of warning indicators	✓	✓	✓	✓	✓
Check/adjust operation of screen/headlamp washers	✓	✓	✓	✓	✓

Operation	1 000	6 000	12 000	24 000	48 000
Check operation of screen wipers and condition of blades	✓	✓	✓	✓	✓
Check security/operation of foot and hand brake; release fully after checking	✓	✓	✓	✓	✓
Open bonnet: fit wing covers	✓	✓	✓	✓	✓
Raise lift to convenient working height with wheels free to rotate	✓	✓	✓	✓	✓
Remove hub/wheel nut caps			✓	✓	✓
Remove road wheels and inspect for damage			✓	✓	✓
Check tread on all tyres		✓	✓	✓	✓
Check tyres for uneven wear	✓	✓	✓	✓	✓
Check tyres for cuts, exposure of ply or cord structure, lumps or bulges	✓	✓	✓	✓	✓
Check/adjust tyre pressures	✓	✓	✓	✓	✓
Check brake pads for wear. Renew if necessary			✓	✓	✓
Check discs for condition if pads are renewed			✓	✓	✓
Inspect rear brake linings for wear			✓	✓	✓
Remove brake drums, wash out dust, inspect shoes and drums for condition			✓	✓	✓
Renew shoes if necessary			✓	✓	✓
Adjust hand brake cable	✓		✓	✓	✓
Grease road wheel mounting spigots if wheels have been removed			✓	✓	✓
Refit road wheels			✓	✓	✓
Check tightness of road wheel fastenings			✓	✓	✓
Refit hub/wheel nut caps			✓	✓	✓
Raise lift to convenient working height	✓	✓	✓	✓	✓
Drain engine oil		✓	✓	✓	✓
Drain automatic transmission oil and remove sump					✓
Check brake hoses, pipes and unions for chafing, cracks, leaks or corrosion	✓	✓	✓	✓	✓
Check visually fuel pipes and unions for chafing, cracks, leaks or corrosion	✓	✓	✓	✓	✓
Check pipes are correctly clipped	✓	✓	✓	✓	✓
Check security and condition of suspension joints and fixings	✓	✓	✓	✓	✓
Check condition of drive shaft gaiters	✓	✓	✓	✓	✓
Check security and condition of steering joints and gaiters	✓	✓	✓	✓	✓
Visually check underbody sealer for damage	✓	✓	✓	✓	✓
Check for fluid leaks from dampers	✓	✓	✓	✓	✓

Operation	1 000	6 000	12 000	24 000	48 000
Renew oil filter element		✓	✓	✓	✓
Check alternator drive belt and adjust or renew		✓	✓	✓	✓
Clean and refit engine drain plug		✓	✓	✓	✓
Clean automatic transmission filter and refit sump					✓
Lower lift	✓	✓	✓	✓	✓
Fit exhaust extractor pipe	✓	✓	✓	✓	✓
Check/adjust torque of cylinder head nuts	✓				
Check/adjust valve clearances			✓	✓	✓
Fill engine with oil		✓	✓	✓	✓
Check/fill automatic transmission with fluid		✓	✓	✓	✓
Check/top up oil/fluid level in transmission		✓	✓	✓	✓
Top up carburettor piston damper		✓	✓	✓	✓
Check/top up power steering reservoir		✓	✓	✓	✓
Renew camshaft driving belt					✓
Check all drive belts, adjust or renew	✓	✓	✓	✓	✓
Renew spark plugs			✓	✓	✓
Check battery condition		✓	✓	✓	✓
Check/top up cooling system		✓	✓	✓	✓
Drain/refill antifreeze				✓	✓
Renew air cleaner element			✓	✓	✓
Replace in-line fuel filter				✓	✓
Renew engine oil filler cap			✓	✓	✓
Clean distributor cap and coil tower			✓	✓	✓
Lubricate distributor advance mechanism			✓	✓	✓
Check operation of throttle	✓	✓	✓	✓	✓
Start engine and leave running		✓	✓	✓	✓
Check sealing of oil filter		✓	✓	✓	✓
Check function of brake pad wear warning indicator	✓	✓	✓	✓	✓
Check function of brake fluid level warning indicator	✓	✓	✓	✓	✓
Check/top up brake fluid level reservoir	✓	✓	✓	✓	✓
Check brake servo hose for security and condition	✓	✓	✓	✓	✓
Check/top up washer reservoir	✓	✓	✓	✓	✓
Inspect exterior paintwork for damage, body panels for corrosion			✓	✓	✓
Remove spare wheel		✓	✓		✓
Inspect wheel for damage		✓	✓	✓	✓
Check tyre tread depth		✓	✓	✓	✓

Operation	1 000	6 000	12 000	24 000	48 000
Check tyre for cuts in fabric, exposure of ply or cord structure lumps or bulges		✓	✓	✓	✓
Check tyre for uneven wear		✓	✓	✓	✓
Check/adjust tyre pressure		✓	✓	✓	✓
Refit spare wheel		✓	✓	✓	✓
Check ignition system, using electronic equipment			✓	✓	✓
Check and adjust fuel system – idle, fast idle speed and mixture			✓	✓	✓
Check automatic transmission oil level and top up	✓	✓	✓	✓	✓
Stop engine: disconnect instruments	✓	✓	✓	✓	✓
Remove wing covers	✓	✓	✓	✓	✓
Fill in details and affix appropriate stickers	✓	✓	✓	✓	✓
Close bonnet	✓	✓	✓	✓	✓
Remove exhaust extractor pipe	✓	✓	✓	✓	✓
Drive off lift	✓	✓	✓	✓	✓
Check front wheel alignment			✓	✓	✓
Report additional work required	✓	✓	✓	✓	✓
Carry out road/roller test	✓	✓	✓	✓	✓

Assuming you are a qualified driver or you are able to tell a driver what you want, then a road test is an excellent way of checking the operation of a vehicle. A check list is again a useful reminder of what should be done.

A typical road test following a service or inspection would be much as follows:

- Fit trade plates to vehicle if necessary.
- Check operation of starter and inhibitor switch (automatic).
- Check operation of lights, horn(s), indicators, wipers and washers.
- Check indicators self cancel.
- Check operation of all warning indicators.
- Check foot and hand brakes.
- Check engine noise levels, performance and throttle operation.
- Check clutch for free play, slipping and judder.
- Check gear selection and noise levels in all gears.
- Check steering for noise, effort required, free play, wander and self centring.
- Check suspension for noise, irregularity in ride and wheel imbalance.
- Check foot brake pedal effort, travel, braking efficiency, pulling and binding.
- Check speedometer for steady operation, noise and operation of mileage recorder.
- Check operation of all instruments.
- Check for abnormal body noises.
- Check operation of seat belts, including operation of inertia reels.

- Check hand brake ratchet and hold.
- Position car on lift.
- Re-check tension if drive belts have been renewed.
- Raise lift.
- Inspect engine and transmission for oil leaks.
- Check exhaust system for condition, leakage, and security.
- Lower lift: drive vehicle off lift.
- Report on road test findings.
- Remove car protection kit.
- Ensure cleanliness of controls, door handles, etc.
- Remove trade plates if fitted.

Effects of incorrect adjustments

As a professional you are expected to make the correct adjustments for the vehicle to operate as smoothly as possible. Anyone can mess with a vehicle and get it wrong, but you'll get it right – keeping the customer and your company happy.

The following table lists a selection of possible incorrect adjustments, together with their effects on the operation of the vehicle. This is intended to be an exercise to help you see why correct adjustments are so important, not so you know how to do it wrong! If you are unable to make the correct adjustments, perhaps due to some parts being worn, you must also be able to tell a customer what effects this could have on vehicle operation.

Incorrect adjustment	Possible effects						
Brake	Excessive pedal and lever travel	Reduced braking efficiency	Unbalanced braking	Over heating			
Drive belts	Over-heating	Battery recharging rate slow	Power steering problems				
Fuel system	Poor starting or non-start	Lack of power or hesitation	Uneven running and stalling	Popping back or backfire	Running on or detonation	Heavy fuel usage	Fuel leaks and smells
Ignition	Poor starting or non-start	Lack of power	Hesitation	Exhaust emission	Running on		
Plug gaps	Poor starting or non-start	Lack of power	Hesitation	Uneven running	Misfire	Exhaust emissions	
Steering system	Abnormal or uneven tyre wear	Heavy steering	Pulling to one side	Poor self centring	Wandering	Steering wheel alignment	Excessive free play
Tyre pressure	Abnormal tyre wear	Heavy steering	Uneven braking	Heavy fuel usage	Tyre life time is reduced		
Valve clearance	Lack of power	Uneven running	Misfire	Excessive fuel usage	Exhaust emissions	Noise from valves or camshaft	

Do a good service

Sometimes customers expect certain tasks to be carried out during servicing which are not actually due to be done. For example, on the 6 000 or interim service, no work is carried out on the ignition system. This will not therefore rectify a misfire. It is important that the customer is aware of what will be done, as well as what was done to their vehicle. This is one good service.

Figure 18.3 A happy customer in reception!

The other good service is simply to do the job well, keep the customer satisfied.

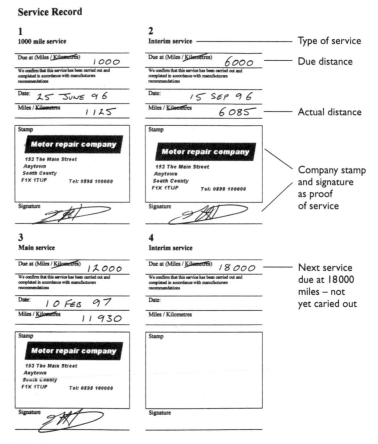

Figure 18.4 Example of a service record

19 The business

1 Introduction

Start here!

Why should you worry about 'the business'? Isn't it somebody else's problem to make sure 'the business' is running all right?

KEY WORDS

- All words in the table
- Company
- Team

We all need to take an interest in the whole business in which we are working. This does not mean interfering in areas we do not understand. It means we should understand that all parts of the business are important. For example, even if you are a really top class technician and your work is always first class, you will soon be without work if you are rude to the customers! When you complete a job and you do not enter all the parts used, or time spent on a job card, how will the person who writes the invoice know what to charge?

'The business does matter.'

Terminology

Customers	The individuals or companies that spend their money at your place of work. Ultimately, your wages come from the customer
Job card	A printed document for recording (amongst other things) work required, work done, parts used and the time taken
Invoice	A description of the parts and services supplied with a demand for payment from the customer
Company system	A set way in which things work in one particular company. Most motor vehicle company systems follow similar rules, but will all be a little different
Contract	An offer which is accepted; payment is agreed. For example, I offer to change your engine oil for £15. You decide this is a good offer and accept the deal. We have made a contract
Image	This is the impression given by the company to existing and potential customers. Not all companies will want to project the same image
Warranty	If within an agreed time a problem occurs with the supplied goods or service, it will be rectified free of charge by the supplier
Recording system	An agreed system within a company so that all details of what is requested and/or carried out are recorded. The job card is one of the main parts of this system

Why 'the business' is important

'The business' is a shorthand way of describing everything that happens at your place of work. Team work is the key issue. We must all play a part in the team. The team is like a chain, each person being an important link. If one link breaks, the chain is no good. For example, let's assume your company has an excellent system for attracting new customers and booking them in to the workshop. If you do not do the work properly, or someone else ordered the wrong parts, the customer will not be happy. More than likely he or she will go elsewhere next time.

Figure 19.1 Two different images projected by a motor vehicle company

The key is that, while you must work to become an expert at your particular job, you must also have some understanding of what others in the team are doing. Besides which, as time goes by you may wish to move into a different type of job in a motor vehicle company. So you will need to know how the team works and what is involved in other areas.

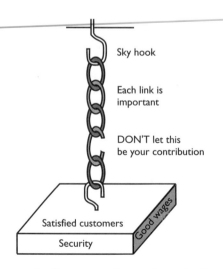

Figure 19.2 Every person in the team makes an important contribution

2   The company

Introduction

KEY WORDS

- Standard times
- Warranty
- Invoice
- Reception
- Job card

This section is about different types of motor vehicle companies and the systems they use to keep the business going. You may be interested in studying some of the issues in more detail as your career in the motor trade progresses. There are lots of opportunities for those who are willing to work hard and move forwards. There are many different types of job, and with a little patience and study you will find one to suit you.

Types of companies

Motor vehicle companies can range from very small one person businesses to very large main dealers. The systems used by each will be different, but the requirements are the same. A system should be in place to ensure the level of service meets the needs of the customer. The following list shows how diverse our trade is, ranging from the 'smallest' to the 'largest' type of business.

Business	Activity
Mobile mechanics	Servicing and repairs at the owner's home or business
Recovery	Some companies just concentrate on recovering vehicles after breakdowns or accidents
Bodywork repairers	Specialists in body repair and paintwork
Petrol stations	These may be owned by an oil company or be independent. Some also do vehicle repair work
Specialised repairers	Business which works only on specific vehicle systems, for example auto-electrical, air conditioning, automatic transmission and ICE
General repair workshop	Servicing and repairs of most types of vehicles
Parts supply	Many companies now supply a wide range of parts. Many will deliver to your workshop.
Fast fit	Supplying and fitting of exhausts, tyres, radiators, batteries, clutches, brakes and windscreens
Non-franchised dealer	Main activity is the servicing and repair of a wide range of vehicles, with some sales
Franchised dealers	Similar to main dealers (as below) but sales, stock and facilities are smaller
Main dealers	Usually franchised to one manufacturer and hold a stock of vehicles and parts. The main dealer will be able to carry out all repairs to their own type of vehicle as they hold all of the parts and special tools. They also have access to the latest information specific to their marque

Company structure

A larger motor vehicle company will probably be made up of at least the following departments:

- reception
- workshop
- parts department
- new and second user car sales
- office support
- management
- cleaning and general duties.

Each area will employ one or a number of people. If you work in a very small garage, you may have to be all of these people at once! Figure 19.3 shows a typical way in which a company could be structured.

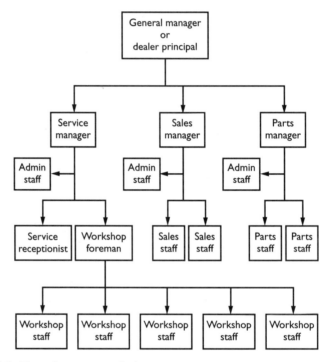

Figure 19.3 Typical structure of a large company

Reception and booking systems

The reception, whether in a large or small company, is often the point of first contact with new customers. Therefore it is very important to get this bit right. The reception should be staffed by pleasant and qualified persons. The purpose of a reception and booking system within a company can be best explained by following through a typical enquiry:

- The customer enters reception area and is greeted in an appropriate way.
- Attention is given to the customer to find out what is required. (Let's assume the car is difficult to start, in this case.)
- Further questions can be used to determine the particular problem, depending on the customer's knowledge of vehicles. (For example, is the problem worse when the weather is cold?)
- Details about the customer, the vehicle and the nature of the problem are recorded on a job card. If the customer is new, a record card can be started; continue an existing card for an existing customer.

Figure 19.4 Customer in reception

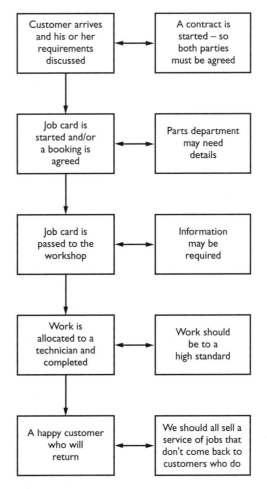

Figure 19.5 A typical reception and booking system

- Explanation of expected costs is given as appropriate. A common and sensible approach is to agree to work up to a set amount, after which the customer will be contacted.
- Date and time when the work will be carried out can now be agreed. This depends on workshop time availability and when is convenient for the customer. It is often better to say you cannot do the job until a certain time, rather than make a promise you can't keep.

- The customer is thanked for visiting.
- Details are now entered in the workshop diary or loading chart, the job card passed to the workshop controller.
- If the vehicle is to be left at that time, the keys should be labelled and stored securely.

Your company may have a slightly different system, but this example will give you an idea of a typical approach.

Parts department Parts are kept and/or ordered in the parts department! This varies quite a lot between different companies. Large main dealers will have a very large stock of parts for their range of vehicles. They will have a parts manager and in some cases several other staff. In some very small garages the 'parts department' may be a few shelves, where popular items such as filters and brake pads are kept.

Whatever the scale of the department, the basic principles are the same:

- A set level of parts or stock is decided upon.
- Parts are stored so they can be easily found.
- A reordering system is used to maintain the stock.

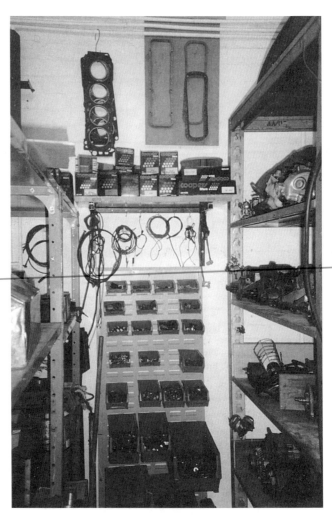

Figure 19.6 Parts department in a very small garage

Security is important, as most parts cost a lot of money. Parts from the parts department or area are

- for direct sale to a customer
- to be used as part of a job
- for use on company vehicles.

In the first case an invoice or a bill will be produced. In the second case the parts will be entered on the customer's job card. In the third case there may also be a job card, if not, some other record must be kept. In all three cases, keeping a record of parts used allows them to be reordered when necessary. If parts are ordered from and delivered by an external supplier, they must again be recorded on the customer's job card.

If you forget to record parts used, who will pay for them? Be warned – it might be you!

Estimating costs and times

When a customer brings his or her car to a garage for work to be carried out, he or she will want to know two things: how much it will cost and when it will be ready. In some cases, such as for a full service, the company will have a set charge and by experience will know it takes a set time. For other types of job this is more difficult.

Most major manufacturers supply information to their dealers about standard times for jobs. These assume a skilled technician with all the necessary tools. For independent garages a publication known as the ICME manual is available. This gives agreed standard times for all the most common tasks on all popular makes of vehicle.

To work out the cost of a job, you look up the required time and multiply it by the company's hourly rate. Don't forget: the cost of parts will also need to be included.

Job cards and systems

The job card is a vital part of the workshop system in a motor vehicle company. Notice the information which is recorded. This is all part of ensuring good communication within the company. Some larger companies now dispense with the 'paper' altogether and use computer systems. These are more expensive to install but allow very fast, easy and accurate communication. Whether job cards or IT systems are used, the principle is the same and consists of a number of important stages.

- Reception – customer's details and requirements are entered on the job card or computer screen.
- Workshop control – jobs are allocated to the appropriate technician using a loading sheet or again via the computer.
- Technician – information is passed directly to the person who will do the work, on screen or on card.
- Parts department – parts used are added to the computer or job card.
- Accounts – invoices are prepared from the information on the job card. Computerised systems may automatically produce the invoice when the job is completed.

When a computer system is used, each terminal will pass information to all the others. With job cards, either the same card must be carried to each stage or copies are kept in each area. The different copies are collected and combined to produce the invoice.

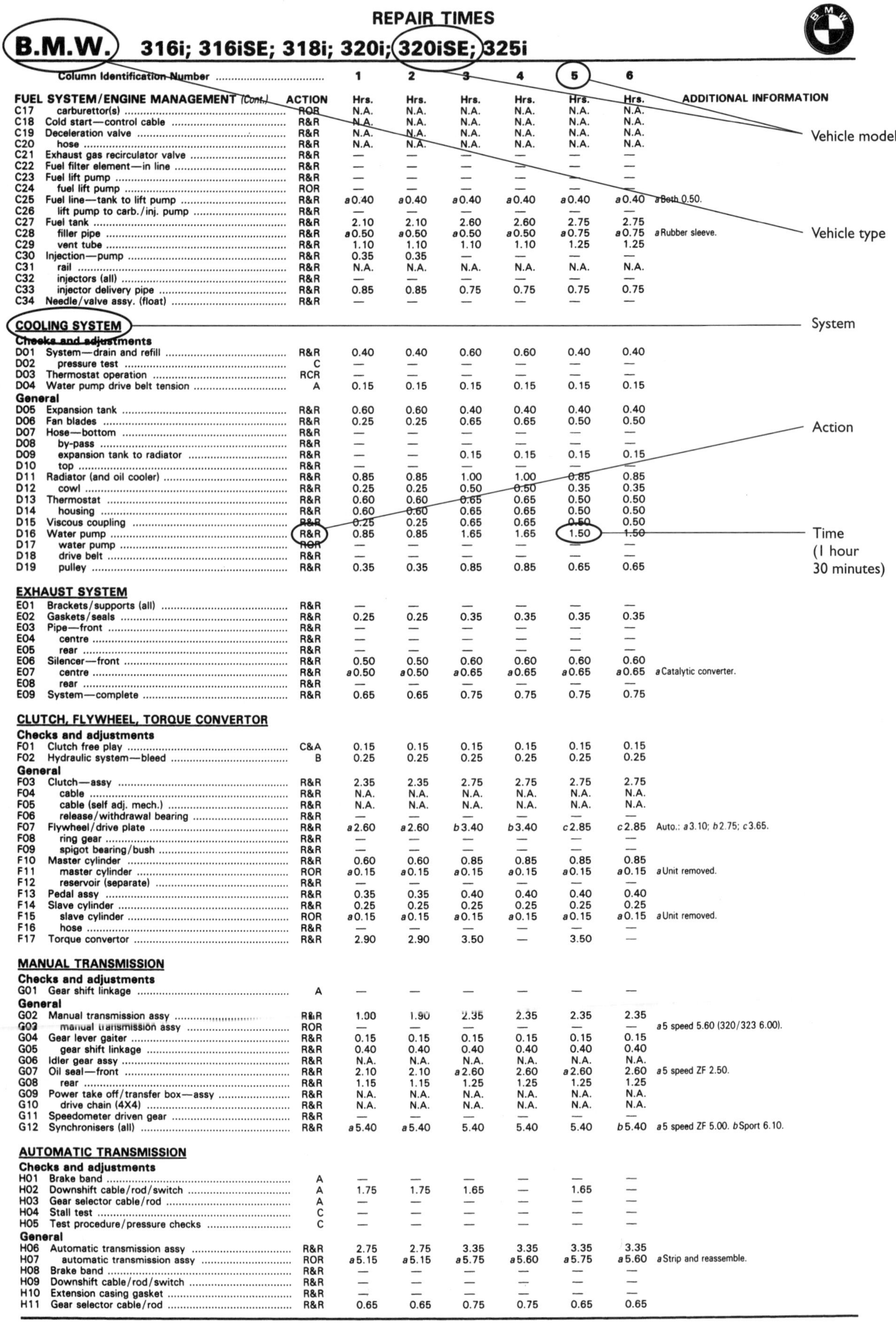

REPAIR TIMES

B.M.W.   316i; 316iSE; 318i; 320i; 320iSE; 325i

Column Identification Number		1	2	3	4	5	6	
FUEL SYSTEM/ENGINE MANAGEMENT *(Cont.)*	ACTION	Hrs.	Hrs.	Hrs.	Hrs.	Hrs.	Hrs.	ADDITIONAL INFORMATION
C17 carburettor(s)	ROR	N.A.	N.A.	N.A.	N.A.	N.A.	N.A.	
C18 Cold start—control cable	R&R	N.A.	N.A.	N.A.	N.A.	N.A.	N.A.	
C19 Deceleration valve	R&R	N.A.	N.A.	N.A.	N.A.	N.A.	N.A.	
C20 hose	R&R	N.A.	N.A.	N.A.	N.A.	N.A.	N.A.	
C21 Exhaust gas recirculator valve	R&R	—	—	—	—	—	—	
C22 Fuel filter element—in line	R&R	—	—	—	—	—	—	
C23 Fuel lift pump	R&R	—	—	—	—	—	—	
C24 fuel lift pump	ROR	—	—	—	—	—	—	
C25 Fuel line—tank to lift pump	R&R	a0.40	a0.40	a0.40	a0.40	a0.40	a0.40	a Beth 0.50.
C26 lift pump to carb./inj. pump	R&R	—	—	—	—	—	—	
C27 Fuel tank	R&R	2.10	2.10	2.60	2.60	2.75	2.75	
C28 filler pipe	R&R	a0.50	a0.50	a0.50	a0.50	a0.75	a0.75	a Rubber sleeve.
C29 vent tube	R&R	1.10	1.10	1.10	1.10	1.25	1.25	
C30 Injection—pump	R&R	0.35	0.35	—	—	—	—	
C31 rail	R&R	N.A.	N.A.	N.A.	N.A.	N.A.	N.A.	
C32 injectors (all)	R&R	—	—	—	—	—	—	
C33 injector delivery pipe	R&R	0.85	0.85	0.75	0.75	0.75	0.75	
C34 Needle/valve assy. (float)	R&R	—	—	—	—	—	—	
COOLING SYSTEM								
Checks and adjustments								
D01 System—drain and refill	R&R	0.40	0.40	0.60	0.60	0.40	0.40	
D02 pressure test	C	—	—	—	—	—	—	
D03 Thermostat operation	RCR	—	—	—	—	—	—	
D04 Water pump drive belt tension	A	0.15	0.15	0.15	0.15	0.15	0.15	
General								
D05 Expansion tank	R&R	0.60	0.60	0.40	0.40	0.40	0.40	
D06 Fan blades	R&R	0.25	0.25	0.65	0.65	0.50	0.50	
D07 Hose—bottom	R&R	—	—	—	—	—	—	
D08 by-pass	R&R	—	—	—	—	—	—	
D09 expansion tank to radiator	R&R	—	—	0.15	0.15	0.15	0.15	
D10 top	R&R	—	—	—	—	—	—	
D11 Radiator (and oil cooler)	R&R	0.85	0.85	1.00	1.00	0.85	0.85	
D12 cowl	R&R	0.25	0.25	0.50	0.50	0.35	0.35	
D13 Thermostat	R&R	0.60	0.60	0.65	0.65	0.50	0.50	
D14 housing	R&R	0.60	0.60	0.65	0.65	0.50	0.50	
D15 Viscous coupling	R&R	0.25	0.25	0.65	0.65	0.50	0.50	
D16 Water pump	R&R	0.85	0.85	1.65	1.65	1.50	1.50	
D17 water pump	ROR	—	—	—	—	—	—	
D18 drive belt	R&R	—	—	—	—	—	—	
D19 pulley	R&R	0.35	0.35	0.85	0.85	0.65	0.65	
EXHAUST SYSTEM								
E01 Brackets/supports (all)	R&R	—	—	—	—	—	—	
E02 Gaskets/seals	R&R	0.25	0.25	0.35	0.35	0.35	0.35	
E03 Pipe—front	R&R	—	—	—	—	—	—	
E04 centre	R&R	—	—	—	—	—	—	
E05 rear	R&R	—	—	—	—	—	—	
E06 Silencer—front	R&R	0.50	0.50	0.60	0.60	0.60	0.60	
E07 centre	R&R	a0.50	a0.50	a0.65	a0.65	a0.65	a0.65	a Catalytic converter.
E08 rear	R&R	—	—	—	—	—	—	
E09 System—complete	R&R	0.65	0.65	0.75	0.75	0.75	0.75	
CLUTCH, FLYWHEEL, TORQUE CONVERTOR								
Checks and adjustments								
F01 Clutch free play	C&A	0.15	0.15	0.15	0.15	0.15	0.15	
F02 Hydraulic system—bleed	B	0.25	0.25	0.25	0.25	0.25	0.25	
General								
F03 Clutch—assy	R&R	2.35	2.35	2.75	2.75	2.75	2.75	
F04 cable	R&R	N.A.	N.A.	N.A.	N.A.	N.A.	N.A.	
F05 cable (self adj. mech.)	R&R	N.A.	N.A.	N.A.	N.A.	N.A.	N.A.	
F06 release/withdrawal bearing	R&R	—	—	—	—	—	—	
F07 Flywheel/drive plate	R&R	a2.60	a2.60	b3.40	b3.40	c2.85	c2.85	Auto.: a3.10; b2.75; c3.65.
F08 ring gear	R&R	—	—	—	—	—	—	
F09 spigot bearing/bush	R&R	—	—	—	—	—	—	
F10 Master cylinder	R&R	0.60	0.60	0.85	0.85	0.85	0.85	
F11 master cylinder	ROR	a0.15	a0.15	a0.15	a0.15	a0.15	a0.15	a Unit removed.
F12 reservoir (separate)	R&R	—	—	—	—	—	—	
F13 Pedal assy	R&R	0.35	0.35	0.40	0.40	0.40	0.40	
F14 Slave cylinder	R&R	0.25	0.25	0.25	0.25	0.25	0.25	
F15 slave cylinder	ROR	a0.15	a0.15	a0.15	a0.15	a0.15	a0.15	a Unit removed.
F16 hose	R&R	—	—	—	—	—	—	
F17 Torque convertor	R&R	2.90	2.90	3.50	—	3.50	—	
MANUAL TRANSMISSION								
Checks and adjustments								
G01 Gear shift linkage	A	—	—	—	—	—	—	
General								
G02 Manual transmission assy	R&R	1.00	1.90	2.35	2.35	2.35	2.35	
G03 manual transmission assy	ROR	—	—	—	—	—	—	a5 speed 5.60 (320/323 6.00).
G04 Gear lever gaiter	R&R	0.15	0.15	0.15	0.15	0.15	0.15	
G05 gear shift linkage	R&R	0.40	0.40	0.40	0.40	0.40	0.40	
G06 Idler gear assy	R&R	N.A.	N.A.	N.A.	N.A.	N.A.	N.A.	
G07 Oil seal—front	R&R	2.10	2.10	a2.60	2.60	a2.60	2.60	a5 speed ZF 2.50.
G08 rear	R&R	1.15	1.15	1.25	1.25	1.25	1.25	
G09 Power take off/transfer box—assy	R&R	N.A.	N.A.	N.A.	N.A.	N.A.	N.A.	
G10 drive chain (4X4)	R&R	N.A.	N.A.	N.A.	N.A.	N.A.	N.A.	
G11 Speedometer driven gear	R&R	—	—	—	—	—	—	
G12 Synchronisers (all)	R&R	a5.40	a5.40	5.40	5.40	5.40	b5.40	a5 speed ZF 5.00. b Sport 6.10.
AUTOMATIC TRANSMISSION								
Checks and adjustments								
H01 Brake band	A	—	—	—	—	—	—	
H02 Downshift cable/rod/switch	A	1.75	1.75	1.65	—	1.65	—	
H03 Gear selector cable/rod	A	—	—	—	—	—	—	
H04 Stall test	C	—	—	—	—	—	—	
H05 Test procedure/pressure checks	C	—	—	—	—	—	—	
General								
H06 Automatic transmission assy	R&R	2.75	2.75	3.35	3.35	3.35	3.35	
H07 automatic transmission assy	ROR	a5.15	a5.15	a5.75	a5.60	a5.75	a5.60	a Strip and reassemble.
H08 Brake band	R&R	—	—	—	—	—	—	
H09 Downshift cable/rod/switch	R&R	—	—	—	—	—	—	
H10 Extension casing gasket	R&R	—	—	—	—	—	—	
H11 Gear selector cable/rod	R&R	0.65	0.65	0.75	0.75	0.65	0.65	

Vehicle model

Vehicle type

System

Action

Time
(1 hour
30 minutes)

Figure 19.7 Example page from the ICME manual

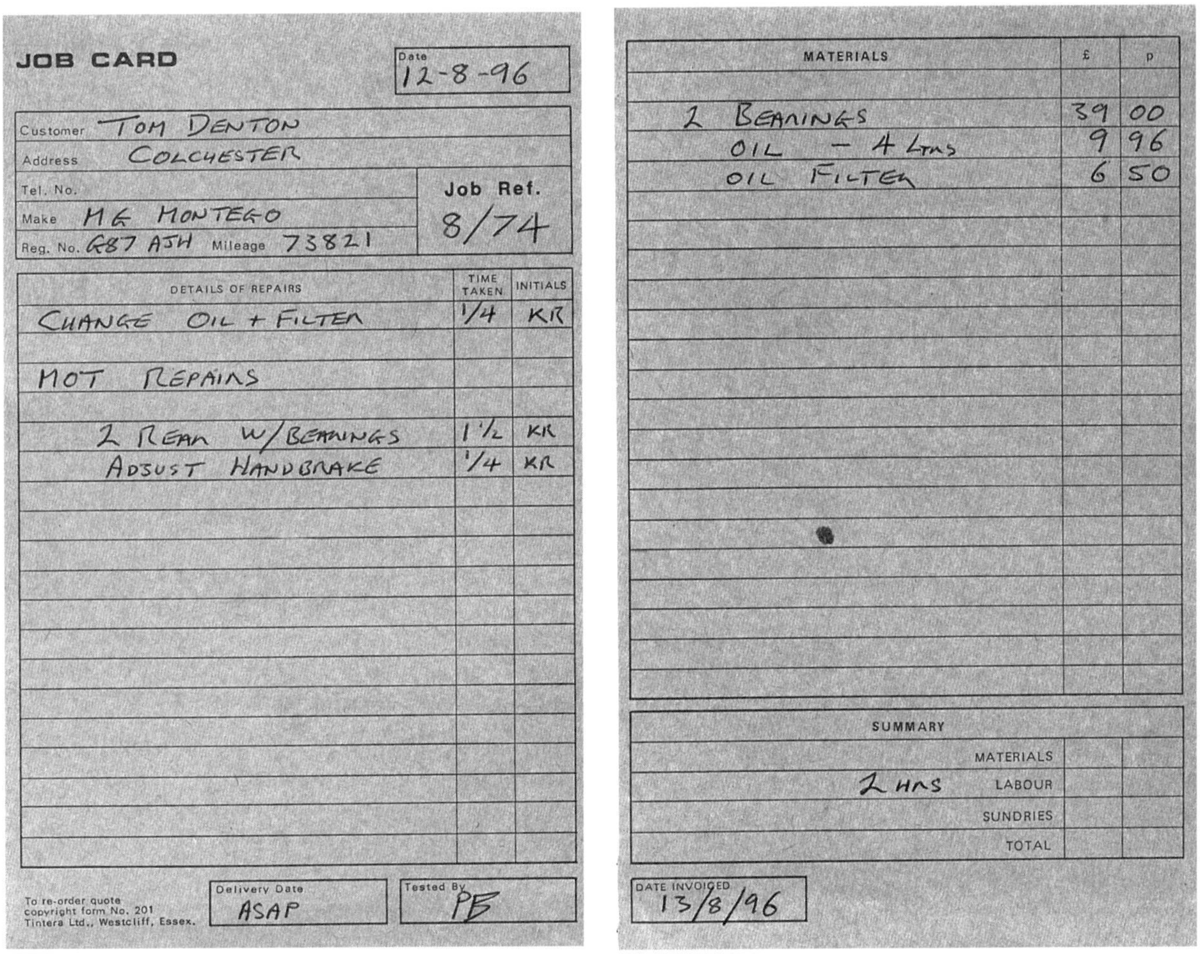

JOB CARD

Date: 12-8-96

Customer: TOM DENTON
Address: COLCHESTER
Tel. No.
Make: MG MONTEGO
Reg. No. G87 AJH   Mileage: 73821

Job Ref.
8/74

DETAILS OF REPAIRS	TIME TAKEN	INITIALS
CHANGE OIL + FILTER	1/4	KR
MOT REPAIRS		
2 REAR W/BEARINGS	1 1/2	KR
ADJUST HANDBRAKE	1/4	KR

To re-order quote copyright form No. 201 Tintera Ltd., Westcliff, Essex.

Delivery Date: ASAP
Tested By: PB

MATERIALS	£	p
2 BEARINGS	39	00
OIL — 4 Ltrs	9	96
OIL FILTER	6	50

SUMMARY		
2 HRS	MATERIALS	
	LABOUR	
	SUNDRIES	
	TOTAL	

DATE INVOICED: 13/8/96

Figure 19.8 A typical job card

Invoicing   As part of the contract made with a customer, an invoice for the work carried out is issued. The main parts of an invoice are as follows:

- Labour charges – the cost of doing the work. Usually the time spent multiplied by the hourly rate.
- Parts – the retail price of the parts or as agreed.
- Sundries – some companies add a small sundry charge to cover consumable items like nuts and bolts or cable ties etc.
- MOT test – if appropriate. This is separated because VAT is not charged on MOTs.
- VAT – Value Added Tax at the current rate, if the company is registered (all but the very small are).

Hourly rates vary quite a lot between different garages. Perhaps the hourly rate your company charges seems rather a lot compared to the rate they pay you. But remember that the hourly rate charged by the company has to pay for a lot more than your wages. Just take a look round in any good workshop: some of the equipment can cost tens of thousands of pounds! Then there are the premises to be paid for, insurance, all your colleagues' wages etc. The money has to come from somewhere.

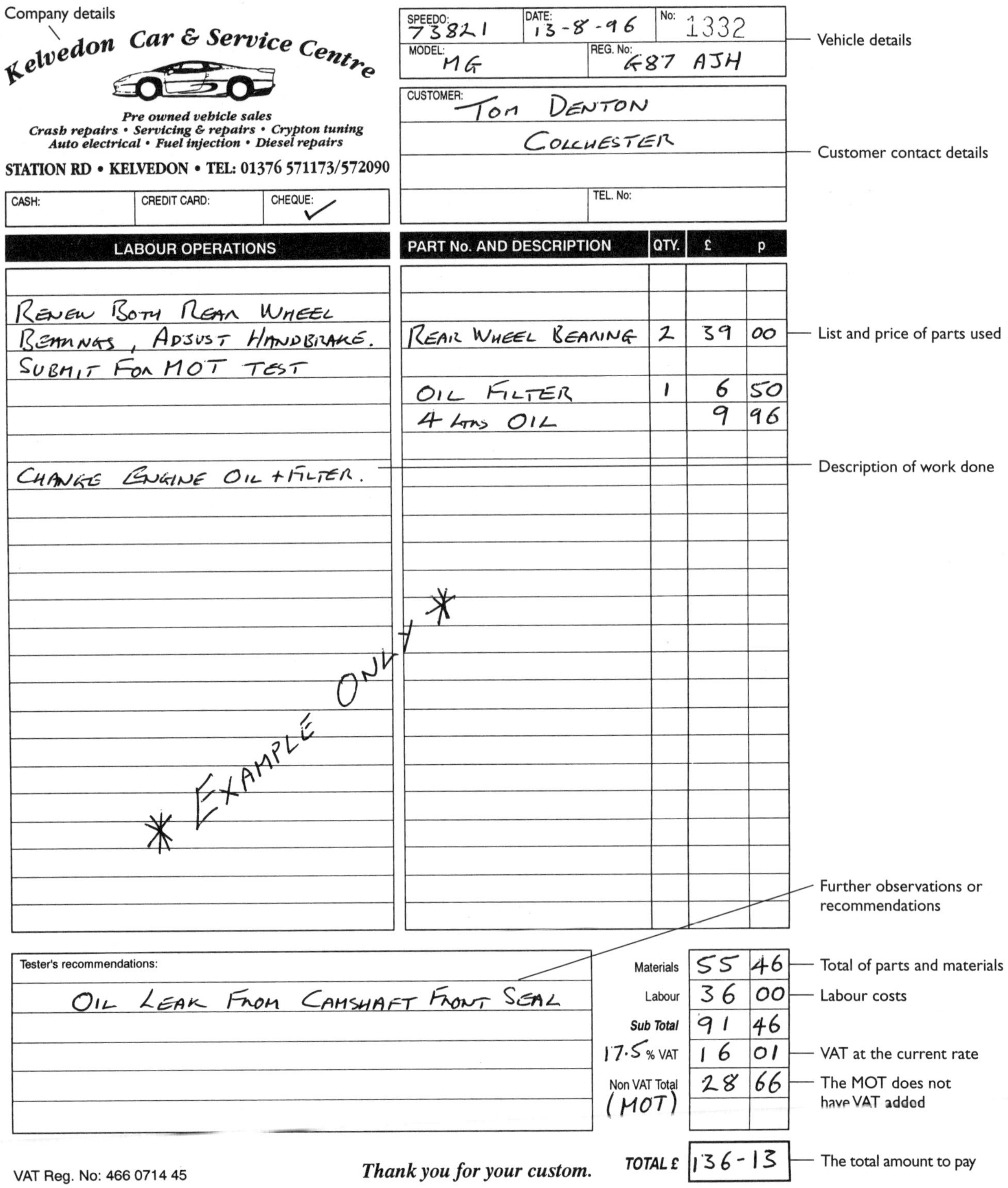

Company details

Kelvedon Car & Service Centre

Pre owned vehicle sales
**Crash repairs • Servicing & repairs • Crypton tuning
Auto electrical • Fuel injection • Diesel repairs**

STATION RD • KELVEDON • TEL: 01376 571173/572090

CASH:	CREDIT CARD:	CHEQUE: ✓

SPEEDO: 73821	DATE: 13-8-96	No: 1332
MODEL: MG	REG. No: G87 AJH	

CUSTOMER: TOM DENTON COLCHESTER

TEL. No:

— Vehicle details
— Customer contact details

LABOUR OPERATIONS	PART No. AND DESCRIPTION	QTY.	£	p
RENEW BOTH REAR WHEEL BEARINGS, ADJUST HANDBRAKE. SUBMIT FOR MOT TEST	REAR WHEEL BEARING	2	39	00
	OIL FILTER	1	6	50
	4 LTRS OIL		9	96
CHANGE ENGINE OIL + FILTER.				

— List and price of parts used
— Description of work done

EXAMPLE ONLY

— Further observations or recommendations

Tester's recommendations:
OIL LEAK FROM CAMSHAFT FRONT SEAL

Materials	55	46
Labour	36	00
Sub Total	91	46
17.5% VAT	16	01
Non VAT Total (MOT)	28	66

— Total of parts and materials
— Labour costs
— VAT at the current rate
— The MOT does not have VAT added

VAT Reg. No: 466 0714 45

Thank you for your custom.

TOTAL £ 136-13 — The total amount to pay

Figure 19.9 Example invoice

Warranties

When a vehicle is sold, a warranty is given meaning that it is fit for the purpose for which it was sold. Further to this, the manufacturer will repair the vehicle at no cost to the customer if a problem develops within a set time. For most new vehicles this is 12 months, but some are now longer. The term generally used for this is 'guarantee'. Quite often manufacturers advertise their guarantee as a selling point.

It is also possible to have a warranty on a used vehicle, or an extended warranty on a new vehicle. These often involve a separate payment to an insurance company. This type of warranty can be quite good, but as with the manufacturer's warranty a number of exclusions and requirements apply, for example:

- Regular servicing at an approved dealer.
- Only recommended parts must be used.
- Wear and tear is not included.
- Any work done must be authorised.
- Only recognised repairers may be used in some cases.

The question of authorisation before work is carried out is very important for the garage to understand. Work carried out without proper authorisation will not be paid for. If a customer returns a car within the warranty period, then a set procedure must be followed.

- Confirm that the work is within the terms of the warranty.
- Get authorisation if over an agreed limit (main dealers have agreements with manufacturers).
- Retain all parts replaced for inspection.
- Produce an invoice which relates to standard or agreed times.

In larger garages one person is often responsible for making warranty claims. You as the mechanic or technician can help by ensuring the job card is correctly completed and that parts removed are returned to the stores for safe keeping. Often these are returned for inspection, both to agree the claim and so the manufacturer can make design changes if necessary.

LEARNING TASKS

- Look back at the key words. Explain each one to a friend, and/or write out a short description to keep as evidence.
- Make a simple sketch to show how each part of your company works together.
- Compare your company systems with the systems used at a friend's company. Are they different? How? Can you work out why?

3 Personnel relationships!

Introduction

KEY WORDS

- Limit of authority
- Responsibility
- Communication

Person*nel* and person*al* relationships are very important for the smooth running of any organisation. The motor trade is no exception. But you will see in this section that dealing with other people in a working situation is mostly common sense. Some further information is given in the next section.

Communication

What is communication all about? Effective communication is communication that is fully understood by the other person. If you use terms the other person can't fully understand, or if you show any kind of impatience, you are not communicating effectively. Do you like it when people tell you things you don't (or can't) understand? What is it like trying to communicate with someone who is impatient with you? Remember that communication is a two way process.

Who do you need to communicate with as part of your normal daily work?

The people you work with

It is vital that you understand what is required of you, and it is also vital that you can make others understand. Here are two ways of asking for the same thing in the parts department:

1. *'Give me the round plastic thing with a spring in it that is at the top of the engine at the front.'*
2. *'A camshaft front oil seal for the XYZ engine, 1995 model please.'*

Need I say more! Practise using the right words and remember: being polite will get you what you want and leave a good impression.

Figure 19.10 Two technicians discussing a problem

The customers

In most cases the secret is to listen carefully, respect what the person has to say and ask questions until you do understand what the customer needs. In other cases you may have to tell the customer about some problem with the car. When talking to customers, try to use language they understand: don't use too many long technical words and try to simplify the subject – but this does mean you will have to understand it well yourself! At the same time don't 'talk down' to the customer. They may not know much about cars, but they won't want to be patronised either!

Your company is also likely to communicate with the customers by letter. A personalised letter from the company will create a good impression. For example, set up a computer to produce a letter, say one month before an MOT test is due.

Getting on with people

How do you maintain working relationships with your colleagues (people you work with)? Here are some basic recommendations:

- Treat others in a way which you would like to be treated.
- Respond promptly to requests from others.
- Offer help to others if required.
- Help new people settle in by offering assistance when needed.
- If problems develop, then speak to your supervisor or manager.

In a company all staff depend on each other and all play an important part in the smooth running of the business. Part of this work will be to present a good image for the company.

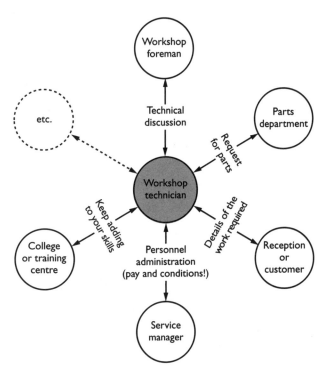

Figure 19.11 Lines of communication

Who is in charge?

Who is in charge? I am in charge! Not me! The boss is! And so it could go on. The main issue here is in relation to the limits of authority and responsibility. We are all in charge and responsible for our own area as it has been delegated to us. The key is to understand the lines of communication and where the limits are. These are often unwritten, but may be stated in your work contract. Common sense is the answer.

The table below shows a few situations and who is responsible or has the authority to deal with them.

Situation	Person with authority
Booking in work	Reception/service manager
Parts ordering	Parts manager
Warranty claims	Reception/service manager
Checking safety	Safety officer
Job card completion	Technician
Authorising FOC work	Service manager
Preparing estimates	Technician/service manager

As a technician or mechanic working in a garage you may be responsible for:

- drawing parts from the stores
- taking care of customers' property
- reporting faults to your supervisor
- safety of equipment
- quality of work
- anything delegated to you!

'If in doubt, ask your supervisor.'

LEARNING TASKS

➡ Look back at the key words. Explain each one to a friend, and/or write out a short description to keep as evidence.

➡ Write a short explanation about why dealing with other people in the correct way is so important.

➡ Practise how you would order particular parts from stores.

---

4   The customer

The customer is always right

KEY WORDS

- Customer
- Profile
- Contract
- Complaints
- Vehicle security

The customer is always right. Sometimes rude, sometimes ignorant and sometimes downright awkward, but always right! The key thing to remember is that we are here to serve the customer, not the other way round. We should also remember that it is the customers who pay our wages.

Dealing with customers

Each customer is a potential user of our services. In other words, we must make them want to have their car repaired at our workshop rather than another. Your garage may have advantages, such as being in a convenient location or holding a franchise, but the customers will not come if they do not like the service and attitude.

The competition in our market today means that dealing with customers is a very important part of our work. If we get it wrong, either by poor work or poor customer contact, we will lose them. Always aim to 'make a sale', that is: secure the job for the company. The process can be divided into four stages:

- A potential customer should be attracted to the service you have to offer.
- Further interest should be encouraged by offering informed assistance.
- A wish to have the services should be created.
- A contract is made (more details later).

This sales technique is more often the work of the reception staff, but you may need to explain some technical issue or answer further questions.

Be polite and know your subject – if you do not know the answer to a customer question, don't bluff or overstep your authority. Find someone who does know the answer.

Finding the problem

When dealing with customers, it can sometimes be difficult to find out what's actually wrong with the vehicle. Misunderstanding can arise because the customer may not understand technical terms. This is our problem, not the customer's.

A customer may simply say 'My car won't start'. Your job is to find out in a little more detail what may be wrong by asking further questions. This will give you a better idea of what you're dealing with; in other words, whether the job will take ten minutes or ten hours. Some questions you could use are as follows:

- What is the make and model?
- When did the problem start?
- Has it happened before?
- Does the engine move when you turn the key (they may not understand the words 'crank over')?
- Have you had any other work done on the car?
- Has it got an alarm fitted?

Ask whatever questions you feel are appropriate to the situation. Remember, it is not an inquisition, just a way of politely finding out the problem.

Making a contract

Making a contract to do something or supply a service is an area you must be aware of. In simple terms a contract means you have reached agreement with another party that something will happen. You agree to change the oil. They agree to pay for it. Once a contract is made, it then is backed by the strength of the law. This is the important thing for you to remember. A contract does not have to be in writing – a verbal agreement is still legally enforceable.

The main parts of a contract are as follows:

Offer and acceptance

This can be verbal or written and is the most important part of a contract. You and the customer agree the deal, possibly after negotiation. You offer to change the oil, the customer accepts and offers to pay £20, which you accept. A contract is made.

Valuable consideration

Valuable or good consideration means 'payment' for the services or goods. The exchange of something of value is the key. Changing the oil has a value, and this passes to the customer. The payment of money, which has a value, in return passes to you.

A contract can be cancelled for the following reasons:

Capacity to contract

Minors (children under 18) cannot make contracts. Further, if somebody is drunk or certified insane, they cannot legally be held to a contract! If an insane sixteen year old drunk wants work done – say no thanks!

Genuineness of consent

This applies if a mistake or a misrepresentation is made, either fraudulently or innocently. If you said the oil would cost £5 but then realise you should have said £50, the contract can be cancelled.

Intention to create legal relations

If duress and undue influence are applied, then a contract becomes invalid. So you can't say to a customer that they must have the oil changed, or their car might get scratched! This does not form a contract!

Legal and possible

If the intention is for illegal purposes or it is impossible to perform, the contract is invalid.

Types of customers

Customers can be divided into six groups, sometimes known as the customer profile.

Profile	Notes
Business	A company car driver who is likely to be more interested in how soon the repairs will be completed than the cost or details about the work to be done
Private	Cost and good service will be particularly important to this customer. Private customers have lots of friends and relatives who could use your garage if recommended
Informed	This person is likely to want to know exactly what will be or has been done to their vehicle. They have a right to know and will also appreciate your technical knowledge
Non-informed	A non-informed person is not stupid or gullible! It means that their skills are not associated with motor vehicles like ours. They will demand and should get respect and a patient description or explanation about the work
New	May be interested in seeing the facilities. Remember that first impressions are long lasting
Regular	Don't become complacent or take regular customers for granted. If customers show loyalty to you, then it should be returned

A customer can fall into several of these groups at the same time: for example, somebody can be a new, business, non-informed customer. The different types of customers will expect and deserve to be treated in different ways. The descriptions in the table are quite general, but the message is still clear: treat all customers politely and with respect. Adapt the way you deal with them to suit their requirements.

Complaints and how to deal with them

The best way to deal with customer complaints is to prevent them! Some understanding as to how complaints arise will help you achieve this objective. Some possible reasons for complaints (not in any order):

- bad attitude of staff
- inaccurate diagnosis of faults
- inaccurate recording of parts used
- incorrect communication of instructions to the workshop

- poor booking in procedure
- unfair charges, slow invoicing, overcharging
- vehicle in unclean condition
- vehicle not collected at agreed time
- warranty work not identified
- work done without permission.

Most complaints are caused by lack of understanding by both parties. A set procedure is therefore a good idea:

- Find out the customer's idea of the problem and acknowledge it; do not admit fault, but do not attack either.
- Gather the relevant information to help you both understand the issues.
- Summarise the problem, using the information you have gathered, so you both agree on the issue.

Respond in a way that does not cause the customer unnecessary worry or problems. If an explanation is required, make sure it is well understood. Do not try to blind the customer with science. If the problem needs further work (paid for or not), try to arrange this as soon as possible. It also helps if you can grow some thicker skin!

Looking after the vehicle and contents
When a customer leaves a vehicle with you for repairs or a service, they are trusting you with, in many cases, thousands of pounds worth of their property. You should respect this:

- Always use protective mats, seat covers, wing covers and other protection as appropriate.
- The vehicle should be returned as clean as, if not cleaner than, when it was left.
- The vehicle should be locked and in a secure area.
- Keys should be labelled and kept safe in the reception area until required.
- Contents must not be disturbed. Encourage the customer not to leave valuables in the car if possible.
- Try to reset the seats and mirrors to the original positions. Do not re-tune the radio unless requested.

Figure 19.12 A vehicle with protection covers fitted

Remember: if you do not take reasonable care of the vehicle you can be held responsible.

LEARNING TASKS

➡ Look back at the key words. Explain each one to a friend, and/or write out a short description to keep as evidence.

➡ The different types of customers will expect and deserve to be treated in different ways. Make notes to say how you would expect to be treated as a customer of a garage.

➡ Write a short explanation about how to treat people belonging to the six different customer profiles.

➡ Practise dealing with a customer complaint.

20 Background studies

1 Introduction

Start here! Well done for even looking at this section! It is often quite hard to see why, when you want to work on motor vehicles, you should study maths, science and drawing. Don't worry, the maths or science in this chapter is at a very simple level to help you learn and understand the basic principles. The drawing section will help you understand information given by technical drawings. And don't worry about remembering formulas; just look them up in this book if you need to.

It may be a good idea to study this chapter in smaller parts, picking out the information you need for the other main chapters. However, please make sure you work through it all!

Don't forget that, to get on well in any job, you need to know your subject to a high standard. For example, if a customer asks why his tyre pressures were higher after a long journey, you could answer in two ways:

1. *I dunno.*
2. *It is because the friction between the tyre and the road, and the materials of the tyre, produce heat. The heat causes the air pressure in the tyre to increase because it can't expand.*

Which answer will make the customer think 'this technician knows his job, I will come here again'? Obvious isn't it!

Finally, properly understanding the basic principles of how something works will allow you to adapt and change when you meet new technologies. Good luck with your studies – it won't be as hard as you think.

Often the words used to describe scientific principles can be confusing. The following table picks out and explains the most important ones. Some of these terms are described in more detail in later sections.

KEY WORDS

- All words in the table
- SI Unit
- Multiplier

Terminology	
SI units	A set of standard units, so we all talk the same language. 'SI' stands for 'Système International'. This is French for 'International System'!
Ratio	The amount of one thing compared to another. E.g. two to one is written as 2:1
Area (m^2)	Amount of surface of anything. E.g. if you know the surface area of a car bonnet, you can work out how much paint would be needed to cover it
Volume (m^3)	Capacity of an object. E.g. 1 000 cc (cubic centimetres), or one litre, of paint to do the job above
Mass (kg)	The quantity of matter in a body. Volume does not matter. E.g. which has the greater mass, a kilogram of lead or a kilogram of feathers? They are both the same, of course, but have different volumes
Density (kg/m^3)	A full paint tin has a greater mass than an empty tin, but the volumes are the same

Terminology

Energy (J)	The ability to do work or the amount of work stored in something. Petrol, for example, contains a lot of energy in chemical form
Force (N)	When you push an object, it moves (if you can apply enough force)
Work (J)	Work is done when the force applied to an object makes it move. Work can also be said to be done when energy is converted from one form to another
Power (W)	The rate at which work can be done. E.g. energy used per second
Torque (Nm)	A turning force, like a spanner turning a nut. A longer spanner needs less force
Velocity (m/s)	A scientific name for speed. E.g. the UK national velocity limit is 70 mph (not an SI unit!)
Acceleration (m/s^2)	The rate at which velocity changes. If positive, the car will increase in speed. If negative (or deceleration), such as when braking, the car speed decreases
Momentum (kg.m/s)	The combination of the mass of a body and its velocity. A large goods vehicle has much greater momentum than a car at the same speed. It must have much better brakes or it will take a lot longer to stop
Friction (μ)	When one surface moves over another, friction tries to stop the movement. It is interesting to note that, without friction, a moving object such as a car would not stop!
Heat (J)	This is a measure of the amount of energy in a body. Heat can only transfer from a higher to a lower temperature, and this will be by conduction, convection or radiation
Temperature (°C)	A measure of how hot something is; this must not be confused with the amount of heat energy
Pressure (N/m^2 or Pa)	This is a force per area. E.g. the old tyre pressure measurement for many cars was 28 psi (pounds per square inch). The current units to get used to are bars: the tyre pressure would be about 1.8 bar. The SI unit is the pascal, or newtons per metre squared (Pa or Nm^2). The pressure in a room is about 1 bar or 1 atmosphere or 100 000 Pa. It may be much more if you have been reading about science for a long time!
Centrifugal force (N)	If you swing a stone on a string round your head, it tries to move outwards and you can feel the centrifugal force on the string. The faster you swing it, the greater the force. When a car wheel is rotating very quickly, a small imbalance in the tyre causes unequal centrifugal force. This makes the wheel wobble
Weight (N)	The mass of an object acted upon by the earth's gravity gives it a weight. When you next go into outer space, you will find that your weight is zero or, in other words, you are weightless. You do still have the same mass, however. The word 'weight' is often used incorrectly but, as gravity is the same all over the earth, it often doesn't make any difference
Centre of gravity	The point within an object at which it will balance. All the weight of an object such as a car can be said to act through the centre of gravity. If the force due to gravity and acceleration acting through this point falls outside the wheels of the car, the car will fall over!
Electricity	This is the movement of electrons known as a current flow in a conductor or a wire. Electricity is a very convenient way of transferring energy
Strength	This is hard to define because different materials are strong in different ways. A material can be strong (provide opposition) to bending, tension, compression or shear force
Corrosion	Corrosion of materials is by a chemical process. E.g. if iron is left exposed to the air or water, it rusts. The chemical process is that the iron is reacting with oxygen in the air and turning into iron oxide or rust
Machines	A machine is something which converts one form of energy into another. An alternator, for example, converts mechanical energy from the engine into electrical energy
Hydraulics	When fluids are used to do 'work', this is described as hydraulics. The braking system of a car is a good example
Oscillation	If you bounce a mass on a spring (a car on its suspension), it will move up and down (oscillate) until all the mechanical energy in the spring has been converted to another form (mostly heat due to friction). Dampers are used on a car to make this time as short as possible

Units

When I go into a café or a pub and ask for a pint of beer or half a litre of coke, I usually get what I want. This is because I ask by using the correct units. When you blow up the tyres on a car, you check the pressure in a book or on a chart and then look at the gauge. They will have the same units, and you can inflate the tyres to the correct pressure.

The best and easiest units to work with are what are known as SI units, sometimes thought of as the metric system. The basic SI units are as follows:

Figure 20.1 A pint of beer!

Unit	Abbreviation	Quantity	Example
metre	m	length	The distance from one point to another
kilogram	kg	mass	The quantity of matter which makes an object
second	s	time	About 300 s to boil an egg!
ampere	A	electric current	The flow rate of electricity through a wire
kelvin	K	temperature	How hot is the radiator of a car
candela	cd	luminous intensity	How bright a headlight shines
mole	mol	amount of substance	A term used mostly in chemistry

Many other units in use are derived from the basic SI units. Many of them are combined and in some cases given new names, for example:

Unit	Abbreviation	Quantity
joule	J	energy
newton	N	force
watt	W	power
square metres	m^2	area
cubic metres	m^3	volume
newton metres	Nm	torque
metres per second	m/s or ms^{-1}	velocity
metres per second per second	m/s/s, ms^{-2} or m/s^2	acceleration

When dealing with units we need a way of describing very large or very small quantities. For example, I would not say that I live 24 000 metres away from where I work. I would say I live 24 kilometres away, normally written as 24 km. The 'k' is known as a multiplier and has the value of 1 000. Likewise, if setting a spark plug gap, I could set it at 0.001 metres; it might be easier to say 1 millimetre, normally written as 1 mm. The 'm' can be thought of as a divider by 1 000, or a multiplier of 0.001. The list of the common multipliers is as follows:

Prefix	Symbol	Value	Long value
mega	M	10^6	1 000 000
kilo	k	10^3	1 000
hecto	h	10^2	100
(none)		10^0	1
centi	c	10^{-2}	0.01
milli	m	10^{-3}	0.001
micro	µ	10^{-6}	0.000001

LEARNING TASKS

➡ Look back at the key words. Explain each one to a friend, and/or write out a short description to keep as evidence.

➡ Make a simple sketch to show what is meant by area, volume and centre of gravity.

➡ Examine a real vehicle and/or look back to other chapters of this book and see if you can say which of the terms in the above tables are used to describe some of the vehicle systems.

2 Science

Introduction

The following sections explain some scientific terms and principles in a little more detail. The figures with some sections show the principle as a picture.

KEY WORDS

■ All words in the table

■ All the section headings

■ Conduction

■ Convection

■ Radiation

Velocity and acceleration

Velocity is the speed of an object in a given direction. Velocity is a 'vector quantity'; this means its direction is important as well as its speed. The velocity v of an object travelling in a fixed direction may be calculated by dividing the distance s it has travelled by the time taken t.

velocity = distance travelled/time taken $(v = s/t)$

Acceleration is the rate of change of velocity (how quickly speed is increasing or decreasing). It is usually measured in metres per second per second. Newton's second law of motion says that a body will accelerate only if it is acted upon by an outside force. The outside force on a car is either the accelerator to increase speed (accelerate) or the brakes to decrease speed (decelerate).

Acceleration due to gravity is the acceleration of an object falling due to the earth's gravity. The value used for gravitational acceleration g is 9.806 ms^{-2} (10 ms^{-2} is usually near enough for our calculations).

The average acceleration a of an object travelling in a straight line over a time t may be calculated using the formula:

acceleration = change of velocity/time taken

or, if v is its final velocity and u its initial velocity,

$a = (v - u)/t$

A negative answer (less than zero, like –2) means that the object is slowing down (decelerating).

Friction   The force that opposes the relative motion of two bodies in contact is known as friction. The coefficient of friction is the ratio of the force needed to achieve this motion to the force pressing the two bodies together.

For motor vehicle use friction is greatly reduced in some places by using lubricants, such as oil and grease. In other places friction is deliberately increased – for example brake shoes and pads, drive belts and tyres.

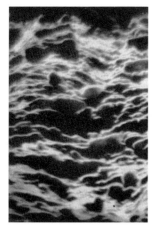

Figure 20.2 The 'smooth' surface of mild steel under a microscope

Pressure   In a fluid or gas, pressure is said to be the force that acts at right angles per unit surface area of an object immersed in the fluid or gas. The SI unit of pressure is the pascal (Pa), equal to a pressure of one newton per square metre. In the atmosphere, the pressure decreases as you go higher: from about 100 kPa at sea level to zero where the atmosphere dwindles into space. The other common unit of pressure you will meet is the bar. One bar (100 kPa) is atmospheric pressure.

Absolute pressure is measured from a perfect vacuum or zero pressure. Gauge pressure is the difference between the measured pressure and atmospheric pressure. A tyre gauge works like this because it reads zero in atmospheric pressure. When we talk about a vacuum or a depression, what we really mean is a pressure less than atmospheric. It is best to use absolute pressure figures for discussing subjects such as the operation of an engine.

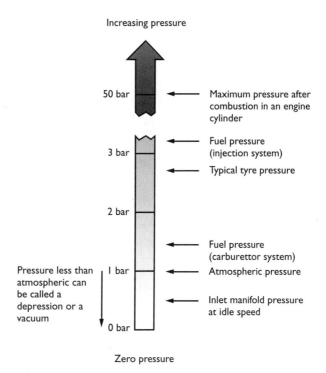

Figure 20.3 Pressure from absolute zero

Centre of gravity or centre of mass

This is the point in (or near) an object about which it would turn if it could rotate freely. A symmetrical object, such as a cube or ball, has its centre of mass at its geometrical centre; a hollow object, such as a glass, may have its centre of gravity in the space inside it.

For an object such as a car to be stable, a perpendicular line down through its centre of gravity must run within the boundaries of its wheel base. If the car is tilted until this line falls outside the wheel base, it will become unstable and fall over!

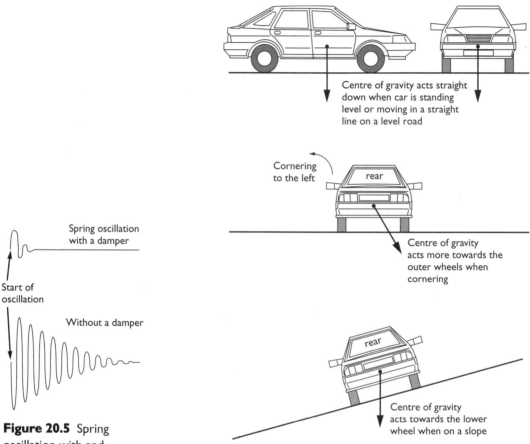

Centre of gravity acts straight down when car is standing level or moving in a straight line on a level road

Cornering to the left

rear

Centre of gravity acts more towards the outer wheels when cornering

rear

Centre of gravity acts towards the lower wheel when on a slope

Figure 20.4 Centre of gravity of a car

Figure 20.5 Spring oscillation with and without a damper

Spring oscillation with a damper

Start of oscillation

Without a damper

Oscillation

An oscillation is one complete to-and-fro movement of a vibrating object or system. The time taken for one complete oscillation is the time period of the vibration. The number of oscillations in one second is its frequency. In most mechanical systems in the car oscillations are damped down. The dampers fitted to the suspension help to prevent the springs oscillating.

Energy, work and power

Energy can be thought of as the ability to do work, or the amount of work stored up; it is measured in joules. When you have no energy, it's hard to work! Energy cannot be destroyed, only converted to another form. It can be stored in a number of forms:

- kinetic or mechanical energy, like the movement of an engine
- potential or position energy; when you lift a hammer, its potential energy increases
- electrical energy, such as that made by an alternator
- chemical energy stored in a battery
- heat energy from burning something

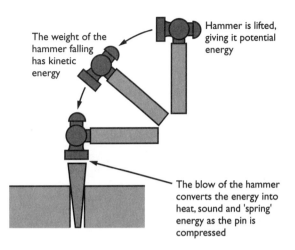

Figure 20.6 Movement of a hammer showing changes of energy

■ nuclear energy which is not yet used on vehicles, fortunately!

Power is the rate of doing work or converting energy. It is measured in watts. If the work done or energy consumed is E joules in t seconds, then the power P is calculated by:

power = work done or energy consumed/time $P = E/t$

Force and torque

A force is thought of as any influence that tends to change the state of rest or the motion in a straight line of an object – just like braking force slowing down a vehicle. If the body can't move freely, it will deform or bend. Force is a vector quantity, which means it must have both size and direction. Its unit is the newton, N.

Torque is the turning effect of force on an object. A car engine produces a torque at the wheels. Torque is measured by multiplying the force by its perpendicular distance from the turning point. Its units therefore are newton metres, Nm.

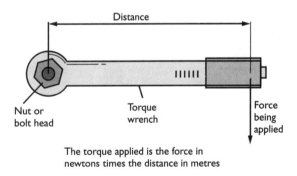

Figure 20.7 Force and torque (a torque wrench)

Mass, weight and force

Mass is the quantity of matter in a body as measured by its resistance to movement. The SI system base unit of mass is the kilogram, kg. The mass of an object determines how much driving force is needed to produce a certain acceleration. The mass also determines the force exerted on a body by gravity. The force F, mass m and acceleration a (or g, if due to gravity) can be calculated by:

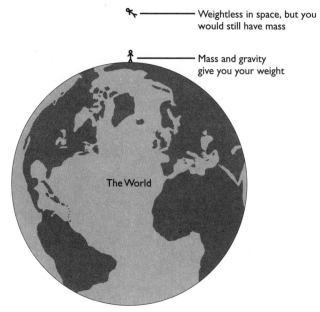

Figure 20.8 Mass and weight

$$\text{force} = \text{mass} \times \text{acceleration} \quad F = ma$$

or

$$\text{force} = \text{mass} \times \text{gravity} \quad F = mg$$

At a given place, equal masses experience equal gravity, known as the weights of the bodies. Masses can be compared by comparing the weights of bodies at the same place.

Volume and density

Density is a measure of the compactness of a substance; it is measured in kg per cubic metre. The density D of a mass m occupying a volume V is given by:

$$\text{density} = \text{mass/volume} \quad D = m/V$$

Relative density is the ratio of the density of a substance to that of water. This is useful for testing older types of battery by comparing the density of the electrolyte to that of water.

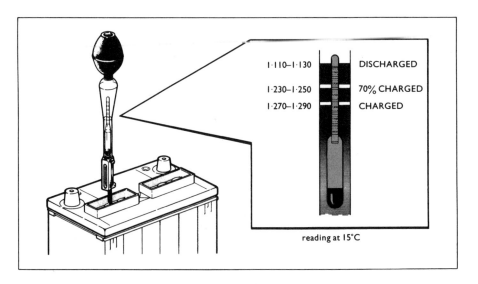

Figure 20.9 Testing the relative density of battery electrolyte

Heat and temperature

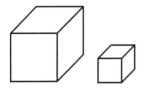

If the small block is heated to a higher *temperature* than the large block, they could both contain the same *heat* energy

Figure 20.10
Temperature and heat

Heat is a form of energy a substance has as a result of the vibrating movement, or kinetic energy, of its molecules or atoms. Heat only flows from a higher temperature to a lower temperature. Its effect on a substance may be simply to raise its temperature, or to cause it to expand. Solids can melt, liquids vaporise and gases, if confined, will increase in pressure. This is much like ice, water, steam and steam pressure in a boiler.

Quantities of heat are usually measured in units of energy, such as joules (J). Specific heat is the amount of heat energy needed to heat a given mass of the substance through a given range of temperature compared to the heat energy needed to heat an equal mass of water through the same range. This is useful for comparing materials.

Heat energy is transferred by conduction, convection and radiation. Conduction is the passing of heat along a medium to neighbouring parts. For example, the whole length of a metal rod becomes hot when one end is held in the flame of a welding torch. Convection is the transmission of heat through a liquid or gas in currents: for example, when the air in a car is warmed by the heater matrix and blower. Radiation is heat transfer by infrared rays. It can pass through a vacuum and travels at the speed of light! For example, you can feel radiated heat from a vehicle headlight just in front of the glass.

LEARNING TASKS

➡ Look back at the key words. Explain each one to a friend, and/or write out a short description to keep as evidence.

➡ Make a simple sketch with an explanation to show all the different energy conversions which take place in a car. Start with the chemical energy in the fuel.

➡ Write a short explanation about why friction is sometimes a problem and sometimes very useful.

3　Electricity

Electrons and things

KEY WORDS

■ Current, voltage and resistance

■ Series and parallel

■ Open circuit and short circuit

■ Induction

To understand electricity properly, we must start by finding out what it really is. This means thinking very small! The molecule is the smallest part of matter that can be recognised as that particular matter. Subdivision of the molecule results in atoms. The atom is the smallest part of matter. An element is a substance which comprises of atoms of one kind only.

The atom consists of a central nucleus made up of protons and neutrons. Electrons orbit around this nucleus, a bit like planets around the sun.

The neutron is a very small part of the nucleus. It has an equal positive and negative charge. It is therefore neutral and has no polarity. The proton is another small part of the nucleus; it is positively charged. As the neutron is neutral and the proton is positively charged, the nucleus of the atom is positively charged.

The electron is an even smaller part of the atom and is negatively charged. It orbits the nucleus and is held in orbit by the attraction of the positively charged protons. All electrons are similar, no matter what type of atom they come from.

When atoms are in a balanced state, the number of electrons orbiting the nucleus equals the number of protons. The atoms of some materials have

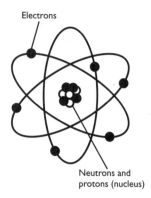

Figure 20.11 The atom

electrons which are easily detached from the parent atom and join an adjacent atom. In so doing they move an electron (like polarities repel) from this atom to a third atom, and so on through the material. This is a random movement. These are called free electrons

Materials are called conductors if the electrons can move easily. In some materials it is extremely difficult to move electrons from their parent atoms. These materials are called insulators.

Electron flow or conventional flow

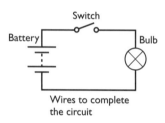

Figure 20.12 A simple electrical circuit

If an electrical pressure (electromotive force or voltage) is applied to a conductor, a directional movement of electrons will take place (like connecting a battery to a wire).

Conditions for an electron flow:

■ a pressure source, e.g. from a battery or generator

■ a complete conducting path for the electrons to move, e.g. wires.

An electron flow is termed an electric current. Figure 20.12 shows a simple electric circuit. The battery positive terminal is connected, through a switch and lamp, to the battery negative terminal. With the switch open, the chemical energy of the battery will remove electrons from the positive terminal to the negative terminal via the battery. This leaves the positive terminal with fewer electrons and the negative terminal with a surplus of electrons. An electrical pressure or electromotive force (emf) exists between the battery terminals.

With the switch closed, the surplus electrons on the negative terminal will flow through the lamp back to the electron deficient positive terminal. The lamp will light, and the chemical energy of the battery will keep the electrons moving in this circuit from negative to positive. This movement from negative to positive is called the electron flow.

However, scientists once thought that current flowed from positive to negative. This convention is still followed for practical purposes and will be used throughout this and other books. So even though it is not correct, the most important point is that we all follow the same convention. We say:

'Current flows from positive to negative.'

Whilst the switch in the above circuit was closed, the chemical energy of the battery was first converted to electrical and then heat energy in the lamp filament.

Effects of current flow

Current flow in a circuit can produce only three effects:

■ heat

■ magnetism

■ chemical action.

The heating effect is the basis of electrical components, such as lights and heater plugs. The magnetic effect is the basis of relays and motors and generators. The chemical effect is the basis for electroplating and battery charging.

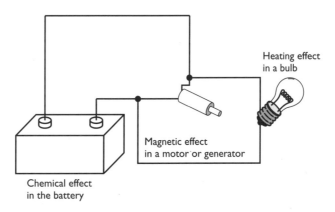

Figure 20.13 A bulb, motor and battery – heat, magnetic and chemical effects

These three effects are reversible. Heat applied to a thermocouple will cause a small emf and therefore a small current to flow. Practical use of this is mainly in instruments. A coil of wire rotated in the magnetic field of a magnet will produce an emf and can cause current to flow. This is the basis of a generator. Chemical action, such as in a battery, produces an emf which can cause current to flow.

Voltage, current resistance and power

In Figure 20.13 the number of electrons through the lamp every second is the rate of flow. The cause of electron flow is the electrical pressure. The lamp produces an opposition to the rate of flow set up by the electrical pressure. Power is the rate of doing work or changing energy from one form to another. All these quantities are given names:

Name	Definition	Name	Symbol	Abbreviation
Electrical flow or current	A number of electrons past a fixed point in one second	ampere	I	A
Electrical pressure	A pressure of 1 volt applied to a circuit will produce a current flow of 1 ampere if the circuit resistance is 1 ohm	volt	V	V
Electrical resistance	This is the opposition to current flow in a material or circuit when a voltage is applied across it	ohm	R	Ω
Electrical power	When a voltage of 1 volt causes a current of 1 ampere to flow, the power developed is 1 watt	watt	P	W

If the voltage applied to the circuit was increased but the lamp resistance stayed the same, then current would increase. If the voltage was maintained constant but the lamp was changed for one with a higher resistance, the current would decrease. This relationship is put into a law called Ohm's Law.

Ohm's Law states that in a closed circuit the current is proportional to the voltage and inversely proportional to the resistance:

voltage = current × resistance   (V = IR) or (R = V/I) or (I = V/R)

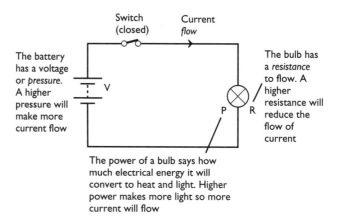

Figure 20.14 An electrical circuit demonstrating Ohm's Law and power

When one volt causes one ampere to flow, the power used (P) is one watt:

power = voltage × current   (P = VI) or (I = P/V) or (V = P/I)

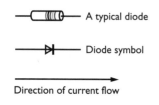

Figure 20.15 Diode and diode symbol

Three terms are useful when discussing electrical circuits:

- Open circuit: the circuit is broken, therefore no current can flow.

- Short circuit: a fault has caused a wire to touch another conductor and the current uses this as an easier way to complete the circuit.

- High resistance: a part of the circuit has developed a high resistance (such as a dirty connection), which will reduce the amount of current which can flow.

Conductors, insulators and semiconductors

All metals are conductors. Silver, copper and aluminium are among the best and are frequently used. Liquids which will conduct an electric current are called electrolytes. Insulators are generally nonmetallic and include rubber, porcelain, glass, plastics, cotton, silk, wax paper and some liquids. Some materials can act either as insulators or conductors, depending on conditions. These are called semiconductors and are used to make transistors and diodes.

Factors affecting resistance of a conductor

In an insulator a large applied voltage will produce a very small electron movement. In a conductor a small applied voltage will produce a large electron flow or current. The amount of resistance offered by the conductor is determined by a number of factors:

- Length: the greater the length of a conductor, the greater is the resistance.

- Cross-sectional area: the larger the CSA, the smaller the resistance.

- The material from which the conductor is made: this is known as the resistivity or specific resistance of the material.

- Temperature: most metals increase in resistance as temperature increases.

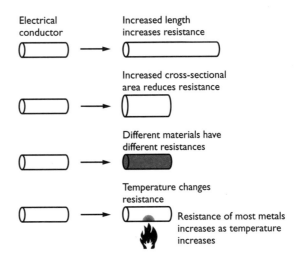

Figure 20.16 Factors affecting electrical resistance

Resistors Good conductors are used to carry the current with minimum voltage loss due to conductor resistance. Resistors are used to control the current flow in a circuit or to set voltage levels. They are made of materials that have a fairly high resistance. Resistors to carry low currents are often made of carbon. Resistors for high currents are usually wire wound.

Circuit networks When components are connected so that there is only one path for the same current to flow through each component they are said to be connected in series. Rules for series circuits:

■ Current is the same in all parts of the circuit.

■ Applied voltage equals the sum of the volt drops around the circuit.

■ Total resistance of the circuit (R_T) equals the sum of the individual resistance values ($R_1 + R_2$ etc.)

When components are connected so that they provide more than one path for the current to flow in and have the same voltage across each component, they are said to be connected in parallel. Rules for parallel circuits:

■ Voltage across all components of a parallel circuit is the same.

■ Total current = sum of the current flowing in each branch.

■ Current splits up depending on each component resistance.

■ Total resistance of the circuit (R_T): $1/R_T = 1/R_1 + 1/R_2$ or $R_T = (R_1 \times R_2)/(R_1 + R_2)$.

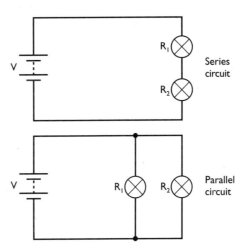

Figure 20.17 Examples of series and parallel circuits

Magnetism and electromagnetism

Magnetism can be created by a permanent magnet or by an electromagnet (remember that magnetism is one of the three effects of electricity). The space around a magnet in which the magnetic effect can be detected is called the magnetic field. In diagrams the shape of magnetic fields is represented by flux lines or lines of force.

Some rules about magnetism:

- Unlike poles attract. Like poles repel.
- Lines of force in the same direction repel sideways; in opposite directions they attract.
- Current flowing in a conductor will set up a magnetic field around the conductor. The strength of the magnetic field is determined by how much current is flowing.
- If a conductor is wound into a coil or solenoid, the resulting magnetism is the same as a permanent bar magnet.

Electromagnets are used in motors, relays and fuel injectors – to name just a few. Force on a current carrying conductor in a magnetic field is caused because of two magnetic fields interacting. This is the basic principle of how a motor works.

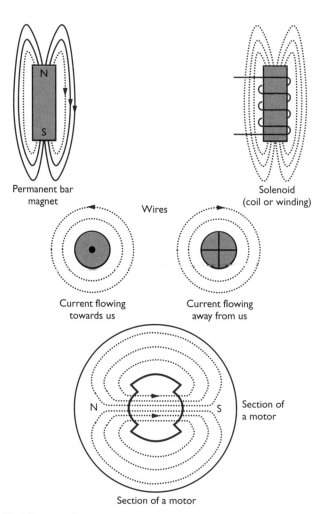

Figure 20.18 Magnetic fields

Electromagnetic induction   Basic laws:

■ When a conductor cuts or is cut by magnetism, a voltage is induced in the conductor.

■ The direction of the induced voltage depends upon the direction of the magnetic field and the direction in which the field moves relative to the conductor.

■ The size is proportional to the rate at which the conductor cuts or is cut by the magnetism.

This effect of induction, meaning that voltage is made in the wire, is the basic principle of how generators such as a car alternator work: a generator is a machine that converts mechanical energy into electrical energy.

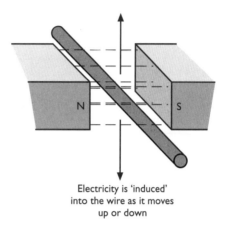

Electricity is 'induced'
into the wire as it moves
up or down

Figure 20.19 Induction

Mutual induction   If two coils (known as the primary and secondary) are wound on to the same iron core, then any change in magnetism of one coil will induce a voltage in to the other. This happens when a current is switched on and off to the primary coil. If the number of turns of wire on the secondary coil is more than the primary, a higher voltage can be produced. If the number of turns of wire on the secondary coil is less than the primary, a lower voltage is obtained. This is called transformer action and is the principle of the ignition coil.

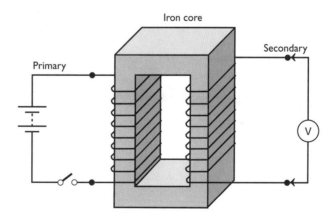

As the switch in the primary is closed and opened, the flow of electricity
makes a changing magnetic field around the iron core. The changing
magnetism mutually induces electricity into the secondary winding

Figure 20.20 Mutual induction

Value of this 'mutually induced' voltage depends upon:

- primary current
- turns ratio between primary and secondary coils
- the speed at which the magnetism changes.

Capacitors A capacitor is a device for storing an electric charge. In its simple form it consists of two plates separated by an insulating material. One plate can have more electrons compared to the other. On vehicles its main uses are for reducing arcing across switch contacts, for radio interference suppression circuits as well as in electronic control units.

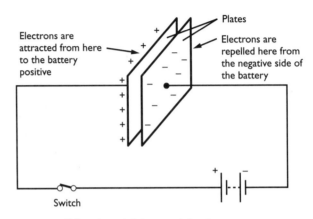

Figure 20.21 A capacitor charged up

LEARNING TASKS

➡ Look back at the key words. Explain each one to a friend, and/or write out a short description to keep as evidence.

➡ Make a simple sketch to show what is meant by series and parallel circuits.

➡ Examine a real system and see where electrical effects are used.

➡ Write short notes to explain what electricity really is.

---

4   Materials

Introduction Because of their properties, different materials are used in different places on motor vehicles. For example, cast iron is normally used for the very hot exhaust manifold, but could plastic be used instead? Well of course not, and it is obvious why. Could you use aluminium instead? This time it is not obvious, and more thought is required to decide the most suitable material. The following table lists several types of material together with important properties. As a rough guide these are given as a number from 1 (best) to 5 (worst) in a kind of league table. This makes the table easier to use for comparing one material to another.

KEY WORDS

- All words in the tables
- Corrosion

Figure 20.22 Exhaust manifold

Material	Ease of shaping	Strength	Withstand heat	Electrical resistance	Corrosion resistance	Cost	Typical MV uses
Copper	2	3	2	1	3	4	Wires and electrical parts
Aluminium	2	3	2	1	3	4	Cylinder heads
Steel	3	2	1	1	4	3	Body panels and exhausts
Cast iron	3	2	1	1	4	3	Manifolds and engine blocks
Platinum	3	1	1	1	2	5	Spark plug tips
Soft plastic	1	5	5	5	1	1	Electrical insulators
Hard plastic	1	4	4	5	1	1	Interiors and some engine components
Glass	3	5	2	5	1	2	Screens and windows
Rubber	2	4	5	5	3	2	Tyres and hoses
Ceramics	4	4	1	5	1	4	Spark plug insulators

This table is just to help you compare properties; the 'league table' positions are only crude estimates and will vary with different examples of the same material.

Corrosion

Corrosion is the eating away and eventual destruction of metals and alloys (a mixtures of metals) by chemical action. Most metals corrode eventually, but the rusting of ordinary iron and steel is the most common form of corrosion. Rusting of iron or steel takes place in damp air, when the iron combines with oxygen and water to form a brown deposit known as rust. Higher temperatures make this reaction work more quickly. Salty road and air conditions make car bodies rust more quickly.

Some materials other than metals, for example rubber based ones, corrode or perish over a period of time. Plastics have the great advantage that they appear to last for ever!

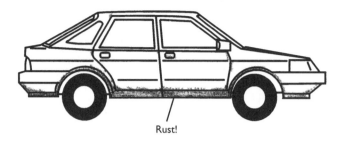

Figure 20.23 Rust!

The following table lists some terms used to describe materials.

Property	Explanation
Hardness	Can withstand indentation (marking)
Softness	Can be easily indented
Toughness	The ability to resist fracture
Brittleness	Breaks or shatters under shock loads (impact)
Ductility	Plastic (deforms and stays that way) under tension or stretching
Malleability	Plastic under compression (squeezing)
Plasticity	The ability to retain a deformation after a load is removed
Elasticity	The ability to return to its original shape when a deforming load is removed
Strength	The ability to withstand a load without breaking

LEARNING TASKS

➡ Look back at the key words. Explain each one to a friend, and/or write out a short description to keep as evidence.

➡ Examine a real vehicle and note some of the materials used in various places. See if you can suggest why certain materials are used.

➡ Copy out the headings in the properties table and, by using other books, see if you can add further types of materials and give them a position in the league.

5 Mechanical machines

Introduction

A simple mechanical machine is a device that allows a small force to overcome a larger force. There are only three basic machines:

■ ramp – such as a wedge

■ lever – such as a lever!

■ wheel and axle – such as pulleys and a belt.

All other machines are combinations of these three. This is a good way of making any complicated machine easier to understand.

The main features of a machine are:

■ mechanical advantage, which is the ratio of load to effort (think of a car jack)

KEY WORDS

■ Mechanical efficiency

■ Gears or cogs

■ Mechanical advantage

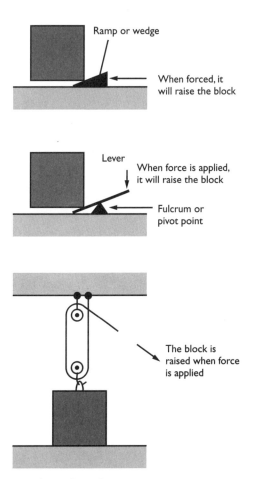

Figure 20.24 Basic mechanical machines

- velocity ratio, which is the velocity input compared to the velocity output (think of a car gear box)
- efficiency, which is the work output divided by the work input as a percentage.

In a perfect machine, with no friction, the efficiency would be 100%. All practical machines have efficiencies of less than 100%, otherwise perpetual motion would be possible!

Gears   Gears are toothed wheels that transmit the turning movement of one shaft to another. Gear wheels may be used in pairs, or in threes if both shafts need to turn in the same direction. The gear ratio, which is the ratio of the number of teeth on the two wheels, determines:

- the torque ratio – the turning force on the output shaft compared with the turning force on the input shaft
- the speed ratio – the speed of the output shaft compared to the speed of input shaft.

Gears with the ratio 2:1 (say 20 teeth input and 10 teeth output) will have an output of twice the speed and half the torque of the input.

A common type of gear for parallel shafts is the spur gear, with straight teeth parallel to the shaft axis. The helical gear (most common in car gear boxes) has teeth cut at an angle in a corkscrew shape The double form of the helical gear is the most efficient for energy transfer. Did you know this is where the shape of the Citroën badge came from?

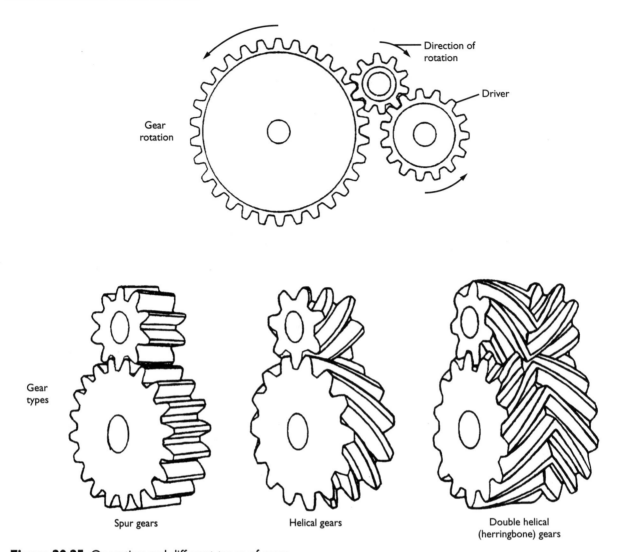

Gear rotation

Direction of rotation

Driver

Gear types

Spur gears

Helical gears

Double helical (herringbone) gears

Figure 20.25 Operation and different types of gears

Hydraulics   Hydraulics means using the properties of liquids to transmit pressure and movement. The best known type of hydraulic machines are the hydraulic press and the hydraulic jack. The hydraulic principle of pressurised liquid increasing mechanical efficiency is ideal for use on vehicle braking systems.

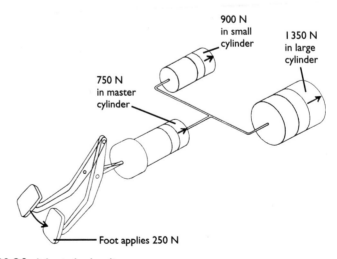

900 N in small cylinder

I 350 N in large cylinder

750 N in master cylinder

Foot applies 250 N

Figure 20.26 A basic hydraulic system

A basic hydraulic system consists of two liquid connected pistons in cylinders, one of narrow bore, one of large bore. A force applied to the narrow piston applies a certain pressure to the liquid, which is transmitted to the larger piston. Because the area of this piston is larger, the force exerted on it is larger. The original force has been increased, although the smaller piston has to move a greater distance to move the larger piston only a little. Mechanical advantage is gained in force, but lost in movement.

> **LEARNING TASKS**
>
> ➠ Look back at the key words. Explain each one to a friend, and/or write out a short description to keep as evidence.
>
> ➠ Make a simple sketch to show gears of different sizes, one driving the other. Work out the torque and speed ratios.
>
> ➠ Write a short explanation explaining why a hydraulic jack makes lifting a car easy.

6   Simple, easy maths

Percentages

KEY WORDS

- Percentages
- Fractions
- Indices
- Ratios
- Areas
- Volumes

Q.   *Give me two good reasons why I need to be able to work out percentages.*

A1.   *So when a data book says the car should have 30% antifreeze, you know how much to put in!*

For example, if the data book says 30% antifreeze and the cooling system holds 8 litres, how much antifreeze should you add? 30% means 30/100, which cancels to 3/10. 3/10 × 8 = 24/10 = 2.4 litres.

A2.   *So when your bonus scheme at work increases your hourly rate by 22%, you know how much you will get!*

For example, the normal pay rate is £5 per hour. How much will you get now? 22% means 22/100. 22/100 × £5 = £1.10. Your new pay rate is £5 + £1.10p = £6.10 per hour. Easy isn't it?

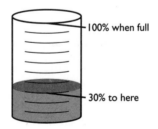

Figure 20.27 Percentages

Fractions

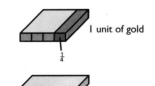

Figure 20.28 Fractions

Q.   *Give me two good reasons why I need to be able to work out fractions.*

A1.   *So you know what you get when your overtime pay is time and a quarter!*

For example, the normal pay rate is £5 per hour. How much will you get now? Time and a quarter means 1¼ × your normal rate. 1¼ × £5 = 5/4 × 5/1 = 25/4 = 6.25. Your overtime pay rate is £6.25 per hour.

A2.   *So you can understand the effect of resistors in parallel circuits!*

For example, if a heater blower circuit has a 2 Ω and a 3 Ω resistor connected in parallel by the speed control switch, what is the combined resistance?

Looking back to the electrical section, you will see the formula is $1/R_T = 1/R_1 + 1/R_2$. This means $1/R_T = 1/2 + 1/3$. To add fractions, the bottom numbers must be the same: $1/R_T = 3/6 + 2/6 = 5/6$. $R_T = 6/5 = 1.2\ \Omega$.

Ratio

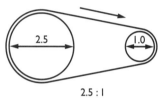

2.5 : 1

Figure 20.29 Ratios

Q.   *Give me one good reason why I need to be able to understand ratios.*

A.   *So you know why things are made as they are!*

For example, if the maximum speed an alternator can run at is 15 000 rev/min and the top speed of the engine is 6 000 rev/min, why is the pulley ratio 2.5:1?

15 000/6 000 = 2.5 (the ratio of the speeds), so the alternator can never be driven too fast.

Areas

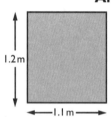

1.2 m

1.1 m

Figure 20.30 Area

Q.   *Give me one good reason why I need to be able to work out areas.*

A.   *To work out how much paint you need to cover a bonnet!*

For example, if the bonnet is 1.2 m long and 1.1 m wide, and the aerosol says it will cover 1.5 m² will it be enough?

The area is 1.2 ×1.1 = 1.32 m². Yes, you have got enough paint (for one coat)!

Volumes

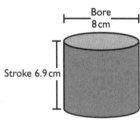

Bore 8 cm

Stroke 6.9 cm

Figure 20.31 Volumes

Q.   *Give me one good reason why I need to be able to work out volumes.*

A.   *So you can understand engine capacity!*

For example, if the bore of a four cylinder engine is 8 cm and the stroke (distance from BDC to TDC) is 6.9 cm, what is the capacity of the engine? The volume of a regular solid is the area × the height. For a cylinder the area is πr^2, so the volume must be $\pi r^2 h$ (r, the radius, is half the bore diameter; h is the stroke). The volume is $3.14 \times 4 \times 4 \times 6.9 = 346.66 \times 4$ cylinders = 1 386.62 cc. This would probably be called a 1 400 cc or a 1.4 l engine.

Indices

$$10^3 = 10 \times 10 \times 10 = 1000$$

Figure 20.32 Indices

Q.   *Give me one good reason why I need to be able to understand indices.*

A.   *So you can write out very large or very small numbers without loads of zeros!*

For example, looking back to the electrical section, to describe completely the current flow of 1 ampere, I should have said 6 000 000 000 000 000 000 electrons pass a point in one second! It is much easier to write 6×10^{18}. This simply means 6 with 18 zeros after it. This quantity of electrons is known as a coulomb. It is about enough electricity to work a heavy duty starter motor for about 0.001 seconds! This could be written as 10^{-3} s. This means moving the 'point' 3 places to the left (dividing by 1 000).

7   Drawings

Introduction

Drawings are an ideal way to pass on important information. Many manufacturers provide information in the form of drawings. It is essential that you can interpret the details you need and are not put off by the amount of information presented. To help you do this, some simple standards are used relating to the type of lines:

■ Continuous thick line _____ Visible outlines
■ Continuous thin line _____ Projection, dimension and hatching lines
■ Short thin dashes _ _ _ _ _ _ _ _ _ _ _ Hidden details
■ Long thin chain __ _ __ _ __ _ __ Centre lines
■ Long chain __ _ __ _ __ _ __ Cutting planes

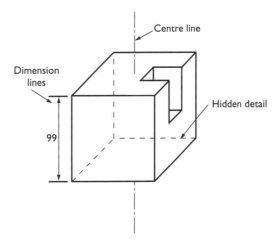

Figure 20.33 Drawing of a basic object using different lines to show details

Terminology	
Sections	When the inside details of an object are important, it is often convenient to show this by sectioning or cutting the object in a suitable place. A sectioned view of a brake cylinder is a good example
Dimensions	Lines with arrow heads, in some cases to simply show the size of the object. This is used more for drawings used to make an item than to pass on information for repair
Tolerances and limits	Dimensions can never be dead on although very close in some cases. A good example of a tolerance or limit on a motor vehicle drawing could be the bore of a cylinder given as 70 ±0.05 mm
Fits	Two types of 'fit' can be used. With clearance fit a pin is slightly smaller and therefore slides into a hole. Interference fit is where the pin would be very slightly too large and would need pressing into the hole
Projection	A term used to describe the way an object is drawn. You can imagine it as if projected on to a screen from different angles
Line diagram	A simplified diagram showing only the most basic of information
Block diagram	Complicated systems can be simplified by representing, say, the fuel system as one block, the engine as another and so on
Exploded diagram	This is often used in workshop manuals. It shows a collection of components spread apart to show their details and suggest their original positions

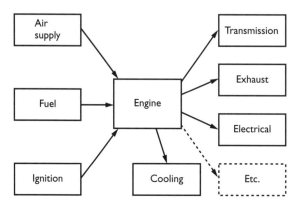

Figure 20.34 Block diagram of an engine and its systems

The following table gives some sources of drawings and other information.

Source	Details
Technical bulletins	Sheets of information sent from manufacturers to dealers outlining the latest repair information
Parts books	The pictures or drawings in parts books can be very useful for repair procedures as they often show all the component parts of an object
Textbooks	This one, of course, but a number of other good books are available
Workshop manuals	This is the traditional source of detailed information on specific vehicles and systems
Microfiche	Pictures and information are often stored on microfilm as a large amount can be stored in a small space. It is like a very small photograph negative which can be read on a viewer
Video	Video tapes are available on many topics. They are ideal training aids
Computer	The computer is increasingly becoming essential in many ways. A large amount of data can be kept on disk and retrieved with a few key strokes

Figure 20.35 Combined information and diagnostic system

Source	Details
Compact disk (CD)	The CD is an extension of the computer storage. One CD can hold a massive amount of information (many workshop manuals full), and this information can be accessed quickly and easily by a computer. Often now CDs are built into test and diagnostic equipment
On line databases	Many sources of information are now available 'on line'. This means that with a computer and modem you can access remote databases. These can be provided by manufacturers for their dealers. Sources are now even available over the Internet

Types of drawings   Drawings can be produced in a number of ways; the best for engineering type drawings, shown in Figure 20.36, are as follows:

- In orthographic projection three elevations are shown: usually a front, plan and end view
- Pictorial projections, such as isometric and oblique, show a representation of what the item looks like.
- The isometric view is often used in workshop manuals to show the arrangement of a complicated system.

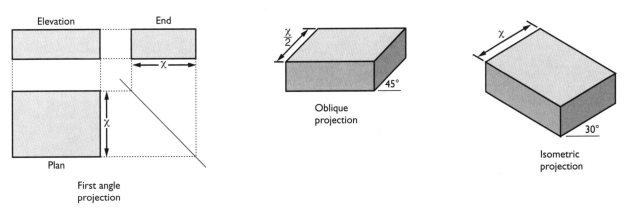

Figure 20.36 First angle, oblique and isometric projections of a simple shape

Summary   Congratulations for working to the end a chapter like this one! To really get to the bottom of some of the details, you will have to keep referring back to look up different things. A great skill to learn in our trade is not to know everything, but to be able to find out anything when you need to! This is another reason why the content of this chapter is important: it gives you the tools to learn new subjects more easily. Well done again and keep at it!

> **LEARNING TASKS**
>
> ➡ Draw a chosen vehicle component in section to show hidden details.
>
> ➡ Make simple sketches to show different types of projections.
>
> ➡ Examine a real system and choose one component. Find further information about this from other sources.

21 Revision and what next?

1 Revision

Stop here!

KEY WORDS

- Revision

If you have just decided to take a look at the last chapter to see if the book has a happy ending – it does. The trouble is that you won't know that until you read it all from the start. Call back here later and all will be revealed!

If you have made it this far from the front of the book – congratulations! If you have not yet completed all your assessments, then now is a good time to do a bit of revision. The best way to revise is not to start again, but to just look back at the key words and learning tasks. Most of them will seem quite easy now. This is because you know the subject so much better than when you started. If some of the key words and learning tasks are still not clear, then a little further reading is needed in that particular area. Also ask your assessor or teacher for some advice.

Well done once again. By now you will understand a lot more about motor vehicle technology and the industry in general. If you have enjoyed learning about the subject, then that is even better.

Figure 21.1 Stop

> **LEARNING TASK**
>
> ➡ Look back through the book at the key words and learning tasks; study again just the parts you are not quite sure about.

2 What next?

NVQ level 3

KEY WORDS

- Money
- Prospects
- Further study

The title of this section says it all. If you have made it this far and completed most of your level 2 assessments for your portfolio, then I'm sure you have the ability to go further. Level 3 will take you more into diagnostic type work, and you will be expected to start working without supervision. Better qualifications mean better job prospects, which mean more money, which means a better life style etc. Look out for the level 3 version of this book.

And now for the happy ending! It's simple: you feel good about yourself, you made it through the course, you made it through the assessments, you did the work – you take the credit.

Good luck with your future studies and work.

Figure 21.2 Go!

> **LEARNING TASK**
>
> ➡ Look back at the key words. Explain each one to a friend, and/or write out a short description to keep as evidence.

Index